D0969063

Communist Parties in Western Europe

Communist Parties in Western Europe

Decline or Adaptation?

Edited by Michael Waller and Meindert Fennema

Basil Blackwell

Copyright © Basil Blackwell Ltd 1988

First published 1988

Basil Blackwell Ltd
108 Cowley Road, Oxford, OX4 1JF, UK

Basil Blackwell Inc.
432 Park Avenue South, Suite 1503
New York, NY 10016, USA

British Library Cataloguing in Publication Data

Communist parties in Western Europe: Decline or Adaptation?
   1. Communist parties — Europe
   I. Waller, Michael II. Fennema, M.
   324.24'075 JN94.A979

   ISBN 0–631–15617–8

Library of Congress Cataloging in Publication Data

Communist parties in Western Europe.

  Bibliography: p.
   1. Communist parties—Europe. 2. Democratic centralism—Europe. 3. Communism—Europe.
I. Waller, Michael, 1934–   . II. Fennema, M., 1946–   .
  JN94.A979C643 1988   324.24'075   87–25003
  ISBN 0–631–15617–8

Typeset in 10 on 12 pt Times
by Downdell Ltd., Abingdon, Oxon.
Printed in Great Britain

Contents

Preface

The history of this book goes back to a workshop entitled 'Inside Communist Parties' which was held as part of the Joint Sessions of the European Consortium for Political Research in Freiburg in 1984. That workshop was attended by both editors of this work. It was concerned almost exclusively with ruling parties, and with problems that were particular to that situation of power.

Disappointed with the restriction of the Freiburg workshop to the ruling parties, one of this book's editors, Meindert Fennema, undertook to organize a further workshop with a similar title, but this time concentrating on the non-ruling communist parties of Western Europe, and involving scholars with first-hand experience of these parties. However, the link with the earlier workshop was maintained by the presence of the book's co-editor, Michael Waller, at the later one, which was held as part of the Joint Sessions of the ECPR in Barcelona in 1985. It was there that the idea of this book was discussed, and where we decided to work together on the venture.

It seemed to us that a serious and fruitful discussion had taken place between scholars of communism and communist scholars, and that the gap between the traditional view of communism from the outside and those from within – both in self-defence and in self-criticism – had been sufficiently bridged to make a homogeneous book not only possible, but desirable.

Although the book in its final form does not contain all the papers presented at the Barcelona workshop, and includes several contributions written specially for the volume, the spirit of the Barcelona workshop has, in our view, been maintained. As the list of contributors will make clear, in almost every case the authors have first-hand knowledge of the country about which they write. In some cases they either have been, or still are, members of the communist party of the country treated. The remainder are political scientists who have had a long experience of studies of communism in Western Europe and elsewhere. Three of the authors are editors of academic journals about communism. The political positions of the contributors range from membership of a central committee to being long-standing critics of communist parties. They share, however, a genuine wish to understand, and to reveal as far as possible what has happened to the West European communist parties over the past twenty or so years, and they all go beyond the political-strategic vantage-point that has for so long dogged the discussion of communism.

The emphasis in this volume is on structural factors that affect the political strength of communist parties: changes in the social composition of the constituency of these parties; changes in the political and economic environment that influence or challenge them as political parties; and, finally, internal factors such as their organizational principles. The treatment overall is comparative. The aim has been to present a living description of the present predicament of the Western European communist parties, and an analysis of that predicament that is informed by experience. As far as we know, this is the first book of its kind; that it has been possible to compose it at all is a mark of the change that has been taking place both within the communist parties and within the academic community's attitudes towards communism. If it has proved impossible to eliminate altogether political preferences of one kind or another, we venture to hope that where they obtrude they will illustrate rather than obscure the points that the book is making.

Finally, acknowledgments are due to those who have helped to prepare the manuscript for publication: Karen Hall and Marilyn Dunn in Manchester, and Do Overtoom and Marianne Pauli in Amsterdam. With authors in eleven different countries involved the task has not been an easy one.

Michael Waller
Meindert Fennema

Abbreviations

Abbreviations are not given here for titles and terms that occur once only in the text.

AES   Alternative Economic Strategy (UK)
APK   *Arbetarpartiet kommunisterna* (Labour Party Communists) (Sweden)
ApO   *Ausser-parlamentarische Opposition* (Extra-parliamentary Opposition) (FRG)
CC.OO. *Comisiones Obreras* (Workers' Committees) (Spain)
CESPE   *Centro Studi Politica Economica* (Centre for the Study of Political Economy) (Italy)
CESPI   *Centro Studi Politica Internazionale* (Centre for the Study of International Politics) (Italy)
CFDT   *Confédération française démocratique du travail* (French Democratic Federation of Labour)
CGIL   *Confederazione Generale Italiana del Lavoro* (Italian General Confederation of Labour)
CGT   *Confédération générale du travail* (General Confederation of Labour) (France)
CISL   *Confederazione Italiana Sindicati Lavoratori* (Italian Confederation of Labour Trade Unions)
CNS   *Central Nacional Sindicalista* (Central National Trade Union Organization) (Spain)
CNT   *Central Nacional del Trabajo* (Central National Labour Organization)
CPGB   Communist Party of Great Britain
CPN   *Communistische Partij van Nederland* (Communist Party of the Netherlands)

CPSU   Communist Party of the Soviet Union
CRS   *Centro per la Riforma dello Stato* (Centre for the
            Reform of the State) (Italy)
DEVA   *Demokraattinen Vaihtoehto* (Democratic Alternative)
            (Finland)
DFFG   *De förenade FNL-grupperna* (The Combined
            FNL-Groups) (Sweden)
DKP   *Deutsche Kommunistische Partei* (German Communist
            Party) (FRG)
EAM   *Ethniko Apoleutherôtiko Metôpo* (National
            Liberation Front) (Greece)
EDA   *Eniaia Dêmokratikê Aristera* (United Democratic
            Left) (Greece)
ELAS   *Ethnikos Laikos Apoleutherotikos Stratos* (National
            Popular Liberation Army) (Greece)
EVC   *Eenheidsvakcentrale* (United Federation of Unions)
            (Netherlands)
FO   *Force ouvrière* (Workers' Strength) (France)
INSEE   *Institut National de la Statistique et des Etudes
            Economiques*
IPSO   *Instituut voor Politiek en Sociaal Onderzoek* (Institute
            for Political and Social Research) (Netherlands)
IU   *Izquierda Unida* (United Left) (Spain)
KFML   *Kommunistiska förbundet marxist–leninisterna*
            (Communist League of Marxist–Leninists) (Sweden)
KKE   *Kommounistiko Komma Elladas* (Communist Party
            of Greece)
KPD   *Kommunistische Partei Deutschlands* (Communist Party
            of Germany) (FRG)
LCDTU   Liaison Committee for the Defence of Trade Unions
            (UK)
MFA   *Movimento das Forças Armadas* (Armed Forces
            Movement) (Portugal)
MUC   *Mesa por la Unidad de los Comunistas* (Platform for
            Communists' Unity) (Spain)
ND   *Nea Dêmokratia* (New Democracy) (Greece)
NVB   *Nederlandse Vrouwenbeweging* (Women's Movement of
            the Netherlands)
PASOK   *Panhellêniko Socialistiko Kinêma* (Panhellenic
            Socialist Movement) (Greece)
PCB   *Parti communiste de Belgique* (Communist Party of
            Belgium)

PCE	*Partido Comunista de España* (Communist Party of Spain)
PCF	*Parti communiste français* (French Communist Party)
PCI	*Partito Comunista Italiano* (Italian Communist Party)
PCP	*Partido Comunista do Portugal* (Communist Party of Portugal)
PCPE	*Partido Comunista de los Pueblos de España* (Communist Party of the Peoples of Spain)
PdA	*Partei der Arbeit* (Labour Party) (Switzerland)
PRD	*Partido Renovador Democrático* (Democratic Party of Renewal) (Portugal)
PREC	*Processo revolucionário em curso* (Revolutionary Process in Progress) (Portugal)
PSOE	*Partido Socialista Obrero Español* (Socialist Workers' Party of Spain)
SAP	*Socialdemokratiska Arbetarpartiet* (Social Democratic Party) (Sweden)
SDS	*Sozialistische Deutsche Studentenbund* (German Socialist Student League) (FRG)
SED	*Sozialistische Einheitspartei Deutschlands* (Socialist Unity Party of Germany) (GDR)
SFIO	*Section française de l'internationale ouvrière* (French Section of the Socialist International)
SHB	*Sozialistische Hochschulbund* (Socialist College League) (FRG)
SKDL	*Suomen Kansan Demokraattinen Liitto* (Finnish People's Democratic League)
SKP	*Suomen Kommunistinen Puolue* (Finnish Communist Party)
SOL	*Sosialistinen opiskelijaliitto* (Socialist Student Association) (Finland)
SPD	*Sozial-demokratische Partei Deutschlands* (Social Democratic Party of Germany) (FRG)
SSV	*Sveriges socialdemokratiska vänsterparti* (Social-Democratic Left Party) (Sweden)
SUN	*Socialistische Uitgeverij Nijmegen* (Socialist Publishing House, Nijmegen) (Netherlands)
TUC	Trades Union Congress (UK)
UCD	*Unión del Centro Democratico* (Union of the Democratic Centre) (Spain)
UCS	Upper Clyde Shipbuilders (UK)
UDP	*Union démocratique et progressiste* (Democratic and Progressive Union) (Belgium)

UGT	*Unión General de Trabajadores* (General Workers' Union) (Spain)
UIL	*Unione Italiana del Lavoro* (Italian Labour Union)
USO	*Unión Sindical Obrera* (Workers' Trade Union) (Spain)
VPK	*Vänsterpartiet kommunisterna* (Left Party Communists) (Sweden)

Introduction
The End of Bolshevism in Western Europe

Michael Waller and Meindert Fennema

The publication of this book highlights the recently celebrated seventieth anniversary of the October Revolution that brought the Bolsheviks to power in Russia.

It is ironical that today, at a time when the Soviet Union's image and standing in the world are possibly better than they have ever been since those revolutionary days, the fortunes of so many of the Western European communist parties should be in a state of crisis. It is ironical, too, that many of these parties, which have always set so much store by organizational unity, should today be beset by factional strife to at least the same extent as their bourgeois counterparts. This book examines the current malaise within Western European communism. It will be seen that this malaise has many sources: declining electoral performances, frequently ambivalent relationships with the Soviet Union, and a tendency towards organizational splits and strains are in fact but symptoms of a much broader and deeper phenomenon. Since the moment when these parties were born, in a multiple birth, of the division in the European Left brought about by the Russian revolution and formation of the Comintern, the political landscape in which they operate has changed out of all recognition. They have therefore had a problem of adaptation, and it will be seen in the chapters that follow that some communist parties have had greater success in adapting than have others.

It is worth spelling out some of the more prominent features of the problem of adaptation, since this will serve to highlight the themes that will be found to recur in the studies presented here of the experiences of individual parties.

First of all, these parties have operated very much in an international context, and have had to take account of international factors much more than have their social democratic rivals. This has introduced complexities into their political stances that are all too familiar, but it has also aggravated the problem of adaptation. It is true that 'internationalism' has been interpreted rather narrowly as support for Soviet positions and Soviet ways of doing things, and it has proved difficult to escape this orientation, given the massive predominance of the Soviet Union, the country of the Great October, in the international movement to which these parties belong. But the tension between national and international goals and orientations, and the tendency since the turning-point of 1956 for the former set to be favoured, is amply illustrated in these pages.

Secondly, these are relatively old parties, old enough for the myths and practices of one generation to be a burden on successor generations. This is a problem for any political organization, but it has been compounded in the case of the communist parties by the defensive position into which they have in general been forced in the period since the Second World War. The tendency to withdraw 'into the fortress' – to quote a phrase that will appear frequently below – has invested the past with a certain aura, and has led often to a fear of change. When the future and the present are uncertain, the past becomes a source of comfort and support.

That the present is so uncertain is a third feature of the problem of adaptation that has faced the Western European communist parties. And this is a most surprising thing for parties that have a radical vocation and a view of the movement of history that is total in its scope. Around them, since the 1960s, has arisen a whole series of movements, parties and groups that share their radical vocation, but which the communist parties have, until recently and with rare exceptions, either ignored or execrated.

There are three reasons why this should be so. One is precisely the fact that the communist parties' view of the world is all-embracing. Since it provides its own answer to – along with everything else – problems of peace, the ecology, gender and ethnicity, there has been a tendency to write off external groups espousing these causes. The second is the 'class reductionism' of the communist parties' – that is, their tendency to subordinate all these problems, and the movements that grew up around them, to the class struggle and in particular to the vanguard organization of the class struggle. And thirdly, the communist parties of Western Europe are quite simply less radical than their basic philosophy would suggest, and in many, if not most, cases they have aided a corporatist process that necessarily casts them in the role of defenders of existing structures, and their policies tend to be derived from this stance. The state and the party systems of Europe stand high in their scale of values.

For these reasons, and no doubt others, the Western European communist parties have so far in most cases allowed a rising tide of extra-parliamentary contestation to pass them by, and the situation is exacerbated by the reinvigoration of the Trotskyist version of the Marxist–Leninist tradition. They have thus come, with few exceptions, to be hemmed in within an increasingly variegated European Left, 'going it alone' not only against the bourgeois political parties (including their long-standing social democratic rivals) but also against a more radical strand of Marxism–Leninism and even, in many cases, against new social groups and movements that are serving increasingly as the foremost channel of protest in Western – and indeed Eastern – Europe.

The Western European communist parties are unlikely to founder, individually or collectively, as a result of their present malaise. The crisis of adaptation through which most of them are passing has in some cases involved, for example, a move towards the 'new social movements', whilst certain parties, most notably the Italian, dealt rather successfully in the post-war period with problems of adaptation. But the malaise raises rather acutely the question of what 'communism' is to mean in Western European circumstances in the closing years of the twentieth century. It is open to any party that sports the Marxist label to claim to be basing its policies on a goal of the 'radical transformation of society'; in fact it is bound to do so. It is a goal, however, that can be interpreted in a number of ways. The question facing the Western European communist parties is to what extent, in addressing themselves to an acute problem of adaptation, they can produce an interpretation that is distinctive from that of their social democratic rivals, and alive to new currents of protest.

In this book the experience of individual communist parties is examined. First, however, a treatment is offered of one particular aspect of the problem of adaptation that the communist parties of Western Europe face. In one area the past appears to weigh particularly heavily – that of party organization. True, the deadening influence of traditional democratic centralism on today's parties is probably exaggerated. The Italian party has managed to combine organizational flexibility with a loose interpretation of democratic centralist norms. The material presented in this book will show, too, that the much-proclaimed organizational uniformity of communist parties accommodates very considerable variation. But there is no doubt that, in general, the practices associated with democratic centralism have worked in such a way as to enable party leaderships to resist challenges to their own power and to the orthodoxy that sustains that power. There is a paradox in the fact that democratic centralism has been defended with the argument that it is needed in order to react swiftly and effectively to events; yet by the way in which it works it acts at the same time as a barrier to change. To that extent adaptation, for communist parties, is no simple matter. It is to the practices associated with democratic centralism, and to the psychology that lies behind those practices, that we turn in the opening chapter.

Before that, however, it should be made clear what the term 'Bolshevism' means in this book. From their origins in the Russian revolutionary movement, and in the revolution itself, the ideas and practices of the Bolsheviks, in the formation of which Lenin played a crucial role, have been carried forward as a broad tradition that has constituted the dominant strand of the communist movement. Bolshevism has been defined, in historical terms, by the task that it has performed, which has been to mobilize the masses for the making of insurrectionary revolution, and for the subsequent process of national development that ruling communist parties have typically addressed. If it was Lenin who presided over the creation of Bolshevism, the Stalinist period in the Soviet Union gave it a particular form in which popular mobilization was attended by abuses of power that have become legendary.

Those abuses of power have overshadowed what was distinctive about the Leninist period, and have made it difficult for innovative spirits in communist parties to restore a form of popular mobilization that is clear of the trammels of Stalinism. The parties of Western Europe now broadly acknowledge the problems that Stalinism has caused them. The question that this book addresses is whether there is any sense in which Bolshevism offers them, as it were, a ledge to withdraw to in their retreat – fitful, and not universal – from Stalinism. Or is there no ledge, and does any retreat from Stalinism lead to a slide either into social democracy or into the abyss?

It would be appropriate in this introduction also to give some advance indication of the key themes that will emerge from the chapters on the individual parties. There is, first, the tension already mentioned between proposals for an increasing integration into the pluralist party systems of Western Europe on the one hand, and on the other the countervailing tendency to hold back from accepting the full implications of that strategy and to withdraw into familiar and traditional strongholds of a local, syndicalist and cultural nature, together with a reaffirmation of the link with the Soviet Union. But secondly, it will be seen that, with a few important exceptions that prove the rule, those strongholds have been undermined, in particular by the shrinking of the traditional working class constituency of these parties in heavy industry. Thirdly, a major shift in the thinking and the assumptions of the Left in Western Europe, especially among the young, took place during and after the 1960s, bringing often volatile new forces – most notably students, and workers in state-dependent sectors – into the communist parties, but bringing also a problem of relationships with new social movements concerned with issues of peace, the ecology, gender and ethnicity, problems that were in part a matter of party structures and in part a matter of attitudes.

If any particular period is worth noting in this story it is the 1970s, when so many of these issues came to a head. It was then, too, that the Spanish, Portuguese and Greek parties emerged into legality. If the experience of these three parties has seemed at times untypical, it is in good part because their circumstances have themselves been untypical, and it will be seen in the chapters devoted to those parties how their individual stories add an important perspective to the more general canvas of the recent development of European communism, of which they constitute an important part.

It was in the 1970s, too, that there emerged another key theme – Eurocommunism – which might appear to be less prominent than expected in this book. If that is the case, it has not been a matter of editorial intervention. The authors of the various chapters have given their accounts using the terminology and the concepts that are current in the parties that they deal with, and Eurocommunism has been much more a term used in works about communism than in the parlance of the communist parties themselves. In a very general sense, the term encapsulates the forces for change within Western European communism. Over-written in Western commentary when the term first appeared, Eurocommunism has never had very precise contours, and apart from a few summit meetings of party leaders and a sprinkling of international conferences (involving parties from every continent) it has never had an inter-party organizational existence. In a few cases, however, the term has been prominent in the internal life of the communist parties treated in this book – for example in the Spanish party in the 1970s, and in the British party more permanently.

The term 'Eurocommunism' is notoriously vague in its reference. It will be found in this book to indicate a strategy along three dimensions. First, and foremost, it has referred to a process wherein communist parties have taken their distance from the Soviet Union. Secondly, it has connoted an acceptance of pluralism before and after the achievement of a radical transformation of society, and has thus involved the abandoning of the notion of the dictatorship of the proletariat. Thirdly, it has referred in general to a greater integration into the contemporary political processes of Western Europe, as opposed to a sectarian, 'go it alone' policy. It is thus best seen as a strategic rather than an organizational matter, a set of assumptions that are shared, in very broad terms, by one side in the general debate that has gripped almost all the communist parties of Western Europe in recent years.

It did, however, have at least two important organizational aspects. The first was that for some communists, integration into the party political life characteristic of Western Europe meant not only accepting the principle of alternation in office, but also a degree of change in the way communist parties had so far run their internal affairs. The second was quite simply that the whole debate about strategy had to be conducted within the framework of the traditional organizational norms. Yet those norms, in the view of increasing numbers within the communist parties, acted as a brake on change, and made it extraordinarily difficult to adapt to new circumstances. At the heart of all the problems of modernization and adaptation that communist parties have had in so many countries lie organizational practices associated with the 'Leninist principle of democratic centralism'. It is to a treatment of those practices and of that concept that we first turn.

1 Democratic Centralism: the Costs of Discipline

Michael Waller

In terms of twentieth-century history, communism and democratic centralism have been inseparable. In a sense they define each other: the touchstone of a communist party is whether it subscribes to the 'Leninist principle of democratic centralism', yet democratic centralism, as it has normally been understood, can only really be defined by the way in which communist parties behave and operate. There is a very simple reason why this should be so – the predominance of the Soviet Union in a world-wide movement that it was able, for a quarter of a century, to lead and to shape. It was the Communist Party of the Soviet Union (CPSU) which, in the aftermath of the Russian revolution, and as a corollary of that event, created the Comintern, and it was the Comintern that transmitted to a world-wide community of communist parties their strategies and their organizational norms. The content of those strategies and the nature of those organizational norms followed the evolution of the Soviet Union itself – an evolution in which a revolutionary force used its political muscle, and arrogated to itself the authority, to drag from backwardness to modernity Europe's largest nation.

The term 'democratic centralism' made its entry into the vocabulary of communism in the revolutionary year of 1905, when it seemed to the Russian Marxists to be at last possible to escape from clandestinity and to introduce truly democratic procedures into the Russian Workers' Social-Democratic Party.[1] After the revolution, although democratic centralism was not invoked to any great extent at the turning-point of the Bolsheviks' tenth party congress in 1921, the term had appeared during the preceding two years in two particular contexts. First, the members of an opposition group that was concerned that party life was atrophying under the pressures of the Civil War styled themselves the Democratic

Centralists in an attempt, by invoking the term, to rally the party to democratic practices that they judged to be under threat. On the other hand, the term was insisted upon in the 21 conditions for acceptance of a party into the Comintern with a different emphasis – on strict 'almost military' discipline. In its infancy, then, and at the point of the creation of the Western European communist parties, the term meant rather different things to different people. It is worth noting, also, that it did not at that time have the resonance within the movement that it has since acquired.

When 'the Leninist principle' appeared for the first time in the CPSU's statutes in 1934, it had come to be associated, in practice, with the organizational norms of that party and of the parties of the Comintern. By that time the Marxist movement had passed through a number of crises and schisms. The 'revisionist' controversy of the turn of the century had been eclipsed by the triumphant assertion of Leninism in the Russian revolution, the corollary of which was the splitting of the Left in Western Europe – at which point the parties that retained the 'social democratic' label had ceased to emphasize any Marxist heritage. The next rift occurred at the heart of the Bolshevik party itself, with the defeat of the Trotskyist opposition in the Soviet Union. From that time onwards, Trotskyisr was to claim the mantle not only of Marx, but of Lenin too. Like the Democratic Centralists before them (for whom Trotsky himself had shown little sympathy), the Trotskyists were to uphold a notion of democratic centralism that they claimed to have atrophied in the Bolshevik party af r 1921.

From the close of the Second World War the communist movement has expanded widely and relatively rapidly. The expansion has, again, been accompanied by schism, but this time the rifts have concerned states rather than individuals or groups. The resonance of such rifts within the movement has been great. The expulsion of the Yugoslavs from the Cominform and the Sino-Soviet split both had a clarity and a finality that have endured. Departures from the established Soviet orthodoxy on the part of the non-ruling communist parties have lacked that clarity and finality, but they have none the less been significant in some cases – for example in the case of the radical parties of the Latin American Left that have emerged as dynamic rivals to the ex-Comintern parties of that continent, and in the case of Eurocommunism. Diversity, in fact, seems to have invaded a movement that once was remarkable for its uniformity.

The fact of the matter is that this question of whether uniformity or diversity is uppermost in communist organization has to be treated with great care, since communist organization exhibits both diversity and a remarkable uniformity, depending on which area of organizational life is under discussion. There is wide variation, for example, in the economic organization sponsored by ruling parties. But as far as communist parties themselves are concerned, what is most striking is the family resemblance in the way in which they are organized, and in the views that they hold –both ruling and non-ruling parties – of their proper relationship with society. They themselves are aware of this resemblance; they take pride in it, and when the dust of schism has settled, these traditional organizational forms are revealed to be still in place.

There can be no doubt that the communist parties have drawn considerable strength, during their formative years, from this uniformity, underpinned as it has been by a sense of common purpose and of the political importance of doctrine, and by a very particular set of organizational arrangements. One of the aims of this chapter is to portray these arrangements, and to examine the problems to which, over time, they have given rise. But it has also the second, and complementary aim, of showing that this uniformity was a long time in the making and has never been complete. Moreover, the world has moved on since the days of the Comintern. The attitude of the Western European communist parties to their home environment has evolved, as has their relationship with the Soviet Union. The Soviet Union itself has changed to a quite considerable extent. Interrelationships and mutual awareness among the nations of Europe as a whole are very different from what they used to be.

In addition, the Western European communist parties are old, as political parties go, and have operated in widely diverse historical and cultural settings. It is one thing to associate communist parties with resistance to change; it is quite another to assume that they are totally immune to change, or each severally incapable of independent development. Whether, or to what extent, each of them can succeed in adapting to changing circumstances is the question to which this book is addressed. This chapter must therefore consider not only the famed uniformity of traditional democratic centralism, but also examples of variation.

There is particular value in taking the Western European communist parties as a case study for these inquiries. The emphasis so far in studies of communism has been above all on the Soviet Union and to a lesser extent on the other ruling parties. This is understandable. Success in revolution gave the Bolsheviks an overwhelming authority in the Marxist movement. With two minor exceptions, the Soviet Union was for a quarter of a century the single established bastion of Marxist – Leninist socialism, and the organizational forms that the CPSU developed during this period became a major point of reference for communist parties. As other communist parties came to power they shared the privileged status of the Soviet Union as the point of focus for studies of communism.

Again with one or two exceptions, these parties, including the CPSU, have come to power in agrarian societies; that is, they have shared a predicament of economic and cultural disadvantage. In addressing themselves to the ruling parties students of communism have been studying the politics of development, in a setting of the struggle of poorer nations against richer. To that extent – and despite the misgivings of Africanists – Mozambique, Angola, even Ethiopia offer the analyst of communism more of the same.

The communist parties of Western Europe also in one sense offer more of the same, in that they have been so heavily influenced by the Comintern, and draw their identity from that. But on the other hand, their profound difference from the ruling parties in terms of the tasks that they face and of their cultural and economic environments should lead us to expect differences also in terms of their organizational behaviour. If we do not find significant differences, then we should expect either that they will emerge, or that these parties will face trouble and possible extinction through failure to adapt.

In order to grasp the particular value that communist parties attach to democratic centralism, it is important, first, to examine what those parties have understood by this cardinal term, and the political practices that have been associated with it.

The question of definition

In view of the frequency with which the concept of democratic centralism is invoked, of its symbolic power, and of the status that it is accorded by friend and foe of communism as the hallmark of communist political organization, it is disconcerting to find that there are very real difficulties in defining it. Within the Western European communist parties particularly, it is frequently defined as 'freedom of discussion, unity of action'. But this rule-of-thumb definition is not distinctive; it gives no indication in itself of the very particular relationship between discussion and action that has been characteristic of democratic centralism in practice.

Interestingly, the definitions set out in the statutes of the various parties offer little more. In most cases these formulations, examples of which are given in the appendix to this book, recommend political practices that conform to the basic notions of liberal democracy: they require accountability through an electoral system and through the revocability of elected representatives, they assert the majority principle, and they conjoin a degree of acceptance of executive authority that is not at all uncongenial to liberal democracy. It is this that enabled Jean Ellenstein to claim that no constitutional revision would be needed to give reality to the French party's statutes; and Althusser has made the same point.[2] The implication is that the statutes lack reality, and that, again, it is to prac- tice rather than to verbal definitions that one must turn in order to discover what the term 'democratic centralism' connotes.

From this point of view, an interview that Paul Laurent gave for *France nouvelle* in June 1977 is more illuminating.[3] As in the case of the party statutes, and of rule-of-thumb definitions (a version of which Laurent gives: 'an intense democratic life, confidence in the leadership, unity in the struggle'), democratic centralism is here associated with the most general democratic processes: 'to enable all communists to partici- pate actively and with political awareness in forming the party's policies and in putting them into action'; 'democratic election'; 'information must circulate in the communist party as widely and as democratically as possible'. But a substantial part of Laurent's definition of democratic centralism if drawn quite simply from the organizational practices of the French Communist Party (*Parti communiste français*, PCF) and is a rationalization of those practices. It is practice that does the definitional filling in, telling us what form 'democratic elections' take and how con- gresses should be run, and leading Laurent to explain that 'between two congresses it is not normally possible for there to be a public expression of different points of view'.[4]

Practice is, in fact, ultimately the most satisfactory basis for a defin- ition of democratic centralism. And that being so, it is often through criticisms from within a party of the way in which it conducts its affairs that a clear understanding is to be had of what democratic centralism has meant in practice. Examples of such criticisms will appear below, but in the practice of communist parties, orthodox democratic centralism is best illustrated not by what it is, but by what it is not – that is, by its opposite or obverse – fractionalism. And fractionalism presents no problems of definition at all.[5]

The taboo on fractional activity has accompanied democratic centralism throughout that concept's history. The two are related as chaos to order, and indeed they are clearly envisaged in terms of chaos and order in what has become the orthodox interpretation of democratic centralism. Fractionalism means setting up an autonomous group in the party subject to a separate discipline, and the emergence of fractionalism in the demonology of the communist movement can be dated precisely to the Bolsheviks' tenth congress in 1921. The ban on fractional activity was to become, in the words of Ralph Miliband, the 'sacred cow' of orthodox communism.[6]

If fractionalism means organizing within the party, democratic centralism then means an emphasis on the collective, on unity and on discipline. The task of definition can then be carried further by enumerating the mechanisms that sustain this collective unity and discipline – an exercise that will be attended to below. Before that, however, a little more must be said on the subject of fractionalism.

First of all, factional strife is a problem for any political party, and any political party must set limits on it if it is to survive at all, let alone achieve its goals. The important question is what is to be the balance between centralism and democracy, and to what lengths the party is prepared to go in order to maintain any particular balance.

Soviet orthodoxy, transmitted in a first stage through the Comintern and in a later stage through the adoption of the Soviet model by the revolutionary elites of a number of less developed countries, clearly involves an unusually marked skew towards executive authority; and since a cardinal feature of that orthodoxy is that it in turn itself values orthodoxy, not much variation is to be expected. All the more interesting, therefore, are the cases among the Western European parties where a categorical ban on fractionalism has either not been pursued, or has been eroded. Thus, the Finnish party has for years managed to live in a state of permanent schism and in a sense to have institutionalized it. The Italian party's ritual invocations of democratic centralism suggest a continued subscription to the orthodox skew towards unity and discipline, yet that party secretes a number of clearly defined groups and alliances. The recent attention that Western European communist parties have been giving to radical groups concerned with issues of peace, ecology and women's liberation may be expected to produce further variation, and has already powerfully affected the Netherlands party.

Worth attention also is the range of political activities that a given party sees as fractional. The establishment of groups with a defined membership and leadership and with an independent programme is the primary target of the ban. At this end of the range there is little to separate a communist party from other political parties. More interesting are the cases where it is not clear that a group is involved at all, but only the expression of an opinion that is judged by the leadership to presage the formation of a group. Thus, in an extreme case the publication of an article or book can be seen as fractional activity: 'A text is a positive act and contrary to our statute. Its target is to contest the policy of the democratic movement which has been worked out at its congress, and to contest the movement's leadership. It is a fractional activity'.[7]

A third consideration requires that a matter of terminology be cleared up. 'Fractionalism' and 'fraction' derive from the Russian term *fraktsiya*, which was used at the Bolsheviks' tenth congress in 1921 in the motion and discussion 'on party unity', and the fractional activity in question has always meant separate organization within the party.[8]

Communist parties have also, however, been characteristically beset by rivalries between *factions*, in the sense of loose alliances within the party's leadership. Whilst these do indeed threaten to divide the party against itself in no uncertain way, they are not usually organized groups subordinated to a separate discipline, and so constitute a rather different phenomenon.

Space does not allow of a full treatment of the subject – nor, be it said, has it ever been fully analysed – but there appears to be a connection between the way in which orthodox democratic centralism works and a tendency for such factions to form. The party centre being the locus of all power and the fount of all doctrine, it is at the centre that contests over power and doctrine will take place. And just as the hierarchical way in which democratic centralism works converts the membership into a support column for the leadership, so it behoves any group or individual that sets out to challenge the leadership group to equip himself or herself with a following within the party, or to take advantage of any dissident forces that are known to exist. The result is a tendency for political life at the centre to resolve itself at times into a tussle between two rival factions. In this situation the 'cult of personality' becomes useful to the leadership group *as a whole*, to secure maximum stability and its own continuance in power.[9]

The best illustrations of such leadership factions are to be found in the history of the Soviet and Chinese parties – with the 'anti-party group' in the Soviet Union during the Stalin succession, and the 'Gang of Four' in China, being good examples of discomfited leadership factions. Strictly speaking, therefore, there is a distinction to be made between 'fractions' and 'factions' in communist politics, but both merit attention in any analysis of orthodox democratic centralism.

This way in which communist parties view fractional activity may serve as a useful introduction to a more positive presentation of democratic centralism, which can now be given.

Democratic centralism involves a set of political practices, but also a particular psychology. The psychology is one that puts a particularly high value on organizational unity. I have illustrated elsewhere how Soviet sources see the party (and in their case society too) as an organism, which is seen as being subject to good and ill health. Fractionalism is seen as a disease, a malfunctioning of the organism.[10]

This psychology informs, legitimates and explains the whole series of political practices associated with democratic centralism in the Soviet Union and in the Western European parties. It is most clear in the taboo on fractional activity; it invests the leadership with an authority that rests on far more than the majority principle; it correspondingly converts a minority into something *less* than a minority – into an 'opposition' that is associated first with blindness to the laws of history and secondly with treachery to the political and social organism. And it goes a long way to explaining why the communist parties of Western Europe have been so resistant to change.

Turning from the psychology to political mechanisms, the following features of the political life of the Western European communist parties are frequently associated with democratic centralism by both dissidents (who object to them) and by party spokesmen (who see most of them as being part of the party's historical identity):

1   The subordination of representative bodies to executive bodies; the limitation of party congresses and conferences to ratification of decisions previously arrived at elsewhere in the party's structure.
2   The prominence within the party of its paid professionals.
3   The control that the party leadership exercises over opportunities for the exchange of opinion, together with a deprecation of 'discussion clubs'.
4   The list system of elections, which allows for the representation of a broad cross-section of the party, but through a filtering of candidates.

These mechanisms represent the uncomfortable resolution of a sharp contradiction between the psychology of democratic centralism and the democratic procedures that are enshrined in the statutes of communist parties. Elections are held, but they are prevented from harming the collective well-being by a filtering of candidates which ensures that a broad cross-section of the party is represented; congresses are held, but if there are to be debates and squabbles, they must take place outside the congress. The collectivist psychology of democratic centralism requires that the question of who is to arrange the filtering of elections, and who is to set the final agenda for congresses is settled 'scientifically', and this has meant in practice by the party leadership, which speaks for the party, though the same composite mechanisms prevent the rank and file of the party from ensuring that the leadership is speaking for it. 'Scientific socialism' is a ghost in the machine in communist party organization, which remains spectre-like only until it is reduced – as Marx reduced the state – to actual people in actual functions.

It is essential for a communist party that history should speak. The question is how it is to do so. Orthodox democratic centralism cannot accept that history should speak through a clamour of discordant voices; but nor can the party leadership accept that, by drowning out all voices but its own, it is doing anything other than speaking for history.

This ability of the leadership to speak for the global interest and to enunciate a 'correct' policy, should be related to what was said above about the tendency for the internal political life of communist parties at the central level to resolve itself into factional struggles between a leadership and an 'anti-party group'. For he who controls the positions of power controls also the word, and can label his rivals renegades, archtraitors, scabs, opportunists, enemies of the people, and the rest of the repertoire of the communist demonology, and thus put them at a distinct political disadvantage.

The matter could be put in another way by saying that there are two modes of decision-making in communist parties. There are, first of all, those procedures that communist parties associate with 'bourgeois democracy' but make use of none the less, in the qualified way described above – elections (but filtered), congresses (which ratify but do not debate). The second mode is not based on formal procedures at all but on the assumption that there is only one proper outcome – that based on scientific socialism, on an understanding of the laws of history, which will enable decisions to be made that conduce to the common good and transcend the bickering of groups and individuals within society.[11]

This combination of two different modes for arriving at decisions explains also the pathological relation between 'renegades' and the party. Expulsions and resignations from the party have taken place in the 'democratic' mode. Those involved have remained active in the second mode, claiming, in fact, that they, rather than the party leadership, have drawn the proper conclusions from the basic tenets of Marxism–Leninism. Maintaining that they have already taken over the intellectual leadership, they have therefore concluded that sooner or later they would replace the party's leadership through the formal 'democratic' channels.

The party leaders, on the other hand, being the symbol of the sole truth in revolutionary matters, clearly cannot tolerate any competition in this area. The more fiercely the renegades cling to the fundamentals of Marxism–Leninism, the more they are considered the source of all evil, of false truth, which is the more dangerous because it so closely resembles the scientific analyses of the party itself. This struggle is fought in absolute terms; the party wants the total annihilation of its former members (ruling parties require physical annihilation, non-ruling parties only their political annihilation). On the other hand, the renegades, in general, go for the scalp of the party leader, who in their eyes is guilty of all the wrongdoings of the communist party in question.

This psychology and these practices have undoubtedly been a source of great organizational strength in certain kinds of situations. But there is no less doubt that they have made for extreme inflexibility, and have rendered it difficult for these parties to adapt to changing circumstances. In the words of MacEwen:

In practice, the insistence on lower bodies submitting to higher bodies and minorities to majorities, the outlawing of 'fractions' . . . and the obligation to fight for majority decisions made it impossible for the membership to change the party's policy or the leadership. All change had to come from the top downwards, and this explains why, even when changes are made in communist parties, they tend to be precipitate (often the result of belatedly recognizing previous mistakes) or too late, or both.[12]

The same point was made by Althusser in his broadside against the PCF's political norms in 1978.[13] The effect of such practices and of this psychology is well summed up by Eduard Kardelj, though this time with reference to the ruling League of Communists of Yugoslavia:

We communists must pose the question of how . . . we can overcome the historical practice . . . under which every political change imposed by the course of events in a socialist state, be it a change of government or of policies, is always attended by political disturbances reminiscent of a *coup d'état*.[14]

The definition of democratic centralism is then, by no means a straightforward matter. If precept is involved it is precept that has grown out of custom. That custom is by now well implanted; and custom is an intricate affair in which practices, attitudes and ritual are all intertwined. The problem of definition – finding answers to the question 'what is democratic centralism?' – cannot be tackled merely by lexicographically providing paraphrases nor by listing a series of practices that have come to be attached to the term. Also very much involved are mental associations that the term evokes, including the negative associations that attach to fractional activity.

It is worth considering, as a coda to this discussion of the definition of democratic centralism, one very important theoretical treatment – the view of the concept that Gramsci set down in his prison cell. Unlike definitions encountered above, this one is not a simple rationalization of the way in which communist parties order their organizational affairs, but amounts, in fact, to a philosophy of democratic centralism. It is also, of course, an indigenous Western European presentation.

Gramsci's view revolves around the basic concept of *organicità*. *Organicità* expresses on the one hand the unity and cohesion of the revolutionary movement, and on the other the movement's forward drive. For *organicità* to prosper, both cohesion and forward drive must be maintained:

Organicità can only be found in democratic centralism which is, so to speak, centralism in movement – i.e. a continual adaptation of the organization of the real movement, a matching of thrusts from below with orders from above, a continuous insertion of elements thrown up from the depths of the rank and file into the solid framework of the leadership apparatus which ensures continuity and the regular accumulation of experience.[15]

Gramsci opposes democratic centralism to 'bureaucratic centralism', when 'the leading group is saturated' and turns into 'a narrow clique which tends to perpetuate its selfish privileges by controlling or even stifling the birth of oppositional forces'.[16]

There is, in Gramsci's idea of *organicità*, a notion of a collective interest, and indeed a collective will, that transcends individual interests and wills. This is important, in suggesting that it is not necessary to father the high value put on collective unity in Western European communist parties entirely on Soviet collectivist thinking and practice. Western European communism itself contains this strand of thought, which has, of course, an earlier manifestation in the ideas of Rousseau.

The historical dimension

Ever since the turning-point of 1956, the Western European communist parties have been engaged in a scrutiny of the Stalinist period and of the chain of events that led from the splitting of the European Left in and around 1920, through the Manichean period of monolithic communism and its unsettling demise, to the emergence of Eurocommunism. This process of introspection has naturally concerned the practices that go on under the rubric of democratic centralism.

The decisive factor in communist history since the Russian revolution has been the confluence of Marxism–Leninism with the search for political and economic independence (or merely the search for legitimacy) by the elites of less-developed countries. An element of the politics of development is clearly discernible in the political forms that the Bolsheviks adopted in the early years of the Soviet regime, but it was powerfully enhanced in the Stalinist period. The impact of this on the Western European communist parties has been a complex matter, since it was the Soviet Union, through the Comintern, that endowed them with their organizational practices. For present purposes it is enough to note that by 1956 these Western European parties had realized the problems that the great detour of communism into the developing world was creating for them. The problems, given the geography and the history of the thing, appeared to them in the form of their relationship with the Soviet Union–a perception that their opponents were only too happy to exploit. No treatment of the transmission of Soviet democratic centralism to the communist parties of Western Europe can afford to ignore the implications of this aspect of the history of communism.

The conventional view that these parties acquired their political forms through the agency of the Comintern is, of course, fundamentally correct. But the manner of that transmission, the period of time over which it took place and the moments during that period that were the most decisive are all questions that are often too little understood. The conventional story of strains and debates around 1920 followed by a process of Bolshevization accompanying the upheavals caused by the internal dispute in the Soviet Union in the mid-1920s is also substantially correct, but again requires refinement. In the account given here, a particular emphasis will be suggested – a reordering of our perceptions of communism in the 1920s and 1930s. The account will make connections rather than offer new evidence. The facts that support it lie in the recent history of the movement and in the recent historiography of the Soviet Union.

Two developments in particular force a new perspective on the 1920s and 1930s. The first is the re-emergence of Trotskyism after 1956. The second is the increasing attention that is being given to the five years that were decisive in the shaping of Soviet political forms – the period from 1928 to 1932, when the politics of development were finally instituted.

A simple chronology will serve as a framework for what follows:

1917	Russian revolution.
1920	The second congress of the Comintern stipulates the '21 conditions' for acceptance of a party into that organization.
1924	Comintern's fifth congress; Trotskyists outcast.
1928–32	First five-year plan; Stalinism takes on its definitive form.
1956 and after	The Western European communist parties rethink the path followed since 1920; Trotskyism re-emerges.

If the decisive moment in the formation of the Stalinist system of politics was 1928–32, are we to continue to see the period 1920–5 as the crucial period in the formation of the politics of the communist parties of Western Europe? Is there a distinction to be made between the 'Bolshevization' of the earlier period and the Stalinization of the latter? These are aspects of the larger question that will now be addressed: how and when was democratic centralism transmitted to the Western European communist parties?

It would be as well to start the discussion by returning to those features of the life of the Western European communist parties that are associated with democratic centralism and which were noted above. It is reasonable to attribute the 'absolute verticality' of democratic centralism in the Western European communist parties, together with the prominent role played by the apparatus within the party, to a transfer of norms that the CPSU acquired during the rigours of its construction drive.

Yet historians more often date the transposition to the process of 'Bolshevization' of 1924–5.

There is, in fact, no conundrum here. It was not a matter of Western Europe's communist parties acquiring the CPSU's political norms in a single package once and for all. The process of transposition was a continuous one. Crudely, what happened was that, through the agency of the Comintern, these parties *followed the evolution* of Soviet democratic centralism. Borrowing a term from the economists, they were indexed to it. The major turning-points of this evolution are listed above: the splitting of the Left in and around 1920 (the date of the Comintern's second congress); the impact of the defeat of the Trotskyist opposition; and the final formation of the Stalinist political system in 1928–32. It was only when Stalin had risen to a position of supremacy in the Soviet Union in 1929 that Soviet control over the parties and the policies of the Comintern became total.[17] Only certain points of interest in this story can be treated here.

First, the initial repercussions of the 21 conditions of 1920 were, of course, momentous in terms of the choice that socialist parties of the time had to make. But despite the call for 'iron discipline bordering on military discipline' in the 21 conditions[18] it was some time before affiliating parties were brought, or brought themselves, to conform with Bolshevik practice. Despite the rigour of the campaign to base party organization on cells in factories, by 1931 only one in 23 members of the Communist Party of Great Britain was enrolled in a cell, whilst in Czechoslovakia the percentage of members in cells actually fell by two-thirds between 1926 and 1930.[19] In 1924 the PCI was still split into three quite distinct factions. In the PCF, in 1925 and 1926 party members were not only contributing to the dissident *Bulletin communiste* and *Révolution prolétarienne*, but were even serving on the editorial boards of these journals. And in 1925 Pyatnitsky was chiding the CPGB and the CPF for having no paid full-time officials.[20]

But if the process of transposition of Soviet norms was a long and gradual one, and was in some areas widely resisted – particularly the insistence that the party be organized in cells – it was helped along precisely by the crises and splits listed above. Already the 21 conditions had caused socialists to take up a position; those who sought affiliation were by that fact predisposed to conform to Bolshevik practice. At the time of the Comintern's fifth congress, the nervousness caused by the rift in the international movement led to further pressure either to conform or to face expulsion. The Conference on Organization, held in Moscow in 1925, is a mark of the tightening of discipline at this time.[21] Then, after 1928 and especially in the 1930s, the Western European communist parties were subjected to the same stringent discipline that was being exacted of the membership of the CPSU, and indeed of all Soviet citizens.

Finally, if this complex story throws up relatively late examples of lingering diversity, it also presents cases of very early reproduction in Western Europe of the psychology that lies behind Soviet democratic centralism, as is illustrated by these words of a French Communist:

In our party, which the revolutionary struggle has not yet completely purged of its old social-democratic deposit, the influence of personalities still plays too great a role . . . It is only through the destruction of all petty-bourgeois survivals of the individualist 'I' that we shall form the anonymous iron cohort of French Bolsheviks.[22]

A second point of interest in the process by which democratic centralism was transmitted to other parties concerns the way in which the revolutionary current ran not westwards into Europe, but into the countries of the developing world. In the debates concerning the Trotskyist opposition it can be seen how a contradiction had emerged between the party as government and the party as agent of revolution. Since 1917, and particularly since 1921, the CPSU had undergone powerful changes that stemmed from its governmental role. The Western European parties did not have to link support for Soviet power to an unconditional imitation of the CPSU's political practices, for they were not subjected to the pressures of government. That they did so, fatefully, is a mark, firstly, of the overwhelming authority that the Bolsheviks enjoyed as a result of success in revolution and, secondly, of their equally impressive success in setting up an authoritative international organization – itself, with its organizational norms, an illustration of the development of orthodox democratic centralism.

What could not possibly have been foreseen at the time was that Bolshevism was indeed to be a revolutionary force, but in the very different framework of poor nations against rich, of the world against the West – a framework in which insurrectionary revolution and a military form of political organization adapted to the tasks of national construction in an unlettered and relatively poor society had a logic that was sure to wrong-foot the communist parties of Western Europe in the end.

By the time this logic became clear, the extension of their support for the Soviet Union to include an imitation of the CPSU's practices had led them into something of an impasse. It had also left the field open for a revolutionary tendency to arise in Western Europe in the 1950s around the figure of Trotsky that could be critical of the Soviet Union, could condemn the CPSU's political practices since 1921 and could invoke a concept of democratic centralism based upon the practices of the Bolsheviks before the exercise of governmental power and the strains of a developmental drive perverted those practices. What is surprising is that it took so long for this revival of Trotskyism to take place.

Thirdly, having in this manner attached themselves to the CPSU's interpretation of democratic centralism, the Western European communist parties then underwent the process of Stalinization that affected their mentor in the years from 1928, and were caught up in the purges of the 1930s and in the tergiversations of Soviet foreign policy which they duly endorsed until the Comintern, having become an embarrassment to Soviet policies, was abolished in 1943. It is probably to this period that the full development of orthodox democratic centralism should be dated. Borkenau puts it in strong terms:

Between 1929 and 1934 the communist parties finally and definitely transformed themselves into quasi-military organizations ready to obey anything. The structure did not change: at the top a bureaucracy from which every single man likely to oppose orders had been weeded out; in the middle a small stratum with an absolute unquestioning faith in every order; at the bottom a shifting mass . . . They had become an obedient army of crusaders.[23]

The question that then arises is what change has taken place since that period.

It is a standard criticism made of their parties by dissident Western European communists that democratic centralism, by its very operation, makes change difficult to propose and to implement. None the less, there has been change, and there is today a degree of variation in the political practices of these parties.

The problem lies in determining how much of what has changed concerns the idea of democratic centralism itself. But it can safely be said that the closer one approaches that notion's core – the psychology and the particular mechanisms previously outlined – the less the change that has actually occurred.

Thus there has been change, for example, in attitudes to the Soviet Union. This affects some parties more than others, and indeed is one of the criteria according to which the label 'Eurocommunist' is attributed. The extreme case is that of the Italian Communist Party which declared in 1981 that the 'phase of socialist development that began with the October Revolution has exhausted its propulsive force'[24], a sally that did not have the cataclysmic effect that might be expected, but has served to mark off the leadership's position from that of Cossutta's pro-Moscow strand in the party. There has also been a change in relations between communist parties and their 'front' organizations, particularly in the trade union field. Many parties also have attempted to shake off a reputation for secrecy by making their operations more transparent. In the British party, for example, local branches have for some time opened some of their meetings to interested members of the public, and in a move that caused no little stir, the French Communist Party permitted a pair of journalists to explore, through interviews and visits, the internal life of the party – an exercise that resulted in the publication of a substantial book.[25] Finally, there has been a widespread adjustment of the traditional rhetoric: the doctrine of the dictatorship of the proletariat has almost universally been abandoned, and certain parties have dropped the term 'Leninist' in self-description.

But when it comes to the actual mechanisms of democratic centralism, change has not been great, and the point of interest is that it has occurred at all, since even slight change, in the situation of strain and intro-spection that afflicts the Western European communist parties at present, must be seen as symptomatic, as a possible harbinger of more significant change.

Of all the Western European parties the PCI is usually offered as the case that has proved the most open to change. It has abandoned the system whereby communist candidates were adopted by imposition from the centre in a secret process based upon the candidate's 'biography'; it has abolished the 'cell' structure of the party, leaving the section as the basic organizational unit; and it has allowed clearly demarcated *correnti* to air their views in the party press.[26] Those who still assume that democratic centralism spells uniformity with Soviet practice might reflect on the election of Alessandro Natta as General Secretary of the PCI by a show of hands in the Central Committee, with a recorded vote (227 for, none against, 11 abstentions).

It is, however, admitted by many commentators, including Gianfranco Pasquino in his contribution to this volume (chapter 2), that considerable impediments to a full democratization of party life in the PCI still remain. Nor is it clear that the PCI is very far ahead of certain other parties in its moves towards developing greater democracy. The material presented in this book – on the Swedish, Netherlands and other parties –will document this. The abandoning of the cell structure, for example, has been fairly common. Nor is voting by a show of hands in the central committee necessarily a better guarantee of democracy than a secret ballot – as the discussion of Mikhail Gorbachev's speech of January 1987 in the Soviet case made clear.

Change, then, at the heart of orthodox democratic centralism has been neither widespread nor deep, but it has occurred. Moreover, a preoccupation with the present should not be allowed to eclipse a more general evolution that has been taking place since Stalin died, and which is not often remarked. One does not have to be very old to remember that there was once a whole vocabularly of deviations and the party line that dominated the discourse of the Western European communist parties, just as it dominated that of the CPSU. It has now more or less vanished from the scene.

Conclusion

In 1924 Ramsey MacDonald said: 'Communism as we know it has nothing practical in common with us. It is a product of Tsarism and of war mentality'.[27] In 1920 Osinskii, a member of the Democratic Centralist opposition in the infant Soviet Union had remarked: 'We do not need militarization [during the Civil War] because within our civilian apparatus there is an organic gravitation towards military methods of organization'.[28] Althusser in 1978, as noted above, claimed that everything in the PCF happens as if it were 'closely modelled on the apparatus of the bourgeois state and on the military apparatus'.[29]

Democratic centralism has been defined in various ways, but, more importantly, it has served various purposes. At the point of its origins in 1905 it acknowledged the dawning in Russia of a chance to organize freely for political ends. That chance proved illusory; and the history of the concept was to be shaped by the pressures to which the Bolshevik party was subjected after its accession to power. The authoritarian practices associated with the concept in the Stalinist system, and the psychology of unity and solidarity that informed those practices were to prove productive as further communist parties came to power in other less-developed countries.

The transposition of the concept to the Western European communist parties through the agency of the Comintern led to a dissonance between that psychology and those practices on the one hand, and the political cultures of Western Europe on the other. Despite that dissonance and despite a certain degree of change in the political practices that are conducted under the rubric of democratic centralism, the communist parties of Western Europe still exhibit a striking degree of uniformity in their political practices. These practices are an important part of their identity: they are also a source of problems today for these parties. It remains to be seen whether an awareness of these problems and of the factors from which they spring, will lead to further and more significant change. Should this happen, the history of the concept of democratic centralism, and also the very statutes that the Western European communist parties have drafted for themselves, offer many points of reference for a renovation of the concept.

Notes

1   I have drawn throughout this chapter on my *Democratic Centralism; an Historical Commentary* (Manchester University Press, Manchester, 1981). For the origins of the concept of democratic centralism, see pp. 21–30.
2   *Le Monde*, 17 June 1978 and 6 April 1978. See Appendix II for the rules of four communist parties.
3   Paul Laurent, 'Oui, le centralisme démocratique', *France nouvelle*, 6 June 1977.
4   Ibid., p. 9.
5   Waller, *Democratic Centralism*, p. 38 et passim.
6   *Socialist Register* (1976) pp. 58 ff.
7   *Le Monde*, 1 June 1978. (The source is Catala of the PCF.)
8   The wording in the motion 'on the unity of the party' at the Bolsheviks' tenth congress was: 'the appearance of groups with special platforms and with the ambition to form in some degree a unit and to establish their own group discipline'.
9   This is the view of J. Arch Getty, *The Origins of the Great Purges* (Cambridge University Press, Cambridge, 1985), p. 205.
10 Waller, *Democratic Centralism*, p. 65.
11 The greater part of this and the following two paragraphs has been contributed by Meindert Fennema.
12 Malcolm MacEwen, 'The Day the Party had to Stop', in *Socialist Register* (1976), p. 37.
13 Louis Althusser, 'Ce qui ne peut plus durer dans le parti communiste', *Le Monde*, 25–28 April 1978.
14 Quoted in Dennison Rusinow, *The Yugoslav Experiment, 1945–1974* (Hurst, London, 1977), p. 216.
15 Quentin Hoare and Geoffrey Nowell-Smith, *Selections from the Prison Notebooks of Antonio Gramsci* (Lawrence and Wishart, London, 1971).
16 Ibid., p. 168.
17 J. W. Friend, 'The Roots of Autonomy in West European Communism', *Problems of Communism*, vol. XXIX, no. 5, 1980, p. 29; Jules Humbert-Droz, *De Lénine à Staline* (La Baconnière, Neuchâtel, 1971), pp. 319–56.
18 The text of the '21 conditions' can be found in Jane Degras (ed.), *The Communist International (1919–1943): Documents* (Oxford University Press, London, 1956–65), pp. 169–72.
19 F. Borkenau, *The Communist International* (Faber and Faber, London, 1938), p. 361. The importance of the cell structure is brought out by Neil McInnes in his *The Communist Parties of Western Europe* (London: Oxford University Press, 1975), p. 100, where he claims that that structure 'constitutes the communist party'.
20 E. H. Carr, *A History of Soviet Russia. Socialism in One Country 1924–26* (Macmillan, London, 1964), vol. 3, pp. 365–6.
21 Ibid., p. 913.
22 Ibid., p. 148.
23 Borkenau, *The Communist International*, p. 375. See also Fernando Claudin, *The Communist Movement* (Penguin, Harmondsworth, 1985). Heinz Timmermann sees a 'second Bolshevization' of the European communist parties as having taken place after the Second World War, in the Cominform period: 'The Cominform Effects on Soviet Foreign Policy' *Studies in Comparative Communism*, vol. XVIII, no.1, 1985.

24 *L'Unità*, 30 December 1981.
25 André Harris and Alain Sédouy, *Voyage à l'intérieur du parti communiste* (Seuil, Paris, 1974).
26 See Ronald Tiersky, *Ordinary Stalinism: Democratic Centralism and the Question of Communist Political Development* (George Allen and Unwin, Boston, Mass., 1985), ch.5. According to Giorgio Ruffolo 'democratic centralism, that mixture of monolithism and secret, has kept its name and its form, but it has, in the PCI, lost its soul', *Politique aujourd'hui*, 13 (1986), p. 97.
27 Carr, *History of Soviet Russia*, p. 136.
28 Quoted in Roger Pethybridge, *The Social Prelude to Stalinism* (Macmillan, London, 1974), p. 116.
29 See n. 13.

2 Mid-Stream and under Stress
The Italian Communist Party

Gianfranco Pasquino

In contrast to most if not all Western European communist parties, the Italian Communist Party (*Partito Comunista Italiano*: PCI) has seemed to be in excellent shape up to very recent events. The PCI has scored important electoral successes. It has been able to channel into its ranks most of the dynamism developed by the students' and the workers' movements, and even the feminist movement. It has kept political recruitment of new members and cadres at a relatively high level and of a good quality. It has governed several local areas in a satisfactory and often innovative way.

On the other hand, most of these features seem to have a negative side to them as well. In the past, the PCI had always been able to consolidate its electoral gains and to move up. Its electoral performance since the impressive advance of 1976 (from 27.2 per cent in 1972 to 34.4 per cent) has shown several ups and downs (30.4 per cent in 1979, 29.9 per cent in 1983, 33.4 per cent in the European elections of 1984, 30.3 per cent in the administrative elections of 1985, 26.6 per cent in 1987). The PCI has also experienced difficulties in recruiting *leading* students' representatives, workers' organizers, militant feminists (it has even been obliged to accept the practice of 'double militancy' through which many women join specific organizations first and the PCI next). In order to keep its membership at a very high level, it has devoted ever greater efforts to recruitment campaigns, with mixed results even in terms of the quality of the emerging members. Finally, its overall performance at the local level, while better than other administrations that exclude the Communists, has recently been found lacking in élan and in new ideas.

All these elements have finally been reflected in a sense of impending crisis, of problems that are considered structural and no longer conjunctural. This is particularly so in the light of the succession to Berlinguer (party secretary for 12 years, but in charge of the party for 15 years), and the advanced age of the entire leadership group; and even more so since the Communists are finding more and more difficulty in creating governing alliances at the local level. As one intelligent commentator, the editor of the leading independent left-wing paper *la Repubblica*, Eugenio Scalfari, put it: the Communists risk becoming ever stronger as they become more isolated.

Indeed, the PCI has based its overall strategy of the parliamentary road to socialism on three legs.[1] A strong parliamentary presence, politico-administrative power at the local level, and a large trade union movement were considered the three legs on which the strategy of political and social alliances advocated by Togliatti could advance, as guided by the party. The party, obviously, was to provide a political synthesis among the different elements. Not simply because it was the repository of the scientific knowledge of socialism (according to the Marxist–Leninist approach), but because it was the collective intellectual (in Gramsci's view) capable of drawing on the ideas, the expertise and the energies of all the intellectuals surrounding it, and also because its democratic centralism allowed a sharp, precise, immediate implementation of decisions once reached.

The political synthesis has proved to be more and more difficult to provide. In order to understand why, we shall look in turn at the parliamentary representation of the PCI, at its local administrative role and at the nature of the trade union movement. Then attention will be focused on the party itself, its internal functioning, the tendencies of opinion within it and the different conceptions held by its members. Finally, we shall analyse the Communist political culture and its adequacy in changing times, with special reference to revisions in the party's strategy of political and social alliances. This ought to provide a broad, but coherent view of the transition from a classic communist party to a new form of radical reformist mass party in a Western European democracy.[2]

Parliamentary representation

Ever since Togliatti fulminated against the *prospettiva greca* – that is, the attempt by a communist party to acquire power through insurrection – the PCI has not only accustomed itself to parliamentary activities, it has thrived on them. The PCI never interpreted its role as simply that of a tribune, which had to protect and advocate the interests of the working class in the manner of the French Communist Party.[3] It always conceived of itself at the parliamentary level as a party committed to the formulation of a national policy, of laws intended to benefit the national community. For this reason, the party used its sizeable parliamentary representation at the same time to reward and promote gifted, hardworking, highly motivated militants and to recruit skilled legislators (who had already acquired some legislative experience at the local level in administrative positions).

In more recent times, however, the turning-point being the 1976 elections, Communist recruitment policy has changed both at the local level and at the parliamentary level. The advocacy of the 'historic compromise' in which the PCI's main partner was to be the Christian Democrats, implied, or was meant to effect, the attraction of more Catholic voters to the Communist ranks and anyway to dissipate the image of being an anti-clerical party (an image revived by the half-hearted stand taken by the PCI in favour of the law allowing divorce and against its repeal through a referendum). Therefore, for the first time, the PCI put up some prominent Catholics and duly elected them to the parliament. Since the PCI had also to dispel its image as an anti-institutional (or anti-régime) party, it recruited and elected to the parliament some representatives of those institutions: a few judges, a general, a prominent federalist. The experience of fishing for visible, competent, outstanding non-Communist candidates representing certain sectors of civil society was repeated at the local as well as at the national level in subsequent elections. So that there were, from 1983 to 1987 for instance, in the Chamber of Deputies and in the Senate two parliamentary groups of the *Sinistra Indipendente* (Independent Left), holding respectively 20 seats out of 630 and 18 out of 315, elected on the Communists' lists and with Communist votes, but enjoying financial autonomy and total independence in voting. The PCI's aim is, of course, to show that it is open to distinguished personalities, that it is indeed capable of attracting them, and that its parliamentary representation is better in quality than any other party's.

While it is difficult to evaluate the net gains for the PCI deriving from the experience of the Independent Left, this phenomenon is certainly unique among Western European communist parties. At the same time, the PCI has tried to open its 'official' ranks and lists to several groups and movements, to the new social and cultural sectors. The party has consistently striven for a larger female representation, again both at the local and at the national level. Its aim now is to reach the 50 per cent threshold, at least in local administrations, for candidates and, gradually, for elected representatives. In addition, the PCI has offered candidacies to representatives of environmental, anti-nuclear and pacifist groups. The electoral results have been mixed (for instance, in many local areas the

Greens have presented their own lists and elected their own candidates, in several cases drawing votes away from the PCI).

What seems particularly striking, and perhaps worrisome, is the tendency of the party to accept this sort of 'quota representation', which is leading in the direction of a fragmentation of the decision-making process. Indeed, female parliamentary representatives have created their own subgroup, exercising almost a veto power on issues affecting women's interests (potentially almost all). On other issues – industrial policy as against environmental interests, defence policy as against pacifist demands, labour relations as against workers' collective power –the party has fluctuated. In the end, it has not been able to produce a coherent decision and has suffered from its own attempt to represent too many diverse interests.

From the point of view of parliamentary representation (though one could extend these considerations to all kinds of elective representatives), the PCI has been extremely open, perhaps too much so. Even the great autonomy enjoyed by its two parliamentary groups (in the House and in the Senate) has in some cases produced tensions with the party leadership and shown that problems of coordination and political synthesis are plaguing a party that is looking for an appropriate balance between the role of an inflexible opposition and that of an active, capable, responsible participant in the decision-making process. Of course, as we shall stress later, the striking of an effective balance between these two roles becomes all the more complicated if, as was the case with the last government before the 1987 elections, the prime minister is an anticommunist socialist (an unprecedented situation).

Politico-administrative power

The functions of political and administrative power at the local level for a communist party are manifold. First of all, of course, power at that level indicates in a visible and tangible way the party's level of success in free competitive elections. It is a measure of its organizational capabilities. Secondly, it allows the party to offer its militants governing roles that are at the same time a coveted reward for the services performed for the party and thus are useful incentives for continued activity within the party organization, and a necessary training ground for greater responsibilities within the party hierarchy and in other elective offices. Finally, politico-administrative power constitutes a major opportunity for a communist party to test its governing capabilities, to legitimate itself in the eyes of even the most adamant opponents, to give them a taste of what a communist party is able and wants to do in terms of policies and reforms. All this, of course, in situations in which the PCI had to collaborate, albeit usually in the position of a senior partner, with the Socialists at the least.

By governing at the local level, in important areas of the country, the PCI has avoided the sense of isolation that might have been felt by the French Communists. The PCI had to get rid of simple approaches. It could reap several political benefits. It did so in a convincing way, so much so that by 1975 the local areas governed with Communist participation amounted to the most developed sections of Italy, including all major northern cities. However, since 1980 a creeping crisis has tarnished the image of the *giunte rosse* (red local governments) curtailed their innovative policies and in 1985 reduced their number and geographical extension to the old, solid Red Belt (Emilia–Romagna, Tuscany and Umbria).

While, of course, much of the responsibility for these developments must be laid at the door of Socialists who challenged their Communist partners with the express aim of getting better power positions, there is no doubt that Communist local governments had lost some of their élan. Had the Communist vote increased, this would have produced a drawing effect. By making it impossible to create local governments that excluded the PCI, it would have obliged even the Socialists to come to terms with the Communists. But the PCI's decline provided a ready-made justification for its exclusion from several local governments, even where it still retains a relative majority of votes. The strategy of social and, especially, political alliances comes into the picture at this point. Reformulation and redefinition are now very urgent for the PCI – indeed, a top priority. But, before proceeding in that direction, we would do better to analyse the role of the trade union movement. After all, the starting point of any communist strategy of social and political alliances was, and still largely is, the organized working class.

The organized working class and the trade unions

By definition, a communist party wants to represent the interests of the working class first and foremost. With all the necessary nuances, deriving from his knowledge of the Italian situation, Togliatti stressed this element with much precision in a famous speech of the autumn of 1946.[4] The PCI, being the party of the working class, was also willing to represent in its concrete activities the interests of other social groups, provided they were compatible with those of the working class. From the point of view of the material development of the country, of its democratic texture (which had to remain republican and anti-fascist), of the goals that society set itself (the achievement of a progressive democracy and then of socialism), the working class was willing to collaborate with other social strata. Obviously, the PCI recognized from the very beginning the difference between the representation of political interests and values (to be performed by the party) and the protection and promotion of workers' rights and living and working conditions (to be advanced by the trade union movement, with a special role for the Socialist-Communist trade union, the CGIL – the *Confederazione Generale Italiana del Lavoro*).[5]

The division of socio-political labour, though never devoid of conflicts and tensions, worked relatively well. Indeed, by 1970 it seemed as if both the party and the union could make gains simultaneously and strengthen each other. To prove the point, the highest gains made by the unions and the workers – almost full protection against inflation with a 100 per cent wage indexation for all workers – coincided in 1975 with the PCI's greatest electoral success. It was difficult not to believe in a mutually reinforcing effect.

But the unions never succeeded in going beyond their role of protection of the organized working class. They proved incapable of becoming protagonists in the process of economic policy-making (in spite of a valiant effort made in 1978 by Luciano Lama, the Secretary General of the CGIL). They were not capable, or not willing, to take into account the interests of white collar industrial employees (who then moved to the creation of their own professional association, with devastating effects on the working class unions). They remained insensitive to the issue of different wages for better skilled workers. They did not grasp the process of differentiation that was at work within the working class at the same time as the number of industrial workers and the percentage of unionized workers over the total work force were rapidly declining. Finally, not only did their long-awaited process of unification – of the CGIL, the Socialist–Republican *Unione Italiana del Lavora* (UIL) and the largely Catholic–Christian Democratic *Confederazione Italiana Sindicati Lavoratori* (CISL) – fail to materialize, but on the fundamental issue of reaching an agreement with the government, in a quasi neo-corporatist fashion, a profound, seemingly irreconcilable cleavage developed in 1983–4 between the CISL, the UIL and the Socialist wing of the CGIL against the Communist wing of the CGIL, which led the PCI to request a referendum on the subsequent decree enacted by the government abolishing the indexation of wages.

On one major occasion, the largest union confederation underwent a split that showed the relative isolation of Communist workers. More than that: it quickly became clear that the working class, reduced in numbers, fragmented in terms of occupational activities, probably expectations and life styles, and moreover politically divided, could not be counted upon any more to constitute the core of a viable strategy of social alliances. Indeed, as a whole the trade unions had lost much of their representational capabilities. This loss was much more damaging to the Communists, who rely on the working class vote to a greater extent than the other parties and who still recruit many of their militants from the labour aristocracy. The results of the referendum on the *scala mobile* (the indexation system) in June 1985 revealed that although the organizational machine of the PCI remains in good shape and is largely capable of turning out the vote, the working class as a whole is not only divided, but is no longer a majority and is incapable of attracting enough support from other social strata in Italian politics.

The government had much politicized the issue, fundamentally requesting a referendum on its overall economic policy. The Communists had been unable or unwilling to accept the challenge that the referendum by its very nature posed. It was precisely in view of this politicization, however, that the results (54.3 per cent in favour of the decree that had reduced the indexation system and 45.7 per cent in favour of its reinstatement) suggested that the PCI and the organized working class each have a long way to go if between them they are to recreate a viable system of social alliances and to recover their strength and unity (if, indeed, that is still possible).

Ten years after a great working class victory, then, came a significant defeat. Two elements are particularly noteworthy. The first indicates that the working class and those favourable to an improvement of its social and political situation in Italy represent a minority, albeit a sizeable one. One immediately thinks of the referendum on the divorce law of 1974 when the results (59.1 per cent in favour of the law and 40.9 per cent against) indicated that the Catholics were indeed a minority. And this had a strong political impact (which, perhaps, the Left, and specifically the PCI, were unable to exploit with enough vigour). The second element points in the direction of the absolute need for the organized working class, but particularly for the Communists, to shape a strategy capable of acquiring the consensus and the active support of other social groups. The weakness of the working class has been reflected in the weakness of the PCI. Since there is no way to strengthen the working class numerically, the only viable strategy would consist in increasing its political strength. But is the Communist (socio-) political culture up to this momentous task?

In order to provide a meaningful answer to this complex question, one must analyse the PCI's organization, the party's change over time, its present situation and the role it plays and will presumably continue to play within the political system. An in-depth analysis of this kind will allow us to identify the present challenges to the PCI and to predict some of the problems it will face in the near future and the alternatives it might be in a position to pursue.

The changing structure of the party

For Italian Communists, the party has always represented more than just the organization entitled to represent their interests. It has always been an object of affection as well. Moreover, it has been and has functioned as the instrument capable of providing the political synthesis of the various demands, preferences and activities initiated and conducted by other flanking organizations. This could be done successfully, of course, not simply because the party was held to be the repository of politics and to enjoy a monopoly in that realm, but because the communist ideology laid due emphasis on democratic centralism.

It must be said from the outset, in order to aid an understanding of subsequent developments, that the Italian Communist Party has always been rather diverse in terms of its socio-political entrenchment and social membership. It has, therefore, always lacked that fundamental sociological, geographical, even political homogeneity (the common origins and the same political experiences among the leadership group) that makes for a rigid attachment to democratic centralism. On the contrary, for reasons related to the previous existence of Socialist organizations and to the toughness of the Resistance movement, the PCI became from the very beginning a heterogeneous party. In fact, it was very strong, organizationally and electorally, in predominantly agricultural Emilia–Romagna and Tuscany (and slightly later in Umbria, which had similar features), rather strong, but in competition with the Socialists, in the industrial triangle (Turin, Milan, and Genoa), relatively weak everywhere else, and especially so in the areas dominated by the Catholics (the north-east of Italy) and to a lesser extent in the south.

While the party has gradually grown, it has never succeeded in overcoming all its initial lagging features. Above all, it has not been able to consolidate its electoral gains in the south and to create a viable organizational network there. It is, indeed, still struggling, against many impediments, to acquire and maintain a stable following (one of the impediments, of course, being the unscrupulous utilization by governing parties of public resources to tie the voters: the well-known phenomenon of clientelism, which the PCI cannot practise owing, apart from ideological reasons, to a lack of an appropriate structure). Thus its political organizational strength is still concentrated in the Red Belt, where it polls around 50 per cent of the vote. It gets about 35 per cent in the industrial triangle; and at the most slightly more than 20 to 25 per cent in the south.

Obviously the differences in electoral showing tell us much about the party's ability to recruit members and to select militants. Where the party is strong, it can choose among a variety of well-prepared, ambitious members representing different backgrounds, activities and groups. So in the north, it is still in a position to attract (and train, if the need arises) working class members. In the south, the difficulties are evident: few resources to offer, few positions to be filled, political power very far removed. At best the PCI is appealing to traditional intellectuals, the radicalized members of the petty bourgeoisie whose ability to interpret and represent the interests of the southern masses remains doubtful.

Purely from the point of view of recruitment problems and of variations in the social composition of the membership, one cannot but notice that the PCI has had increasing difficulty in artificially keeping the percentage of working class members at around half of the entire membership. Moreover, the inclination of old workers to renew their membership card after retirement so that they are still counted as workers and not as 'retired people' has transformed the PCI into a party of working class families (this is due also to the fact that it is customary for the wife to join her husband's party). Unfortunately for the PCI, its working class families have found it increasingly difficult to convince their children to join the party. Thus there has been first of all a dramatic decline of the Communist Youth Federation (FGCI) – now undergoing a major transformation in trying to open up its ranks to youngsters in a more flexible and appealing way, working on an issue approach to political activities – and then a remarkable decline in the percentage of student members of the party, at a time when the student population has been expanding.

All this said, the major point still stands: the PCI was and is a rather diversified party. Moreover, the initial decision by Togliatti to create a *partito nuovo* (a new party), that is a mass party and not a sectarian party of professional revolutionaries, had already introduced some difficulties in the concrete working of democratic centralism. Not that the party was not a disciplined body of loyal Communists willing to accept and enforce the decisions coming from the top. But from the very beginning, and increasingly so, those decisions took into account, if not the opinions of all the rank and file, at least those of a wide cross-section of the militants. On a few occasions, democratic centralism was invoked and applied, in a more or less ruthless way, such as between 1964 and 1966 to weaken the impact of Ingrao's challenge to the official party line of accommodation with the socio-economic trends of the Italian capitalist system. And indeed democratic centralism blocked both Amendola's right wing ascent and Ingrao's left-wing alternative, opening the way to the centrist Enrico Berlinguer.[6] In 1969, democratic centralism led to the expulsion of a fraction of Ingrao's former left wing, known as the Manifesto group, who were guilty of not stopping publication of their journal and, therefore of 'fractional' activities. They were readmitted into the party in 1984, but not all the top leaders have rejoined.

Anyway, probably the most important consequences of democratic centralism in the Italian Communist Party have been at the same time both positive and negative. On the positive side, a diversified party has maintained its unity in spite of the existence of different tendencies, based on different analyses of the Italian situation and diverging prognoses about the future. Still on the positive side, by stressing both poles of democratic centralism (centralism and democracy) a better educated, politically committed rank and file has recently pressed for a profound revision of the model of internal organization and has achieved significant results. In 1981, the groundwork was laid for more open, franker, explicit debates recording differences of opinion and therefore establishing the bases for the formation of alternative policy options. During the long preparation for the 1983 national party congress, secret voting was allowed, both in elections and on motions, if it was requested by a small percentage of the members. At last, internal democracy was recognized, and in some cases actually hailed as a functional necessity. A complex and diversified party needs a democratic internal life in order to collect all the information necessary for its decision-making process. This principle has recently led to a wide process of consultation and to a series of voting occasions for the nomination of candidates. While, as many Communists still complain, the process of internal democracy has not yet gone far enough, and indeed may have suffered some reversals in recent periods, the real problem may be that orthodox democratic centralism cannot be revived, whilst at the same time party leaders have not been able to find an alternative model or to push all the way for full internal democracy. This could have undesirable results: increasing difficulties in the decision-making process; slow, tentative and complex bargaining among the different positions; inability to manoeuvre quickly. And still the old process of cooptation of party leaders lives on; even though the new Secretary General, Alessandro Natta, was chosen after a wide consultation of the most influential members of the party, with dissenting opinions being frankly expressed, the choice seemed to reflect an internal stalemate.

In all likelihood, the most negative consequences, not yet overcome, of democratic centralism concern the procedure through which the most important political strategies of the party were formulated and implemented. It was Berlinguer's decision (and responsibility) to launch the 'historic compromise' in September 1973, in the wake of Allende's overthrow in Chile.[7] This policy of giving conditional support to

Christian Democrat governments was a defensive strategy, at a time when Italian society was becoming more secularized and more mobilized, more inclined to accept change. The most important decision-making bodies of the party were afterwards informed and duly ratified the decision to launch the policy. But the militants always retained their reservations and the implementation of a strategy that had not been discussed with the militants and was not liked by them (and was, obviously, also rejected by the Christian Democrats) proved very difficult *et pour cause.*[8] Berlinguer certainly had a degree of aristocratic disdain for internal democracy. In all likelihood he thought that the militants were some steps behind the evolution of the domestic and international political system. He may have been right, especially when he started distancing the PCI from the Soviet Union and then launched Eurocommunism, and afterwards, in the wake of the Polish military coup d'etat in 1981, declared that the 'propulsive force' of the October revolution was exhausted. Again, without any previous deliberation by the Central Committee and after having only informed, not consulted, the members of the Executive Committee, in November 1980 Berlinguer moved the party along the path of the 'democratic alternative', indicating his preference for a governing coalition that would exclude the Christian Democrats. Unprepared for this sudden change, the party, its militants and core of activists, took a while to formulate all the subtleties of the new strategy and, perhaps, found themselves once more in mid-stream. By that time, the Socialists, the indispensable partner, were approaching the Christian Democrats for an alliance which has led them to isolate the PCI and to conquer the coveted position of prime minister.

At a time when strategic imperatives make it even more necessary to widen the internal debate and to address a clear appeal to potential partners, the problem of overcoming the last remnants of democratic centralism (those psychological inclinations and anticipated reactions that die so very hard) looms large within the party. Democracy is more than a functional necessity; it is being advocated by some party leaders, though still a minority, as the winning card in a complex democratic society if the party really wants to offer meaningful representation and considerable political influence to its cherished old and revered new groups, movements and interests.

This appears to be the bone of contention: whether the party can and should retain its monopoly over political interests, demands and preferences, and provide *the* synthesis between them, or whether it ought to be conceived more as a referee among competing interests, demands and preferences, an organization among others, even though with some specific political (and elective) responsibilities. Not even the 'extraordinary' party congress of April 1986 was able to provide a totally satisfactory solution to these recurring issues. The congress reaffirmed the indispensability of a mass party and at the same time advocated the creation of a more responsive and flexible party structure. Be that as it may, the PCI has gone a long way towards recognizing the validity of all organizations representing progressive interests and views, accepting to act as their reference point, and conceiving of itself as one instrument (in the minds of many – probably still the majority of the members of the party – *the* most important and anyway the best placed instrument) for the transformation of the Italian political system.

Changing conceptions of the party

The transformation just described suggests how far away the PCI has travelled from the orthodox conception of the communist party as the repository of the entire ideological truth and as the only organization possessing class consciousness and therefore capable of initiating a transition to socialism. A more secularized view of ideology and politics has ensued, though not without reservations and criticisms. As a matter of fact, traditional Communist leaders had been trained in the Gramscian perspective, that is in the belief that cultural hegemony is indispensable for the acquisition and the successful exercise of political power. The more a party, or a social bloc, is capable of acquiring cultural hegemony, the less it will have to rely on coercion.[9]

This tradition was correctly interpreted and duly implemented by Togliatti. Since culture and ideas must be spread, Togliatti paid great attention to the vectors through which the Communist culture could be made to travel and to shape the minds of militants as well as the actual and potential Communist electorate. For these reasons, Togliatti founded *Řinascita*, at first a fortnightly, later a weekly publication, as early as 1946. The main objective was to create a shared political culture offering a tribune's platform for the debate of ideas among Communist leaders and intellectuals (many of the former being intellectuals themselves), to attract other progressive intellectuals, and to expose the militants to new political ideas. There is no doubt that *Rinascita* succeeded in all of these tasks and is today a well-established political weekly. Obviously, even during the Resistance and for some years during the Fascism period, the PCI did not relinquish publishing its official daily *l'Unità*, or at least some special editions. Today, the PCI is one of the very few left-wing parties in Western Europe that publishes a national daily. *l'Unità*'s daily circulation is almost 200,000 copies. On Sundays, helped by door-to-door sales, it reaches 500,000 and in some exceptional circumstances even 1,000,000 copies (however, costs are running high and *l'Unità* still has a deficit).

The continued existence and the wide circulation of a Communist daily constitute an important factor in the battle of ideas in Italy. Because the state TV system is in the hands of governmental parties, because most of the so-called independent press thrives on governmental subsidies and the rest has very moderate leanings, it is extremely important for the PCI to counteract quickly the information provided by the mass media and to put forward its own views. This is important for the militants and the voters, and also in order to exchange ideas and rebuttals with governmental parties and opinion-makers. The PCI is fighting hard against the mass conformity that is produced by the information system in Western European countries. It does so also through an innovative policy, which Gramsci might have liked because it appeals to all citizens and voters and tries to blend politics with leisure; this is, *l'Unità*'s festivals. Organized both to spread political ideas and to finance the party and the paper, these festivals have acquired national recognition and importance. In addition to many local and provincial events, there is a national festival, large and imposing, which is traditionally the occasion for a major speech by the party's general secretary. These festivals have been very successful both in terms of their overall number and of the quantity of visitors (some Communists, however, wonder why the visitors do not translate their interest in PCI's activities into party membership . . .).

Finally, in keeping with the Gramscian tradition and its cherished image of an intellectual party (the party being, according to a famous expression of Gramsci, 'the collective intellectual') – and perhaps also a party of intellectuals – the PCI has founded a national institute for scholarly research now called, appropriately, the Gramsci Foundation. This foundation, with its many local branches, is largely autonomous of the PCI. Other more specialized research institutes deal with economic policy (the *Centro Studi Politica Economica*, CESPE, which also publishes a monthly, *Politica e economia*); institutional and legal problems (the *Centro per la Riforma dello Stato*, CRS, which publishes a bimonthly, *Democrazia e diritto*); and foreign policy (the *Centro Studi Politica Internazionale*, CESPI). And of course the party has a theoretical bimonthly *Critica marxista* and from the very beginning has sponsored a journal for historical analysis, *Studi storici*. All these publications cater to very many left-wing intellectuals and scholars, not only Communist ones.

Obviously, the PCI never was an *ouvrièriste* party (though a wing of this kind always existed and some of these positions still play a role). The overwhelming respect enjoyed by Togliatti and the way in which democratic centralism worked allowed a blending of the various threads of diversified cultural experiences and approaches. Berlinguer, much less of an intellectual himself than Togliatti, tried in a famous public meeting with progressive intellectuals in 1977, at the height of the controversy over the 'historic compromise', to revive the PCI's ties with the intellectuals. Whether he was successful or not is still a moot point. However, what is more important is that in a famous article published in *Rinascita* in 1978, Giorgio Amendola complained of, or rather denounced, in his customary blunt and outspoken manner, the fragmentation of the Communist political culture.[10]

Himself a representative of a specific intellectual wing within the party, identified with Marxist historicism and strongly tinged with Crocian idealism, Amendola fulminated against a decline of Marxist thinking within the party, against an inclination rashly to accept revisionist ideas, to introduce within the party's culture traditions of thought extraneous to it, to accept social science theories, to be unwilling and probably unable to provide a new, fertile synthesis. According to him, the PCI risked becoming a pragmatic, reformist party. Some of these criticisms have been revived recently because, according to some left-wing spokesmen, the PCI has overemphasized its acceptance of democracy ('a universal value' as Berlinguer put it repeatedly) at the expense of socialism. In fact, the analysis of socialism, its contemporary meaning, the steps to be undertaken to move in that direction seem to have passed into oblivion. The PCI itself has lost, its internal critics say, its propulsive force. Be that as it may, Communist political culture in Italy is certainly divided on many questions (the most important being what is a reformist–revolutionary party today in the Western context and what is the alternative to a capitalist democratic regime) and in painful search for a coherent blending of its diversified perspectives. 'Unity in diversity' may be an appealing solution, but it is not in sight.[11]

This is all the more true for the fact that Communist militants are divided on the very conception of the party today.[12] That is, while the differences should by no means be exaggerated, there are three views of what the Communist party is and ought to be. First, there is the classical view of the party as the most important object of allegiance: the party in itself is a value. Secondly, there is the conception of the party as the necessary, most useful instrument for a socialist transformation. Thirdly, there is the perspective based on the role of the party as the bearer of a project, as the interpreter of ideas and proposals for change. While there are generational differences (the younger and the more recent militants supporting the third view; the older ones being closer to the first conception), the relevant point is that there has been a major internal differentiation among Communist militants. This may go a long way, together with the fragmentation of Communist culture, towards explaining the difficulties that the PCI has encountered in shaping and implementing its strategy.

Conclusions

A party regularly polling over a quarter of the national vote, governing about one-third of the Italian population and territory, with more than 1,600,000 members, some 300 parliamentary representatives, a widely read daily national paper, an audience among intellectuals, international recognition and respect, is obviously not undergoing a major crisis. Neither in terms of its internal organization nor in terms of its political culture can the PCI be correctly defined as being in crisis. However, it would be very inappropriate and misleading to deny, or even underestimate, the fact that the PCI is facing serious problems. These problems are well known to party leaders and militants and constitute the object of a lively and anxious debate.

Paradoxically, one can say that the PCI has been very successful in Italy because from being a rather separate and exceptional organization (most Communists have been very proud of their 'diversity') it has come to embody and to reflect most of the complexity of a society that has grown, changed and matured. Most of the problems of the PCI are the product of the complexity of the Italian socio-political system, and, of course, of the accompanying difficulty of managing such a complex system. This might not be very much of a problem for the conservatives and the moderates who want to retain control and who are willing to adjust to the existing complexity. But it is a major problem for the progressives and the reformists who want to control the dynamics of the system and to guide it in the desired direction.

The process of guidance needs a powerful and cohesive organization (and we have seen that the PCI is under stress from this point of view), a coherent and widely shared political culture (which has not yet emerged within the party) and above all powerful and reliable allies. Of all the problems that the PCI will have to resolve, the most difficult will concern the reformulation of its strategy of social and political alliances. Indeed, it is the crumbling away of the two pillars upon which the strategy had been built that has shown up in a dramatic way all the other problems. Social alliances will be more difficult to create than at any other time in the past not only because the working class is not becoming the 'general' class and the unions are divided among themselves, but because the working class is now very fragmented, and its unity cannot any more be taken for granted. Therefore, from the perspective of social alliances, the PCI will have to work hard to identify those needs, preferences and values capable of tying together a progressive coalition (which will have to be formed and reformed in the light of the acceleration of social, economic, and political changes among Western publics in the 1980s and 1990s).[13]

But, in all likelihood, the biggest problem of all will be the reformulation of a strategy of political alliances. Unless Italy moves towards the utilization of a different electoral system, with fewer elements of proportionality (the debate is open and lively, with the party so far opposing any such reform), in a system characterized and shaped by proportional representation, all parties will need allies in order to govern. In the past, the Communists could confidently count on the Socialists, faithful and indispensable allies. In recent times, however, under the leadership of Bettino Craxi, the Socialist Party has adopted clear and tough anti-Communist positions and has tried – often with some success – to exclude it from governmental power at the local level. It has, in a word, pursued a policy of deliberate isolation of the PCI. Since the Socialists enjoy a pivotal position within the Italian party alignment (very few coalitions being possible without their participation, and none at the national level), the duel within the Left[14] has badly damaged the PCI.

The Socialists are certainly attempting to show that in a modern, democratic, (almost) post-industrial society there is no place for a Communist party. They hope to inherit all or most of the votes of those who have supported the Communists as a protest against the establishment and against coalitions dominated by the Christian Democrats. While the Socialists' socio-political analysis might be wrong in many respects, their political clout has been utilized in a rather ruthless way so far; and the question they raise is a real one – whether there is still place for a Communist party. Once Togliatti explained the surprise of many analysts in the face of Communist strength and resilience by saying that the PCI is like a giraffe, an animal that many zoologists believe should not exist. More critically, some progressive scholars are afraid that the PCI might be or might become a unicorn, an animal that quite certainly does not exist in reality.

Since, however, the PCI exists and may not be disappearing in the short run, the central question concerns its viability, its possibilities of playing an important, governing role in the Italian political system in the near future, and its potential for producing major changes in a democratic capitalist regime.[15] It would be too easy to conclude simply that the PCI is not in a state of crisis but in one of transition. A comparative look at other Western European socialist parties, at their socio-political problems and at their debates would probably be more illuminating for understanding the present plight of the PCI than a comparison with minor or declining Communist organizations. Indeed, the real problem might be that the PCI has to revise its political culture, reform its organization, redefine its strategy of alliances and cease to be a traditional Communist party (which it has not been for some time anyway) without thereby becoming a traditional socialist party.[16] The starting point of the transitional phase is reasonably clear; the ultimate goal remains to be precisely defined. The experiment, therefore, deserves the utmost attention and also, perhaps, sympathy.

Postscript

In the national elections of 14–15 June 1987 the PCI lost 3.3 per cent of the vote. Its 26.6 per cent represented a jump backward to its level before 1968. The losses were particularly severe in the ten largest cities. Political (the tough competition mounted by the Socialist Party which gained 2.9 per cent and was clearly perceived by many as a concrete, real, viable alternative to the Christian Democrats) and structural factors (the absolute decline of working class voters and the inability to reach the new young voters) explain the electoral defeat.

During an agonizing reappraisal of its role, the Communist Party divided openly for the first time in the election of a vice-general secretary, eventually to succeed Alessandro Natta. The centre-left of the party supported Achille Occhetto, while the moderate, 'social democratic' sectors led by Giorgio Napolitano opposed him. Structurally and politically, the Italian Communist Party remains very different from the French one and extrapolations from the recent history of the latter are not fully appropriate. Several, deep worries as to the future of the PCI emerged, however, within its rank-and-file and leadership, most of them justified. *Chi vivrà, vedrà* (he who stays alive will see).

Appendix

Table 2.1 PCI membership in absolute numbers in selected years

	1968	1976	1984	1986
Men	1,148,195	1,378,899	1,188,965	1,129,939
Women	354,667	435,438	430,070	421,637
Total	1,502,862	1,814,317	1,619,035	1,551,576

Source: Official party figures, by courtesy of the PCI Statistical Section

Table 2.2 Changes in the social composition of PCI membership in selected years

Social categories	1968 (%)	1977 (%)	1984 (%)
Industrial workers	40.1	40.1	38.7
Farmhands, salaried agricultural workers	10.3	5.3	4.0
Small farmers, sharecroppers	12.5	5.4	3.0
Shopkeepers	2.0	1.9	2.9
Artisans, small entrepreneurs	4.6	9.1	6.5
White collar employees	3.3	8.3	9.7
Cottage workers	—	0.7	0.8
Housewives	12.8	10.3	7.6
Retired people	11.8	17.4	21.0
Students	0.6	2.1	1.0
Others	2.0	0.3	4.8

Source: Official party figures, by courtesy of the PCI Statistical Section

Table 2.3 Membership of the Communist Youth Federation (FGCI) in selected years

1968	1971	1980	1984
125,438	85,960 (10,825)[a]	73,874	45,000 (16,000)[a]

[a] Numbers of women.
Source: Official party figures, by courtesy of the PCI Statistical Section (the figures for 1984 are estimates)

Table 2.4 Miscellaneous data on the composition of PCI Federal Committees in 1983

Gender (no.)	
Men 5,557	
Women 1,199 (17.73%)	
Total 6,756	
Social composition (%)	
White collar employees	22.1
Industrial workers	19.3
Teachers	18.0
Professionals	11.2
Students	10.2
Technicians	3.7
Shopkeepers, artisans, small	
Entrepreneurs	2.9
Pensioners	2.6
Agricultural workers	2.1
Other categories	3.1
Missing data	4.0
Education (%)	
Elementary school	7.3
Junior high school	18.1
High school diploma	38.4
University degree	30.9
Missing data	5.3
Age (%)	
< 25	5.7
26–30	17.9
31–40	41.6
41–50	16.5
51–60	10.2
60 +	3.1
Missing data	5.0

Source: Official party figures, by courtesy of the PCI Statistical Section

Table 2.5 Geographical distribution of the vote for the PCI in national election years

	1968 (%)	1972 (%)	1976 (%)	1979 (%)	1983 (%)	1984[a] (%)	1987[b] (%)
North	25.8	26.4	33.5	30.5	30.1	32.2	26.1
Centre	34.2	34.4	41.4	37.8	37.6	41.5	34.3
South	24.7	24.4	32.4	26.4	25.4	30.2	23.1
Islands	22.8	22.2	29.5	23.7	23.4	28.3	21.3
Italy	27.0	27.2	34.4	30.4	29.9	33.4	26.6

[a] European elections.
[b] From *La Repubblica*, 17 June 1987.
Source: Official party figures, by courtesy of the PCI Statistical Section

Notes

The author gratefully acknowledges the assistance of Oreste Massari in collecting the data for the tables.

1 The best overall analysis remains the one provided in the essays collected by Donald L.M. Blackmer and Sidney Tarrow (eds), *Communism in Italy and France* (Princeton University Press, Princeton, NJ, 1975).

2 On this specific point see Robert D. Putnam, 'The Italian Communist Politician', in Blackmer and Tarrow, *Communism in Italy and France*, pp. 173–217.

3 As Georges Lavau tells us in 'The PCF, the State, and the Revolution: an Analysis of Party Policies, Communications, and Popular Culture', in Blackmer and Tarrow, *Communism in Italy and France*, pp. 87–139.

4 'Ceto medio e Emilia rossa', delivered at Reggio Emilia, 24 September 1946. See also Steven Hellman's excellent analysis of the contradictions implied in this strategy: 'The PCI's Alliance Strategy and the case of the Middle Classes', in Blackmer and Tarrow, *Communism in Italy and France*, pp. 373–419.

5 On these aspects see Peter Lange, George Ross and Maurizio Vannicelli, *Unions, Change and Crisis: French and Italian Union Strategy and the Political Economy 1945–1980* (Allen and Unwin, London, 1982).

6 On these developments see the account provided by Grant Amyot, *The Italian Communist Party. The Crisis of the Popular Front Strategy* (Croom Helm, London, 1981).

7 On this point see the analysis by Stephen Hellman, 'The Longest Campaign: Communist Party Strategy and the Elections of 1976', in Howard R. Penniman (ed.), *Italy at the Polls. The Parliamentary Election of 1976* (American Enterprise Institute, 1977), pp. 155–82.

8 For empirical backing see Marzio Barbagli and Piergiorgio Corbetta, 'After the Historic Compromise: a Turning Point for the PCI', *European Journal of Political Research*, vol. 10, no. 3, September 1982, pp. 213–39.

9 For an excellent synthesis of Gramsci's contributions see Joseph V. Femia, *Gramsci's Political Thought* (Clarendon Press, Oxford, 1981).

10   Giorgio Amendola, *Rinascita*, 4 August 1978, no. 31.
11   See the debate on 'Le nouve idee della sinistra' ('The New Ideas of the Left') launched in *Rinascita*, 1984, no. 44 and continued in nos. 46, 48, 50 and 51 of 1984 and nos. 2, 4, 5, 6, 7 and 9 of 1985, and concluded by the editor himself (Giuseppe Chiarante): 'Risposta al reaganismo e prospettive riformatrici' ('Response to Reaganism and Reformist Perspectives'), *Rinascita*, 1985, no. 11. No working consensus was reached.
12   See the findings of a large empirical research on Communist Party militants carried out at the end of the 1970s in Aris Accornero, Renato Mannheimer and Chiara Sebastiani (eds), *L'identità comunista. I militanti, le strutture, la cultura del Pci* (Editori Riuniti, Rome, 1983).
13   My own analysis, 'Il Pci nel rompicapo italiano' ('The PCI in the Italian Puzzle'), can be found in *Rinascita*, 1985, no. 26, pp. 40–2.
14   As it has been defined by two infuential Socialist intellectuals and policy-makers – Giuliano Amato and Luciano Cafagna, *Duello a sinistra. Socialisti e comunisti nei lunghi anni '70* (Il Mulino, Bologna, 1982).
15   The best contribution so far can be found in a short article by Alberto Jacoviello, former correspondent of *l'Unità*, 'Il silenzio del Pci' ('The Silence of the PCI'), *la Repubblica*, 21 June 1985, p. 6. See also Aldo Schiavone, *Per il nuovo Pci* (Laterza, Bari, 1985).
16   I have dealt with these problems in 'Il Partito comunista nel sistema politico italiano', now in Gianfranco Pasquino (ed.), *Il sistema politico italiano* (Laterza, Bari, 1985), pp. 128–68.

3 From Decline to Marginalization: the PCF Breaks with French Society
The French Communist Party

Stéphane Courtois and Denis Peschanski

In a remarkably short space of time, in fact in less than five years, a succession of electoral setbacks has brought about the eclipse of the French Communist Party (*Parti communiste français*, PCF) and its effective marginalization, a turn of events that is all the more striking because the PCF has for long been such a major feature of the French political landscape.

In this situation, perceptions of reality are as important as reality itself. In the kaleidoscope of memory certain images predominate – a party deeply implanted in society with the arrival of the Popular Front, the leading organizer of the Resistance, from which it emerged with full honours, attracting at that point over a quarter of the electorate and sharing in governmental power, enjoying a position of hegemony in the working class and in the intelligentsia from the 1940s to the mid-1970s, and then, in the company of the Italians and the Spaniards, making its 'Eurocommunist' *aggiornamento*. This is how the party's image appears although an examination of the facts would require refinements to be made. But the present crisis in the PCF is all the more profound for the fact that the party's self-image throws the reality into sharper relief. The crisis gives rise to at least two series of questions: how far-reaching is it, and what is its real nature? Are we dealing with a passing setback or is this the sign of an irreversible decline?

The following conclusions can be drawn from the material presented in this chapter and particularly from the explanatory factors that will be suggested below:

1 For the first time in the history of the PCF and of its crises, all the elements of those crises converge.

2   The present short period of crisis (1981–6) has highlighted and accelerated deep-seated tendencies that have been taking shape over many decades.
3   The crisis is all the more serious in bringing into question the party's communist identity, as a result of the problem – always difficult – of reconciling the anchoring of the PCF in French society with the external nature of the goals and practices associated with communism.

To measure the strength of the PCF is first and foremost to count its electorate, its members and its militants. This counting process, however, does not yield immediate results. It meets obstructions of all kinds: differences in the sources of information and the elastic nature of the indicators that one has to deal with. Secrecy within the party is an essential factor in the internal cohesion of the group, and has a function that is more ideological than practical. This rule stems from the 'logic of war',[1] the class war that is continued in the war of ideology. This complicates the task of anyone trying to assess the party's strength (apart, of course, from its simple electoral strength). The party's participation in political life, the continual opinion surveys, the crises and successive waves of resignations that have studded the history of the PCF provide, or suggest, a wide spread of sources, with an equally broad range of reliability. Nor should it be imagined that all the indicators are subject to simultaneous shifts; each evolves according to its own rhythm and has its own degree of elasticity.

The electoral collapse

From 1978 to 1986, from election to election, the PCF has seen its support fall away. If we take only national legislative elections, in 1978 it took 20.7 per cent of the poll (index 100), 16.1 per cent in 1981 (index 78) and 9.8 per cent in 1986 (index 47). With 9.8 per cent of the poll and 7.2 per cent of the electorate it has come full circle to its original performance in 1924, and only just over its historical minimum in 1932 (see table 3.3). In gross figures, the PCF had about 6 million electors in 1978, 4 million in 1981 and 2.7 million in 1986. If figures for the 96 *départements* of metropolitan France are examined, it can be seen that the PCF took more than 25 per cent of the vote in 23 of them in 1978, but in none of them eight years later, whilst it took less than 10 per cent of the poll in nine *départements* in 1978, as against 58 in 1986.

The first conclusion is clear: the communist electorate has been subject to an erosion that is spectacular both in its scope and its rapidity.

Table 3.1 Electoral results of the PCF in the 96 *départements* of metropolitan France, 1978–86

Percentage of vote	Leg.[a] '78	Eur.[b] '79	Leg. '81	Eur. '84	Leg. '86
Under 10	9	6	30	45	58
10–14	15	19	24	31	27
15–19	27	29	17	15	8
20–24	22	22	13	5	3
25+	23	20	12	0	0

[a] Legislative elections.
[b] European Assembly elections.
Source: Le Monde

The geographical and sociological calculation is no more encouraging. It was not the working class and urban *départements* – the traditional strongholds – that headed the list in 1986, but heavily rural *départements* of central France, far removed from the places where economic and social change has been taking place, for example in the Cher, the Allier, the Haute Vienne and the Corrèze. In most recent years, whilst the decline has been general, and whilst the political weight of well-known local figures complicates the picture when it comes to municipal, cantonal or legislative elections (though not in presidential and European elections), the PCF has stood up better in the rural areas of Central France and in the 'red south' or in certain urban zones marked by industrial decline.[2]

The so-called 'poll exit' surveys, which take the form of confronting electors on election day itself with a very precise and anonymous questionnaire on the way they have voted, confirm that this reduction in the vote has been accompanied by an ageing of Communist electoral support (see table 3.2), which a priori limits the potential for change. Comparing the Communist vote of 1978 with that of 1986, it can be seen that:

1 The decline in the vote correlates strongly with the age of Communist voters.
2 The percentage vote remains stable only for the 65 and over age group.
3 There is a steep decline in the figures for the 18–34 age group, and in particular for the 18–24 age group.

It cannot, however, be assumed that this is an entirely new phenomenon. The curve that traces the evolution of the Communist vote since 1924 shows that after a spectacular expansion over 15 years, the PCF's performance has declined steadily over the past 40 years, with two

Table 3.2 The Communist vote according to age

Age range (yr)	Communist vote as percentage of total		
	1978	*1984*	*1986*
			6 (under 25)
18–34	21	11	12 (25–34)
35–49	20	11	10
50–64	16	11	9
65 +	11.5	12	10

Source: 1978 and 1984, IFOP; 1986, SOFRES

long plateaux of relative stability – around 25 per cent before the coming to power of General de Gaulle in 1958, and again between 20 and 22 per cent before the shock of the presidential election of 1981 (see table 3.3). Whilst, in its period of expansion, the PCF drew its strength from the living forces of the nation, it did not succeed in attracting the rising social categories in the '30 glorious years'[3] – workers in service industries, the new working class, white collar workers and so on. Electoral disaster has struck the party only in recent years, but it cannot be separated from latent tendencies for the vote to come progressively to rest with the social groups and geographical areas that were in the process of marginalization.

Table 3.3 The Communist vote since 1924 as a percentage of the poll

Year	%	Year	%
1924	9.5	1967	22.5
1928	11.4	1968	20.0
1932	8.4	1969[a]	21.5
1936	15.4	1973	21.4
1945	26.3	1978	20.7
1946 (June)	25.7	1979[b]	20.6
1946 (November)	28.6	1981[a] (May)	15.5
1951	26.9	1981 (June)	16.1
1956	25.9	1984[b]	11.2
1958	19.2	1986	9.8
1962	21.8		

[a] Presidential elections.
[b] Elections for the European Assembly. All other figures are for national legislative elections.
Source: Electoral records

Fluctuations in membership

The party's membership represents another essential mark of its presence in society. Twenty years ago Annie Kriegel published a pioneering work on PCF membership between the wars.[4] If the secrecy of the party makes any estimate of total membership arbitrary, there are sufficient sources today to allow an overall picture to emerge – such as that of Philippe Buton, which has recently been joined by numerous regional or contemporary studies.[5] Without embarking on methodological digressions, it can be said that the curve for 'membership cards sold' shows that party members are more sensitive to the immediate political circumstances than is the Communist electorate, where fluctuations are traditionally more random, at least until very recent times.

The strong initial start of 100,000 members dwindled rapidly during the 1920s to sink in 1933 to the historical low of 30,000, when the 'class against class' strategy was in full swing. But although their numbers were small, these Communists were entirely different from the Socialist Party as it had been before the 1921 split. After the strategic turning-point of 1934, these working class cadres were able to integrate into the Communist Party the influx of new members that the Popular Front brought. In September 1937 the PCF had more than 300,000 members. Once it had put behind it the tergiversations of the beginning of the Second World War, the PCF reaped spectacular results from its activities in the French Resistance and from the prestige of the Soviet Union. It emerged from the *maquis* with 60,000 members, but the figure rose 14-fold to 814,285 in 1946. The onset of the cold war had an immediate effect on the party's strength, but the electoral decline at that point was limited (see above). Between 1952 and 1972 membership levelled off at between 300,000 and 400,000. With the signature of the Common Programme and an increasing disassociation from the Soviet Union – what came to be called the 'Eurocommunist period' – membership rose sharply to achieve a new peak of 520,000 in 1978 (the PCF's leadership was claiming at that time a membership of 700,000).[6]

The collapse of the union of the Left in September 1977, and the new rapprochement with the Soviet Union witnessed by the theses proposed by Marchais for the twenty-third congress and his report to that congress,[7] by the television speech that the same general secretary broadcast from Moscow in January 1980 endorsing the invasion of Afghanistan, and by the stance adopted when the military assumed power in Poland in 1981, spelled a fresh departure of members, accompanied this time by electoral reverses. Philippe Buton estimates that between 1978 and 1984 membership fell from 520,000 to 380,000, that is, a drop of 27 per cent.[8] If one follows Jean Ranger,[9] and if one takes account of calculations made at the level of cells or sections, or even federations, and also of an analysis made of a sample of the 1979 members,[10] the peak of 1978–9 could not in fact have surpassed 450,000 members, to sink to a maximum of 230,000 at the end of 1985. This gives an indication, at all events, of the extent of the crisis as measured by this particular criterion of Communist strength (see figure 3.1).

The crisis of militancy

Militant activity, the third element of the Communist political presence, is even more difficult to measure. As in any mass party, there are very many who limit their commitment – despite the sincerity of their convictions – to buying a card and paying for some stamps. Militancy is to be located in the number of posters put up, the demonstrations, the weekly door-to-door sales of *Humanité dimanche* or taking part in the running and direction of organizations that defend the interests of one group or another (trade unions, tenants' associations, parents committees in schools, and the like).

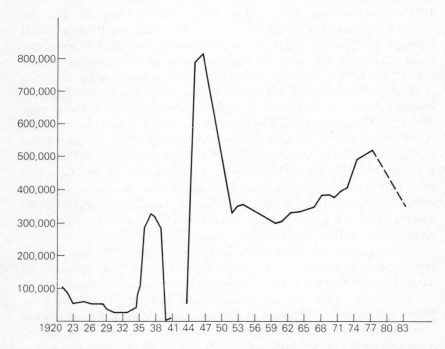

Figure 3.1 Membership of the French Communist Party, 1921–84 (from Philippe Buton, 'Les effectifs du Parti communiste français, 1920–84, *Communisme*, no. 7, 1985, p.9)

This is enough to show that no precise measure is possible. All we have to go on are the accumulated facts in these various domains, and, more often, the observer's impressions. But the outlines are clear. On the one hand, it is subject to extreme variation (which we shall term the 'degree of elasticity'). On the other hand, it is strongly conditioned by political circumstances, and by the high level of a shared, and unchanging, consciousness of a common identity; in other terms, in proportion to the number of members, militancy can be at a high level as long as a strong ideological cohesion is maintained. Finally, militancy inevitably increases in pre-electoral periods, as is required by the political system.

The contrast with the 1970s, when the militant presence of the party was massive and constant, is stark for any observer of French political life. The virtual disappearance of door-to-door selling, walls bereft of posters, and abandoned sales pitches are the all-too-evident signs of a sagging militancy. The appearance of opposition groups at one and the same time reflects and explains this situation.

A tenacious dissidence

Successive defeats have provided the impetus not only for a flood of resignations, but also for an increase in dissidence. Incidents since 1978 have included: a petition signed by hundreds of Communists, chiefly intellectuals, effectively condemning the leadership's refusal to countenance any real debate after the legislative elections of 1978; the revolt of the majority of the editorial teams of the weekly *France nouvelle* and the monthly *La Nouvelle critique* in 1979, which led to the closure of these publications and their replacement by the weekly *Révolution*, the management of which in turn had to be reshuffled in 1985; the crisis in the important Paris *fédération* in 1979–80 in which Henri Fijzbin played the leading role; the creation of a vast movement in 1980–1 grouping together Communists, Socialists and Trotskyists in order to demand unity at the base and at the summit of the party; the formation of an opposition – half internal, half external – around the editorial team of *Rencontres communistes* (editor, Henri Fijzbin) in 1981–2.

The results of the European elections of 1984 (11.2 per cent of the poll and 6.3 per cent of the electorate) and the breaking-off of Communist participation in government (the Fabius government lost its Communist ministers) led to the birth of a new internal offensive, which affected even the Central Committee. A preparatory document for the twenty-fifth party congress was put to the vote on 30 October 1984 but six members of the Central Committee abstained – a thing hitherto unheard of. More, three federations (those of the Haute Vienne, the Hautes Alpes

and Corse du Sud) were soon thereafter to reject the draft; in 25 federations abstentions and adverse votes together exceeded 15 per cent. Some
of these passed substantial amendments to the draft, whilst others strove
to protect the embattled dissident leaderships of the federations in
question by tactical voting. In all its various forms, dissent was concentrated in certain regions: central France, the Mediterranean south and
Lorraine. At the congress itself, on 6–10 February 1985, the debate was
at times fierce.

Faced with this new offensive, large in numbers but diverse in its
motivations, the leadership chose (or had to choose) to conduct a purge
in stages rather than to launch an all-out one. When the Central Committee
came to be elected, 24 members failed to secure re-election, 20 of them
for political reasons. The three principle dissidents, however, had to be
retained – Pierre Juquin, Marcel Rigout and Félix Damette, even if Pierre
Juquin was removed from the Political Bureau, whilst Claude Poperen,
who sympathized with the dissidents, lost his principle responsibilities on
that body. During the following months, the dissidents' chief bases were
reduced, with the replacing of recalcitrant federation secretaries and with
the reorganization of the weekly *Révolution*'s editorial team. But the
electoral returns of 1986 (see above) brought about a new petition which
garnered the signatures of more than 3,000 Communists.

The organizational rules of the PCF make it very difficult for an
opposition of any sort to express its views, by forbidding horizontal
structures to operate and through the selection of party officials by the
level above. But the opposition groups are themselves divided. However
profoundly he opposes the party's policies, the Communist militant is
imbued with certain fundamental principles, such as the primary importance of the defence of the revolutionary weapon against the attacks of
the class enemy (the 'embattled fortress' syndrome) or the need to respect
the rules of democratic centralism. The development of an oppositional
tendency normally takes place gradually and, for each individual, at his
own rhythm, and this makes it all the more fragile. Diversity of motivations also reduces the organizational possibilities.

Since working class members of the party prefer to 'vote with their
feet' and leave in silence, whilst intellectuals express their oppositional
views before leaving, it is the latter who have at all times provided the
main body of dissent in the party. It was the case also in the crisis that
started in 1978. But the haemorrhage has been severe, to the extent that
the PCF now has only a marginal influence with the intelligentsia, whilst
it still had a dominant, if not hegemonic, influence in the 1970s. By
reading the lists of signatures at the foot of petitions it can be seen also,
over the past few years, that a significant part has been played by the
Communist parliamentary deputies, people whom it is hard for the

leadership to attack, since they draw their legitimacy from outside the party, from their electorate. Moreover this externally determined legitimacy, whilst it registers the extent of the party's integration into society, is itself brought into question by the party's decline.

The party's presence in society founders

With a crisis in its electorate, a crisis of recruitment and a crisis of militantism, the party's presence in society has suffered a severe blow simultaneously in these three crucial areas. But the institutions that have traditionally guaranteed the continuity of that presence – the municipalities and the trade unions – have been equally affected.

The severe defeat in the municipal elections of 1983 gashed the tissue that had once provided such rich associational bonds. Analysis of the results is impeded by the fact that Communists stood very often on joint lists with other parties of the Left, but it can be seen that the PCF, in a setback which affected the entire Left, lost on that occasion control of the councils of one-third of its towns with more than 30,000 inhabitants. The implications of losses on this scale are often underestimated, in terms of the enormous number of jobs that can be allocated to the party's officials, or semi-officials, and the preference that can be shown to party-controlled companies when it comes to awarding municipal contracts. The financial dimension of the crisis that the PCF is passing through is not lightly to be neglected.[11]

In the realm of industrial strength, it would be just as absurd to see the *Confédération générale du travail* (CGT), the leading French trade union organization, as nothing more than a 'Communist trade union' as to deny the preponderant role that Communist Party members play in it and the place that the PCF accords to trade union action in its overall strategy. The CGT's problems date back a long way since, if the results of elections to place-of-work committees since 1966 are examined, they reveal that the CGT won 50 per cent of the votes in that year and a little over 37 per cent in 1977–8.

A good deal of this decline is accounted for by the powerful rise of the *Confédération française du travail* (CFDT). In 1984–5, the CGT's vote was scarcely 30 per cent.[12] During the past few years *Force ouvrière* (FO – led by André Bergeron), and electoral lists without a party affiliation have made advances. It should be noted, too, that the results for the first three months of 1986 seem to show a stabilization, and even a slight rise for the CGT. A study of the union's membership is more complicated, owing to a lack of reliable information. Nevertheless, it can be done more easily than for the political parties. We know that French unions are particularly weak and that less than one worker in seven is unionized; and moreover that this proportion has declined in recent years. That is to say, the crisis in the CGT is a crisis that affects all the French trade unions. But, according to René Mouriaux, whilst the FO seems to have gained members, and the CFDT to have lost about 15 per cent, the losses of the CGT amount to 40 per cent over the past ten years.[13]

The special links that exist between the CGT and the PCF cost the latter dear, simply because the crisis in which the PCF finds itself is gaining in complexity and showing a tendency to snowball. This multi-faceted crisis is reflected in the party's decreasing standing in the eyes of the public.

The party's public standing falls

The SOFRES opinion poll and the *Figaro* newspaper (and then the *Figaro Magazine*) have since 1972 provided a monthly survey into the 'good' and 'bad' opinions of French people on the various political parties. The trends are well worth studying, but we can only deal with certain features here. In 1974 33 per cent of people in France held a favourable opinion of the PCF, whilst in 1985 the figure was 15 per cent; in 1974 48 per cent had a poor opinion of the PCF, against 74 per cent in 1985.

But the curve is irregular. The break-up of the union of the Left at the end of 1977, which brought about the joint failure in the legislative elections of 1978, or the spectacular speech by Georges Marchais broadcast direct from Moscow, in which he defended the Soviet intervention in Afghanistan (what Jean-Luc Parodi and Olivier Duhamel termed 'the Kabul effect'),[14] had an immediate detrimental impact. Participation in government brought an improvement, which was checked by the application of the austerity programme (which cost the Left as a whole dear, though the PCF more than the Socialist Party), and by the position that the party adopted on Poland in December 1981.

As for the initial drop in 1974, this can be related to the 'Gulag effect' that attended the publication, with wide publicity, of Solzhenitsyn's *Gulag Archipelago*, and to the forward policy of the Soviet Union in Africa. The spectacular deterioration of the Soviet Union's image in French public opinion thus accompanies, and to an extent explains, the decline of the PCF, to the extent that the latter, from 1979, dropped its critical attitude towards the Soviet Union. Comparison with the upshot of events in Budapest in 1956 and in Prague in 1968 has led Jean-Luc Parodi and Olivier Duhamel[15] to generalize and to say that, whilst such events have had immediate repercussions, a longer-term deterioration sets in if at the time the PCF is in a close relationship with the Soviet Union and if there exists a destination for Communists who have fallen out with their party (in the case in question, a Socialist Party leaning sufficiently to the Left). Thus the problems of the union of the Left and of the PCF's relationship with the Soviet Union are inextricably linked, and have contributed to a crisis that has, since 1978, profoundly shaken the PCF.

This convergence of multiple factors with their cumulative effects emphasizes the weakening of the PCF, but leaves open the question as to what is the real nature of the crisis that the party is passing through. Is this a passing malaise, possibly still reversible? Or is the setback we see today a harbinger of an ineluctable and slow decline, or even of a rapid collapse and a marginalization '*à l'espagnole*'?

We have said that the weakening of the PCF cannot be put down to a single factor, whether social, political, or other. It must rather be explained by the convergence of four major crises. Two of these are structural and are quite beyond the party's control: the crisis of the working class and the crisis of the communist eco-system. The other two are internal to the PCF: the crisis of leadership and that of the communist identity.

The crisis of the working class

One of the principal historical characteristics of the PCF is to have been the only Stalinist party to have succeeded in the inter-war period in becoming a mass workers' party, and one that was capable of maintaining this position for more than 50 years. The PCF based its strength – between 1935 and 1937 – on a firm implantation in a working class that had three essential characteristics.

First of all, for some 60 years the working class has been a numerically expanding social force. The process by which the PCF came to take root among the workers during the Popular Front period coincides with the apogee of the second French industrial revolution which, from 1900 to 1930 brought about a massive increase in the working class. From 4.3 million in 1906, the number of industrial workers leaped to 6.3 million in 1931.[16] The most rapid rise was in the metallurgical industries, which passed from 600,000 to 1.2 million, and in the railways, which stood at 500,000 in 1931. The metal worker and the railway worker are two emblematic figures of the communist party member and party leader. Moreover, this rise in numbers was accompanied by a radical change in the class structure. Whilst in 1906 60 per cent of workers were employed in factories with a work force of under 100, in 1931 more than 50 per cent were employed in factories with a work force of over 100.

This evolution was to bring in its train, secondly, a pronounced homogenization of the working class world, which until then had been composed for the greater part of workers with trades that were often close to those of the artisan. Now the working class world came to be dominated in a few decades by the specialized worker–the *ouvrier spécialisé* (OS) – a pure product of the rationalization of work and of the big firm, and whose role, as we know, was essential to the Communist successes of 1935 and 1936.

Finally, this emerging working class in the process of construction had a driving impulse to strike social, territorial and cultural roots. For the greater part this new working class was composed of immigrants, immigrants from the interior, the product of a rural exodus which, in the 1920s, drained away towards the cities and large-scale industry over a million of the rural population, mostly from Britanny and the Massif Central.[17] But there were also immigrants from abroad who, in 1931, formed 15 per cent of the working class. Concentrated above all in the worst jobs, those that the French no longer accepted, they made up at the time 42 per cent of mining workers, 38.2 per cent of those in heavy industry and 29 per cent of those in construction.

It was to this working class in course of formation, and in the ascendant, that the economic crisis, from 1933 on, was to administer a shock that struck at two of its initial and cherished aspirations. In the short term, this working class was firmly set on establishing a strategy of collective defence of its chief gains – jobs and aid in the event of unemployment on the one hand, and on the other an improvement in its immediate living conditions. In the middle and long term, it sought stability, an identity and integration into the nation (this was true both for the internal and external immigrants).[18]

It was to these aspirations that the PCF responded in 1935 at the time of the municipal elections which saw the rise of the 'red suburbs' around Paris, and in the spring of 1936 during the legislative elections of the Popular Front. This first response from the summer of 1936 was doubled by the reunited CGT, which was soon taken in hand by the Communist militants. The role of the PCF as the means whereby a new working class sought to establish itself in society was consecrated in the sacrifices of the Resistance and the Liberation. The PCF preserved this heritage without great difficulty from 1945 to 1974.

Since 1974, however, the situation of the working class has been quite turned round by the blows of a new economic crisis. It is today a numerically declining force. Between 1975 and 1985 industry lost 1.2 million jobs and in 1985 a further loss of one million was foreseen for the coming decade. The workers alone – not counting foremen and administrators – have shrunk by one million, mostly from among the non-qualified. From 1975 to 1984 the car industry registered a decline in its overall work force of 6 per cent, but of 22 per cent among unskilled workers. In public construction works the figures were 13 and 34 per cent respectively, and in electrical construction 5 and 29 per cent.[19] Within the working population the working class has been quite outstripped by workers in the tertiary sector which, between 1975 and 1985, made a net gain of one and a half million jobs and thus formed some 60 per cent of the employed work force.

Moreover, the working world is becoming ever more heterogeneous. There has been a strong diversification in industry, where the tertiary sector accounted for only 20 per cent of the work force in 1962, but for 37 per cent in 1985. Engineers and technicians leaped from 270,000 in 1954 to 1.3 million in 1983. The working class itself has become fundamentally heterogeneous, to the extent that the INSEE has had to separate out two broad categories within it: on the one hand workers of an industrial type, who amounted to 3.2 million in 1985, almost 800,000 of them being immigrant workers; and on the other hand artisans, of whom there are 2 million, the product of a rapid increase, especially in the large towns, of the maintenance and repair sector. Often these are more qualified workers – motor mechanics, service agents for electrical and electronic household appliances, and workers employed in the domestic installation of such alliances.

Finally, this working class of the years from 1920 to 1970, for which social and territorial establishment had become a basic collective requirement, was precipitately and unceremoniously plunged during the period 1975–80 into an economic crisis that required the restructuring of industry and implied territorial mobility and retraining for the workers. This process was particularly apparent in the mines of the Nord and the Pas-de-Calais, and in the mines and steel works of Lorraine.

All these factors, converging, have, by atomizing it, splitting it and reducing it in size, brought about a radical change in the working class within which the PCF was establishing itself. Furthermore, there has been, since the 1960s, a complete change in the habits of blue collar workers, stemming from the rise in the standard of living. In 1953, 8 per cent of workers owned a car, against 73.6 per cent in 1975; 0.9 per cent had a television set, against 88.4 per cent in 1975; 3 per cent used a refrigerator against 91.6 per cent. Above all, 19.8 per cent owned their house or flat in 1953 against 37.5 per cent in 1975 and 44 per cent in 1985 (the same percentage as for white collar workers).

The Communists are themselves conscious of these changes. Here is Viviane, an unskilled worker, and a Communist militant: 'Before, the good life was having enough to eat. Nowadays, the good life is a holiday, labour-saving machines at home, the car, the sitting-room, skiing holidays, the computer for the kid, evenings out at the theatre. It's a fuller life than 40 years ago. The party doesn't realize it.'[20] This is confirmed by a party official from the Puy de Dome, Jean-Pierre Antignac:

For a long time the workers, for us, were conditioned to spending 90 per cent of their time at work. But now, for wage earners, the job is only half their time – and what's more, with completely different working relationships and economic results – and the other half of the time with their eyes open on a whole lot of other concerns – individual, family, cultural and so on . . .[21]

In parallel with this, the workers have undergone a crisis of identity. A SOFRES survey shows that from 1975 to 1982 'the percentage of French people who felt that they belonged to the working class sank from 27 to 22, whilst in the same period the share of the working class in the active population sank from 36 to 31.[22]

Finally, the traditional political representation of the working class has, in turn, entered a period of crisis. In one decade the traditional working class has been much reduced in numbers. Its more qualified members have gone on to be integrated into society and to be assimilated to the middle class. Its older members have been the particular victims of increasing unemployment and deindustrialization and have been unable to convert to other occupations before retirement. Its least qualified members are for the most part its least well protected layers – immigrants, women, and non-qualified young people. The social foundation on which for 50 years the Communist edifice rested is in the process of dissolution. Through a shock-wave effect, this dissolution has triggered a destabilization of the Communist eco-system.

The crisis in the Communist eco-system

In the 1930s French society found a certain equilibrium – in economic, social and political terms – which lasted until the end of the 1960s. Within this framework the PCF had established and maintained a stable position. It drew support, certainly, from a nationwide constituency, but both electoral geography and an examination of the way in which the party's electorate developed show that its strength rested, from the 1930s, on three zones where it was particularly well implanted: the industrial regions, the *départements* of the Mediterranean coast, and the west and north of the Massif Central.[23] In each of these zones, between 1935 and 1945, a sort of political and social eco-system was established, largely dominated by the PCF, and organized around the Communist municipalities. In this way a number of mass bastions were created, which showed a formidable cohesion and allowed real local and regional identities to emerge, attuned to the Communist phenomenon.[24] The Paris suburbs, or the valley of the Longwy basin where the steelworks were located, were veritable prototypes of this eco-system. Today, however, not only has the PCF lost a great part of its national influence, but it has suffered a serious crisis in these its traditional bastions.

It is obviously in the industrial regions that the party has been hardest hit. In the Nord, the Pas-de-Calais, the Somme, the Ardennes, the Seine Inférieure, the Aisne, the Allier, the Moselle and the Meurthe-et-Moselle, the traditional industries are in full decline. These regions now have the highest rate of unemployment – more than 12.5 per cent of the active population in 1984.[25]

In the Paris region, deindustrialization has proceeded apace after 1974. According to Jean Lojkine, between 1962 and 1976 Ivry-sur-Seine lost 50 per cent of its industrial jobs, Saint-Denis 46 per cent, Saint-Ouen, Bois-Colombes 44 per cent, and so on...; it is impossible not to relate this 'deindustrial' revolution to the palpable collapse of the Communist eco-system in the 'red suburbs'. In the legislative elections of 1986, the PCF won only 11.8 per cent of the poll (against 26.4 in 1978) and ten seats (against 27 in 1978).[26] Massive unemployment and early retirements are destabilizing the working class communities and provoking an upsurge of xenophobia and racism that benefits the National Front of Jean-Marie Le Pen. Many workers have lost hope in the strategy of collective defence – as is borne out by the general crisis of French trade unionism and the decline of the CGT in particular.

Although less industrialized, the Mediterranean littoral has also seen its Communist eco-system severely affected. Together with the industrial regions of the north, it has had the highest rate of unemployment in France – over 12.5 per cent of the active population. In this region, the 'disgruntlement vote' that was once given to the PCF seems now to go to the National Front, which has had its best result there (of over 20 per cent) in the Bouches-du-Rhône and the Alpes-Maritimes. Dismayed by the economic crisis, the poorer sections of society that have traditionally inclined to an oppositional stance seem now to have swung towards either abstention on a massive scale or the National Front.

It is in the north and west of the Massif Central that the PCF is holding its own best. Paradoxically, these are the most rural areas of France (with a population over 17.5 per cent agricultural), where the population is older (less than 28.5 per cent of people under 25 years old), more static (in 1982, over 55 per cent of inhabitants were dwelling in the same housing they had occupied in 1975), and the most Malthusian (less than 1.75 children per woman on average).[27] As early as 1849 these regions were the most republican and anti-clerical but also the most opposed to the process of modernization imposed by Paris. The PCF replaced the Republicans and became the mouthpiece of this France *profonde* soon to be condemned.

The crisis affecting the PCF, however, is not due solely to the blows administered by the evolution of French society. The party must bear its own share of responsibility, in particular in an area where it is supposed to excel – that of politics, of strategy and tactics. Here, it seems, it leadership has let it down.

The crisis of leadership

One of the crucial tasks of a communist leadership is to conduct what Lenin termed 'a concrete analysis of concrete situations', so as to judge whether the moment is favourable or not for a given action – in short to establish a line of policy for the short, medium and long terms. In all these realms, however, the PCF's leadership has shown itself quite incapable of innovation.

On the one hand, since 1961 it has blocked all timid attempts to learn the lessons of the evolution of socialism. The weight both of Marxist–Leninist doctrine and of the mythology of the Popular Front imposed on the party an untouchable equation: PCF = working class = proletariat = the eternal and unalterable reality. It is for this reason that the PCF to a great extent failed to understand the movement of May–June 1968, representing as it did the aspirations of young working people (including women and immigrants) for consumer goods, for culture, and more generally for liberty, in particular in the moral realm; and for democracy, in particular spontaneous and anti-authoritarian democracy.

At the same time, rallying in 1965 behind the presidential candidature of François Mitterrand, the PCF embarked on a strategy of a union of the Left. This strategy was based on an incorrect estimate of the balance of political forces. In fact, in the presidential elections of 1969, the PCF, thanks to Jacques Duclos, had won over 21 per cent of the poll, whilst the socialist Gaston Deferre scored no more than 5 per cent. Over-hastily the PCF decided that 'social-democracy', being moribund, would make a fine ally, controllable and open to influence. But this was to leave two things out of account; the prominence since 1968 of the middle classes, their way of behaving and their values; secondly, François Mitterrand sensed that the time had come to build a solid party apparatus to base himself on, and staged a takeover bid on the old SFIO. At the congress of Epinay in 1972, he transformed it into a 'brand new' socialist party which made immediate inroads into the middle classes so scorned by the PCF.

At the very moment when the Common Programme was signed (1972) the balance of forces had already potentially swung in favour of the Socialist Party. Underestimating the influence of the institutions of the Fifth Republic on the political game, the PCF understood too late that by being directly elected, the President of the Republic has been since 1962 the hub of the political scene. It thus contributed directly, by supporting a single candidate of the Left in 1965 and in 1974, to the forging of Mitterrand's presidential image, and to the implanting in the mind of left-wing voters – Communists among them – a reflex towards avoiding a 'wasted vote', thus reducing the Communist votes to a mere supporting role.

On the other hand, in taking part in the union of the Left, the party leadership had realized that the double ballot system would allow it to appear much more often in the second round, when it could win the consolidated votes on the Left. The calculation paid off, in particular in the municipal elections of 1977. But by that time the Socialist breakthrough was becoming clear enough to enable the Socialist Party to gain from the same mechanism in 1977 and after. Until 1978 the PCF maintained by and large its normal vote, and won an appreciable number of seats – 10 in 1958, 73 in March 1967, 73 in March 1973 and 86 in March 1978 (against 115 for the Socialists). But once the Communist vote began to fall, the mechanism worked entirely against the party: in the legislative elections of 1981, the Socialists won an absolute majority with 222 deputies, the PCF winning only 37 deputies. At the same time, because of its poor analysis of the balance of forces the PCF fell into the trap that François Mitterrand had, no doubt, deliberately laid for it.

Once it had realized what had happened, the PCF tried to free itself. Having been enthusiastic enough for two in its support of unity, it now attacked the Socialists so vehemently that it appeared as the 'shipwrecked' partner of the union of the Left, and a part of its electorate abandoned it in 1981. Furthermore, the breakdown of the union coincided with a spectacular return of the PCF to the Soviet allegiance. In March 1979 Georges Marchais made his celebrated announcement that the record of 'real socialism' was 'globally positive', and went on, in January 1980, to give his approval, on television from Moscow, of the Soviet invasion of Afghanistan. The 'Kabul effect' brought about a sharp drop in the PCF's image in French public opinion.

As François Hincker has pointed out, the PCF has missed two historic opportunities:

From the end of the war in Algeria in 1962 to the congress of Epinay in 1972, a wide political space opened on the left for the PCF, and with the benefit of hindsight one can image the party occupying it in the same way as the Italian Communist Party had done in Italy. But until Maurice Thorez died there could be no question of this, and thereafter the party's progress was slow and uncertain. By 1972, it was too late.

Between 1974 and 1981

. . . being unwilling to settle for the most that it could hope to achieve, given the changes in the social structure of France and the fact that the Socialist Party had already managed to reoccupy the political space on the non-communist left, the PCF was to lose the whole of its stake.[28]

In 1979

the PCF fell back on a non-strategy – for the first time in its history. Up until 1934 the revolutionary strategy retained a certain credibility in the small communist movement (in France), and after 1947, union of the Left became the point of reference. The first was no longer tenable – the party having itself repudiated it – whilst the second had been abandoned. The party had nothing left to it but 'being there'.[29]

It is therefore a 'globally negative' balance that the PCF has had to record for the period of 16 years that opened with the presidential elections of 1965 and closed with its serious defeat in those of 1981. Since 1981 the party has strung together in a continuous chain four phases that are entirely contradictory. Until 26 April 1981 (the first round of the presidential elections) it attacked Mitterrand and the PS with all it had. From 27 April it declared itself for Mitterrand in the second round, and then signed an agreement with the PS for a reciprocal withdrawal in the second round of the legislative elections, and accepted four ministerial portfolios in a government completely dominated by the PS, after having signed a 'political agreement for governing' with the latter on 23 June.

On 19 July 1984, the PCF abruptly decided to leave the government and embarked forthwith on an increasingly violent criticism of the Socialist government. Since 26 March 1986 (the date of the Right's victory in the legislative elections) the PCF has persistently maintained that the Right and the PS are as a like as two peas in a pod. This hardly coherent policy could not but throw the party's militants into increasing disarray whilst decreasing its credibility.

The PCF and the crisis of the Communist identity

The Communists in France have always been presented as forming a homogeneous and uniform whole, endowed with a great organic unity. But the party's recent decline shows clearly that around a working class core that has guaranteed its stability, the PCF has managed to collect a congeries of elements that are diverse in social terms – blue collar workers, agricultural workers, people from the middle classes and the intelligentsia – and also in terms of generations and political experiences. The great strength of the party's historic leaders – Maurice Thorez, Jacques Duclos, Bernard Frachon – was that they showed considerable skill in managing this very variegated amalgam.

It is this blending of the old with the new, the traditional with the modern, that the generation of leaders represented by Georges Marchais has been unable to achieve. For the past quarter of a century it has not succeeded in putting life into a revolutionary movement that stems from the nineteenth century. The sources of this failure lie in the social evolution of the party, which shows up three major imbalances.

The first derives from the social origins of the Communists. Since the end of the 1970s the PCF has been a party as much of the working as of the middle class,[30] but the party's apparatus is more and more dominated by the latter, and this conflicts with a Communist history of more than 50 years marked by a great homogeneity of members, militants and leaders. The non-manual workers come from a very different, indeed opposed, culture from that of the workers of the inter-war and post-war periods. They do not share the strong working class values that once characterized the PCF. It was only a matter of time before they would come into conflict with a leadership drawn almost entirely from the working class and much attached to the status of working class politician that this provided.[31] The end of the working class monopoly, or at least dominance, in respect of the apparatus opened up a fundamental crisis of identity between the apparatus and the leadership, and between the apparatus and the rank and file. White collar workers are in the majority in the federal apparatuses, but they are in the minority among congress delegates and even more so among the first secretaries of the federations. This blocking to white collar workers of the access routes to the highest posts in the party has no doubt much to do with the crises since 1977/8 in which 'intellectuals' have opposed the leadership.

The second major imbalance concerns the age structure of the party. At the twenty-third congress in 1979, 76.8 per cent of the delegates were under 39 years of age whilst at that time 51.3 per cent of party members were over 39. The strong advantage that was thus given to young militants of the 1968 and 1974–8 generations has emphasized the contrast between a party base that has its roots in the France of before 1968 and an intermediate apparatus very largely made up of people who joined the party after 1968.

Finally, and most important of all, a major imbalance has appeared between the political generations and the various levels within the party. Whilst in 1979 the majority of members (59.1 per cent) had joined the party during the upswing of the union of the Left (between 1972 and 1979), most middle-level apparatus workers (55.7 per cent) joined in the aftermath of 1968 (1968–74). In the great majority of cases, however, the party's leaders are still drawn from the Thorez generation (77 per cent of federation first secretaries in 1982 had joined before 1967). Since 1979 a fourth generation must be added, one that joined after the collapse of the Common Programme and is thus extremely hostile to the Socialists. The PCF is thus in a totally novel situation; by its very diversity it bears the seeds of a collapse of its homogeneity at the level of the political generations it comprises. 'Managing' these four generations, which are not only diverse, but potentially antagonistic, looks likely to prove an extremely tricky exercise for the leadership, and all the more so because there is a risk that the differences of behaviour and viewpoint that can arise between political generations might be compounded by rifts between militants occupying differing positions in the party's hierarchy.

Conclusions

The PCF today then has two major problems of an internal nature. On the one hand there has been a breakdown in the homogeneity of its membership due to a change of political generations. This has meant that relations are now difficult between the political generations and at the party's various levels – rank and file, cadres and leadership. France's oldest political party is in the completely novel situation of having to integrate and manage political generations that are very, if not too, diverse, and to some extent mutually antagonistic. Yet no leader seems to have emerged with an authority such as would enable the party to surmount these difficulties and to weld the generations together, as Maurice Thorez succeeded in doing from 1930 to 1964 thanks to the homogeneity of the working class and to the Stalinist myth.

This dual internal change which, we have suggested, affects the core of the party, throws the central problem wide open – that of the party's communist identity. The PCF's great strength from 1934 until 1981 was to base its identity on the closest possible relationship between its two major dimensions: first, the social dimension – that is, everything in communism that concerns more or less explicitly the interplay of social, economic, political and cultural forces in French society with the institutions and organizations that aspire to represent them. And secondly, the teleological dimension – everything in communism that concerns the functioning of the world communist system, i.e. doctrine (Marxism–Leninism), strategy (solidarity with the Soviet Union and proletarian internationalism), the functioning and defence of the revolutionary mode of organization (democratic centralism).

These two dimensions work as part of a single system but, in the last resort, it is the teleological dimension that commands at all times, even if it means the breakdown, provisional or permanent, of the social dimension. Today, everything indicates that the PCF is sacrificing its social dimension. Because of its more or less unconditional solidarity with the Soviet Union, its image in public opinion continues to deteriorate. Under the impulse of its anti-socialist and *ouvrièriste* tradition, the PCF is departing each day a little further from the realities of French society. It proclaims itself the party of the working class alone, at a time when that class is in the process of 'evaporating' as a social reality; it proclaims itself the sole revolutionary party and rejects the notion of 'the Left' when a large part of its electorate wants left-wing unity. Charles Fiterman, who had become the party's second-in-command, was not abashed, at the twenty-fifth congress, to talk of 'the external situation of the PCF in relation to the political system', ingenuously wondering whether that implied an external situation in relation to society itself.

The PCF appears complacent in the face of this process of external and internal deterioration. It refuses, in the full knowledge of what is happening, to heed the anguished warnings of its various dissidents. Can it be that it is sailing, all flags flying, towards a foundering that it suspects is inevitable, or is it hoping to be able to select, during a sectarian period, 'Bolshevik' cadres who will preserve its revolutionary purity and at the same time will be able, when the moment comes, to provide the leadership for a popular movement, just as the cadres chosen during the 'class against class' period made possible the triumph of the Popular Front and the Resistance?

Notes

1 Georges Lavau, *A quoi sert le PCF?* (Fayard, Paris, 1981).
2 See in particular, among the more recent and detailed electoral studies, François Platone and Jean Ranger, 'L'échec électoral du Parti communiste' in *1981: Les élections de l'alternance* (Presses de la Fondation nationale des sciences politiques, Paris, 1986); and Jean Ranger, 'Le déclin du Parti communiste français', *Revue française de science politique*, vol. 36, no. 1, February 1986, pp. 46–63.
3 The expression is Jean Fourastier's and refers to the long period of marked growth, and the profound changes that French society and the French economy went through, from the end of the 1940s to the mid-1970s.
4 Annie Kriegel, 'Le Parti communiste français sous la IIIe. république (1920–1939). Mouvement des effectifs et structures d'organisation'. *Revue française de science politique*, vol. 16 no. 1, 1966; and *International Review of Social History*, vol. 9, part 3, 1966, reprinted in Annie Kriegel, *Le pain et les roses* (PUF, Paris, 1968).

5   Philippe Buton, 'Les effectifs du Parti communiste français (1920–1984)', *Communisme*, no. 7, 1985, pp. 5–30.
6   Ibid., pp. 5/6.
7   It was on this occasion that the expression 'a globally positive record' was used.
8   Philippe Buton, 'Les effectifs du PCF', pp. 23–8.
9   Jean Ranger, 'Le déclin du PCF', p. 57.
10 François Platone, 'Les adhérents de l'apogée. La composition du PCF en 1979', *Communisme*, no. 7, 1985, pp. 31–64. This very thorough study was made on the basis of a sample of questionnaires drawn from the entire collection of records on individual members held by the federations of the PCF.
11 cf. Raymond Pronier, *Les municipalités communistes*, (Balland, Paris, 1983).
12 For an examination of these results see the 'Chronique de la vie communiste' regularly included in issues of the journal *Communisme* (nos. 1–8 published by PUF; no. 9 et seq. published by L'Age d'Homme).
13 René Mouriaux, 'Le syndicalisme frappé de langueur', *Politique aujourd'hui*, no. 9, March/April 1985.
14 Olivier Duhamel and Jean-Luc Parodi, 'Images du communisme', *Pouvoirs*, Pt 1: no. 21, 1982, pp. 169–79; Pt 2: no. 22, 1982, pp. 159–72.
15 Ibid., Pt 2, p. 172.
16 Gérard Noiriel, *Les ouvriers dans la société française, 19e.–20e. siècle* (Seuil, Paris, 1986).
17 Stéphane Courtois, 'Enracinement des populations et implantation politique; triomphe et décadence du communisme français', Paper delivered to the workshop on Sociétés ouvrières et monde communiste, Université de Paris X, April 1986.
18 Annie Fourcaut, *Bobigny, banlieue rouge* (Editions ouvrières, Presses de la FNSP, Paris, 1986); Gérard Noiriel, *Longwy, immigrés et prolétaires, 1880–1980* (PUF, Paris, 1984).
19 Jacques Broyelle, 'Des ouvriers de plus en plus bourgeois', in *Valeurs actuelles*, 3 March 1986.
20 Michel Cardoze, *Nouveau voyage à l'intérieur du PCF* (Fayard, Paris, 1986), p. 178.
21 Ibid.
22 Gérard Noiriel, 'Les ouvriers'.
23 Philippe Buton, 'Les effectifs du PCF'.
24 Raymond Pronier, *Les municipalités communistes*.
25 Hervé Le Bras, *Les trois Frances* (Seuil, Paris, 1986).
26 Jean Lojkine, *Classe ouvrière, société locale et municipalités en région parisienne* (Centre d'étude des mouvements sociaux, Paris, 1984), p. 1–160.
27 Hervé Le Bras, *Les trois Frances*.
28 François Hincker, 'France: le PCF divorce de la société' *Communisme*, 11–12 (1986), pp. 86–98.
29 Ibid.
30 Stéphane Courtois, 'Les délégués aux congrès du PCF et l'évolution de l'appareil communiste (1956–1985)' *Communisme*, 10 (1986), pp. 92–116.
31 Bernard Pudal, 'Doctrine stalinienne et légitimation du personnel politique communiste (1920–1939)' *Communisme*, 10 (1986), pp. 53–69.

4 Spanish Communism in Crisis
The Communist Party of Spain

Juan Botella

Since 1980, the word most often used to refer to the Communist Party of Spain (*Partido Comunista de España* – PCE) has certainly been 'crisis'. A mere list of recent top-rank PCE leaders and of their present political positions is truly remarkable: Santiago Carrillo has created a *Partido de los Trabajadores de España–Unidad Comunista* (Spanish Workers' Party–Communist Unity: PTE–VC); I. Gallego and J. Ballesteros are leaders of a clearly pro-Soviet *Partido Comunista de los Pueblos de España* (Communist Party of the Peoples of Spain); names as prominent as Manuel Azcárate, Pilar Brabo, Vicente Cazcarra, Eugenio Triana or Carlos Alonso Zaldívar have joined the *Partido Socialista Obrero Español* (PSOE), while others, such as Jordi Solé-Tura, Ramón Tamames or Jordi Borja are close to, but clearly outside, the PCE.

Split into three different groups, with an electoral influence reduced to one-third of its previous already low results (and with perhaps a heavier loss of influence in other political, not merely electoral, fields) and forced to survive under a Socialist government more solid than its counterparts in other Southern European countries, the situation of the PCE seems to be one of the most difficult among the Western European communist parties.

Paradoxical as it might seem, one can recall here how the PCE was viewed, even as late as 1979, as a leading party in the Eurocommunist wave, as the party that had gone furthest in accepting democracy and in moving away from the Soviet model (for example by rejecting Leninism and by dropping 'democratic centralism' and workplace-centred 'cells'). All its strategic moves in that period, aimed at making the PCE the leading party of the Left in Spain, are confronted ironically with today's realities: Spanish Socialists have won two successive general elections with a majority of seats and a near-majority of the popular vote, while the PCE now has to fight desperately to avoid disappearing from the political arena.[1]

It would be misleading to search for a single, individual factor that would explain the PCE's evolution, just as it would be wrong also to speak about a single crisis: in fact, from at least 1980 until 1985 the PCE underwent an almost continuous series of crises which, although largely independent from and unrelated to each other, have made its very survival problematic. The usual interpretations tend to lay the emphasis on internal factors, on a struggle for power within the party, as the main explanation for the crisis. From this point of view, it is often stressed how the adoption of Eurocommunist policies, and of political orientations more generally, was paradoxically made in a completely top-down way, with the leadership (or part of it) taking steps that would subsequently be approved by the party. This line of argument identifies in Carrillo's personality and style of leadership the main cause of clashes within the PCE, that were to damage the party's image among the mass electorate and even among party members, opening the way for a massive defection towards the PSOE, the Socialist Workers' Party, which was younger, more attractive and better qualified to win.[2]

Without arguing against the validity of such an explanation (which is certainly true as a description of the PCE's own critical view of the process) certain other aspects have also to be taken into account: on the one hand, it is not clear why so much has to be attributed to personal, psychological factors; and, what is more important, these personalized interpretations are of little use in a comparative setting. In the following pages special attention will be devoted to the social and electoral base of the PCE, to its strategic and programmatic definitions and to the peculiar interplay between the former and the latter (which is, I think, an essential point in understanding the crisis in the PCE).

The PCE's social base

The party

The PCE has one particular feature in common with other Spanish political parties – namely its fragility as a political organization. Even at its peak, during and after the transition to democracy, figures for membership have been rather low. At its ninth congress in April 1978 the PCE claimed a membership of 240,000; according to my own partial estimates, this figure should be reduced to around 175,000, which, whilst still making the PCE the Spanish party with the highest membership, compares poorly with its 1.6 million votes in the 1977 general election.

Although no independent estimates are available for the critical period after 1980, official estimates of membership have decreased sharply: 132,069 at the tenth congress (July 1981), and 84,652 at the eleventh (December 1983).

From a geographical point of view, membership distribution closely follows the electoral results, and does not differ from the traditional map of the Spanish republican and leftist tradition: the party is strong on the Mediterranean littoral, from France to Portugal, in central and western Andalusia, Madrid, and Asturias in the north. The Basque country, in spite of a relatively important Communist presence in the 1930s, is an exception, quite clearly because of the Basque political situation and the overwhelming predominance of the national cleavage. Communist presence is very low in the rural regions of central Spain, in the traditional north and in the islands.

As shown in table 4.1, PCE members offer a profile not widely different from other Western European communist parties: mainly young, with a working class majority (but with a strong representation of technicians, professionals and non-manual employees), a low presence of women, and so on. These data, however, refer to the period preceding the most acutely critical moments, which may have changed some elements of that profile. Nevertheless, it is quite possible that, losses and crises having appeared at both ends of the spectrum, those changes may have cancelled each other out, leaving the general profile more or less

Table 4.1 PCE membership (percentages)

Gender	
Men	87
Women	13
Date of joining	
Before 1939	9
1940–60	14
1961–70	32
1971–78	45
Occupation	
Industrial workers	39
Non-manual workers	15
Professionals	32
Small businessmen, self-employed	3
Agrarian workers	3
Students	4
Others	4

Source: PCE (Comisión de Credenciales), 'Los delegados asistentes al IX Congreso', *Nuestra Bandera*, 93 (1978), p. 11; and J. Botella (1982)

unaffected (except for a certain ageing); as mentioned, no recent independent data are available, which makes any assumption merely hypothetical.[3]

The same fragility is visible in other aspects of Spanish Communism. As for the press, the party's weekly, *Mundo Obrero*, became a daily newspaper in 1978; its low sales (reaching a maximum of around 30,000) and subsequent financial difficulties led to a suspension of daily printing in July 1980, when sales had fallen to a little above 10,000, at which point weekly publication was resumed.

However, the most important point here concerns the changes made in some central elements of the Leninist tradition of party organization. Since the summer of 1976 (that is, one year before its legalization) the PCE shifted from a cell model, based on small units in the workplace, to a residential arrangement based on 'groups' (*agrupaciones*), which were larger units of up to 100 members each. A further step was taken in 1978, when 'democratic centralism' disappeared from the party statutes, being replaced by 'democratic rules'. Although the latter change may be considered as merely formal (as the definition of 'democratic rules' reproduces the traditional one of democratic centralism), the former has certainly had important consequences for the PCE, such as the reduction of internal discussion, the priority given to more general and ideological (and thus more divisive) issues, and a growing distance between the party and the trade unions at the grass-roots level, which has led to a clear gap opening between trade unionists and the rest of the party activists.[4]

The voters

As can be seen from table 4.2, the PCE received 1.6 million votes in the first democratic elections held in Spain (a result which was at the time considered low), reaching a high point of nearly 2 million in 1979, slightly above 10 per cent of the vote, and falling subsequently to less than 1 million in 1982 and 1986.

Interestingly, Communist electoral results have been best in senate, regional and especially local elections. Although aggregate general results for the 1979 and 1983 local elections make little sense (because no Spanish party has fought local elections in all Spanish cities), both elections registered visible increases in the PCE vote; even after its serious defeat in the 1982 general elections, the PCE was able in 1983 to keep more than half its previous local power positions, including the control of almost one hundred local councils (among them only one main city, Córdoba), with results often involving up to 60 per cent of the vote. Of course, the popularity of some local personalities explains this increase in the vote, but this does not, however, seem to have an influence on general election results in those same cities.

As mentioned above, the PCE's best results are obtained on the Mediterranean coast, in central and western Andalusia, Madrid, and Asturias. Catalonia, which in 1977 and 1979 was the electoral stronghold of Spanish communism, ranked below Asturias and Andalusia in the 1982 and 1986 elections, as electoral losses have been stronger here than elsewhere. The PCE's results are higher in industrial areas; in the red belts of important cities (such as Madrid, Barcelona, Valencia or Seville) but not in the main cities themselves; and also in some rural areas in Andalusia and Tarragona. Survey data show a strong influence among young people, skilled workers, migrants and professionals (see table 4.3).

From an attitudinal point of view, PCE voters (as compared with those of other parties) are better informed, more politically interested, with a higher degree of attitude formation and closer to the party they vote for. It is interesting to note that PCE voters have been differing markedly from other parties' voters in their stronger acceptance of democracy, tolerance and civil rights, and rejection of Francoism. Although past repression of Spanish communism can be an explanation for this, it is, in my opinion, an important element for understanding the Communist vote in Spain and also, as I will suggest, in understanding the crisis of Spanish communism after 1982.[5]

The party and trade unions

In this respect, the Spanish situation is perhaps unique. While the PCE, even in its brighter moments, has been since the democratic transition a small party as compared with the PSOE, this relation is inverted at the trade union level, where the *Comisiones Obreras* (CC.OO., the Workers' Committees) have always had more influence than the Socialist-directed General Workers' Union (*Unioń General de Trabajadores* – UGT). Only

Table 4.2   PCE electoral results at general elections

	1977	1979	1982	1986
No. of votes	1,655,744	1,940,236	824,978	930,223
Percentage of vote	9.1	10.6	3.8	4.6
Seats	20	23	4	7

At the 1986 General Election, Carrillo's group, MUC, received 225,571 votes, 1.1 per cent of the total vote, without winning any seat.
Source: Electoral records

in the 1982 shop steward elections did the UGT gain a slight advantage over the CC.OO., without doubt as a consequence of the general pro-Socialist wave related to the PSOE's victory in the October 1982 elections (see table 4.4).

The reasons for the CC.OO.'s preeminence over the UGT have to be looked for in the past, and basically in the last years of Francoism. The two important labour organizations of the 1930s, the anarchosyndicalist CNT and the socialist-directed UGT, disappeared almost completely from Spanish society after the end of the Spanish civil war and the political repression that followed; only the UGT was able to survive as an externally based organization, and with a small traditional, almost sub-cultural presence in the Basque country (around Bilbao) and Asturias.

Table 4.3 Profile of PCE voters (percentages)

Gender	
Men	73
Women	27
Age	
Under 25	31
26–35	24
36–45	14
46–55	25
56 +	7
Education level	
Below primary	33
Primary	29
Secondary	23
Technical	6
University	9
Occupation	
Businessmen, managers, professional	2
Small businessmen, farmers, self-employed	9
Agrarian workers	10
Skilled workers	35
Non-skilled workers	8
Non-manual	30
Technicians, engineers	6
Religion	
Practising Catholics	15
Non-practising	44
Indifferent	23
Non-religious	18

Source: As table 4.1

Table 4.4 Results of *elecciones sindicales*, as percentage of elected delegates affiliated to each trade union

	1978	*1980*	*1982*	*1986*[a]
CC.OO.	34.4	31.8	33.4	34.3
UGT	21.7	29.4	36.7	40.2
Others, unaffiliated	43.9	38.8	29.9	25.5

[a]Elections were not held in 1984. Provisional results for 1986.

As Spain developed economically, becoming an industrialized country in the 1960s, with enormous population transfers from rural to urban areas, a new labour movement emerged. Because of police repression, it could not have a permanent mass organization or a bureaucratic structure; in fact, it was only active at special times, such as collective bargaining, solidarity actions, strikes and so on. Early in the 1960s, during a miners' strike in Asturias, this movement was given its name – *comisiones obreras* (workers' committees). It must be borne in mind that the CC.OO. was not formally a trade union (not even a clandestine one), but rather a movement (a sociopolitical movement), a label that was applied to the only possible forms of labour action under Franco's rule. This explains their main outlook during the period: flexibiiity, low level of centralization, discontinuities in action, rather charismatic leaders, and so on. In fact, the term 'CC.OO.' became synonymous with 'labour movement' in Spain between 1962 and 1975. And since the PCE was the only organized and active political group in Spain, its members were to become, almost necessarily, the leaders of the CC.OO. movement.

As could be expected, the CC.OO. was born outside and against the official trade union organization, the CNS (*Central Nacional Sindicalista*). In 1958, in order to give a democratic facade to the CNS, the Spanish government introduced a partially representative system, with direct elections of employees' delegates at the firm and local level. As the CC.OO. grew and gained more and more influence, it began to accept the idea of participating in such elections. Although this possibility divided CC.OO. militants, it was progressively adopted, in an attempt to *copar* (fill up) the official trade union system. Results were successful in 1971 and, more markedly, in 1974/5, when Francoists were quite simply expelled from the CNS in all industrial regions, and replaced by the best known CC.OO. leaders.

This situation, along with the example of the way in which the Portuguese *Intersindical* was created after the 1974 April revolution, led a certain number of CC.OO. leaders to embark on a provocative project – the transformation of the CC.OO. into a unitary democratic trade union organization, similar to the British TUC, in order to avoid a partisan division of the Spanish trade union movement. This strategy aimed at the calling of a *Congreso Sindical Constituyente*, which would democratize CNS from the bottom, turning it into a class organization, as the CC.OO. leader Camacho put it, 'without stopping the lifts'.

However, this project did not succeed. First of all, during the tolerant months of 1975/6, other trade union forces appeared, notably the USO (*Unión Sindical Obrera*) and in particular the UGT (heavily supported by the PSOE and the West German trade unions), which did not accept the proposal, suspecting that such a process, and the trade union that would be created, would mean control by former CC.OO. activists (and, subsequently, the PCE). But difficulties also appeared within the PCE: whilst an important sector supported the project, another group, together with the party's apparatus, held that it was necessary to maintain a separate labour organization, tied to the PCE, that would give the party a strong influence among the working class. This latter position eventually won, which meant that the most liberal and open-minded group of working class Communist leaders was defeated, and in some cases disappeared from the leadership.

This explains how the CC.OO., once it accepted the role of a normal trade union competing with others in a pluralist context, became an uncomfortable partner for the PCE, although its main leaders were members of the PCE, and in spite of the fact that, at the party's ninth congress in April 1978, the only visible change introduced in the latter's leadership was the election of a significant number of CC.OO. leaders. The separation of the Eurocommunist sector from the trade union leadership left the CC.OO. in the hands of the more traditional groups, which often turned the CC.OO. into a shelter from (or a challenge to) the Eurocommunist orientation taken by the PCE. Unavoidably, this situation led to the appearance of what can be properly called a CC.OO. lobby within the PCE, the core of the so-called Leninist tendency.

A further factor has complicated the relations between the PCE and CC.OO: the trade union's political pluralism. On the one hand, an important number of ultra-left groups are present in the CC.OO., with an important presence in CC.OO.'s directing bodies, and with more radical views than the PCE. On the other hand, and perhaps more importantly, the PCE has never been the main electoral choice for CC.OO. members: as surveys have repeatedly shown, even in the 1977–9 period, a majority of the trade union membership voted for the PSOE, and thus prevented the CC.OO. from adopting clearly partisan positions, while the situation was not symmetrical for the other great trade union, the UGT, which was able to define itself as the Socialist trade union and give its clear support to the PSOE.

The PCE's strategy

The PCE's strategic and programmatic choices had been conceived for the most part during Francoism; and this is by no means merely a chronological coincidence. Rather, as the party's 1975 Manifesto–Programme shows quite well, Francoism has been a central element in shaping the PCE's political analyses.[6]

Spanish capitalism is perceived, in the PCE's analysis, as very fragile, both economically (because of the great control that the banks have over industry and because of its heavy dependence on foreign firms), politically (it is unable to accept a moderate liberal system and to produce truly representative bourgeois parties) and ideologically (it leaves this area almost entirely to the Catholic Church, without ever seriously trying to create a good educational system, not to mention a good university or research structure). For Spanish capitalism, military authoritarian rule was the sole way of governing the country. Since it was impossible to produce democratic legitimacy and to integrate working and popular classes into the system, a mixture of paternalism and repression appeared to offer the best possible political system. The long cycle of political instability since 1898 (with the loss of overseas colonies and the emergence of a working class movement) until the 1930s, including the attempted revolution in 1917 and Primo de Rivera's dictatorship in the 1920s, was the main basis for this analysis.

Somehow, Francoism appeared to be absolutely necessary for Spanish capitalism; or, to put it in other words, there seemed to be an incompatibility between Spanish capitalism and democracy: capitalism would not, and could not, afford democracy (divergences between Carrillo and Claudín, leading to the departure of the latter from the party, concerned precisely this point). Therefore, the growth of democratic pressure against dictatorship was not only a push towards democracy, but also (even if some of its components were unaware of it) towards socialism. The proof, almost tautologically, was the central role played by the PCE in the democratic opposition to Franco's regime.

The breakdown of authoritarian rule would be brought about by a peaceful national strike, which meant not only a general working class upsurge, but also the participation of peasants, the middle classes and the non-monopolistic bourgeoisie. This would lead to political democracy, defined in classical liberal terms; but the traditional inability of the Spanish bourgeoisie to accept loyally a democratic system, and the growth of popular mobilization through democratic means would turn the balance in favour of socialism.

Thus, political democracy would open the road to social and economic democracy, in which small and middle-sized property would still be recognized, but large firms, banks, insurance companies and other main centres of economic power would be nationalized and democratically managed. Politically, this phase would be one of an enlargement and deepening of democracy; the increase of participation and the depth of the social and economic changes that would take place would lead to the creation of a new type of political formation which, although very vaguely described, would mean some kind of merger of popular and working class parties through free discussion and consensus, and not through coercive means. Politically, democracy and pluralism would be the keywords to describe this process, as the PCE's programme put it.[7]

It is clear, then, that the crucial hypothesis underlying the PCE's strategy was the inability of Spanish capitalism to create, accept and sustain a process of democratization and a stable democratic system. Thus, transition to democracy would be the touchstone for the PCE's future, not only in a narrowly political sense (for example legalization of the party, and the first free elections) but also from the strategic point of view. Would the course of events validate the PCE's analysis and prospects?

We cannot, of course, discuss here the full process of transition to democracy in Spain. However, as far as the PCE is concerned, two elements are of central importance. First, the transition to democracy was not brought about by a rupture, a clear and definite (although not violent) political break with the Franco regime, but through a process of reform, largely negotiated between Franco's heirs and the democratic opposition. Although this reform went beyond its promoters' plans (as the legalization of the PCE itself showed), it clearly was not the kind of political change that the PCE had sought. As its early acceptance of the monarchy and of the 'national' flag showed, the PCE was aware of this, but did not seem able to re-adapt its analysis to the newly created situation. Secondly, if the general process of transition to democracy did not follow the PCE's designs, nor would the political balance within the Spanish Left. At first, when the PCE was the main (not to say the sole) party in democratic opposition, the PSOE had virtually disappeared from Spanish realities. Badly split between a leadership in exile, which held to a cold war attitude towards communists, and a few inside militants, active only in some areas (Madrid, Seville, the Basque country), it had almost no presence or influence among the working class or other opposition groups, such as in university and intellectual circles. In these circumstances, it was almost natural for the PCE to assume that it was to become the leading party of the Spanish Left in the new democratic system.

But the situation started to change in 1972, when González and a brand new set of leaders defeated the Socialist old guard and, with the support of the Social Democratic Party of Germany (SPD) and, more generally, the Socialist International, progressively turned the PSOE (and its trade union, the UGT) into an important political force. We cannot discuss this process here, but what is important is its result – the feelings of surprise and the dismay experienced by the PCE when the 1977 elections showed that the PSOE had tripled the PCE vote.

The predominance of the PSOE within the Left was perceived by the PCE as an historical injustice, but the way in which the PCE tried to compete with the PSOE (pushing for consensus policies in the making of the constitution and in the Moncloa agreements in autumn 1977) was at least ambiguous, permitting of the interpretation that it was trying to catch the PSOE in a cross-fire between the UCD (*Unión del Centro Democratico*) and the PCE itself.[8]

In sum, neither the kind of transition to democracy that Spain had experienced nor the role assumed by the PCE validated the party's previous analyses. The attempted military coup of February 1981 showed that political reform had not fully reached certain central points of the state machinery but also, and certainly more importantly, that authoritarian temptations were by no means followed by the core of the army, nor did they have any support among financial or political conservative circles. Perhaps democracy was not completely consolidated, as the PCE insisted, but the road was open, in the electorate's perception, for a deeper change, the change the PSOE would promise at the 1982 general elections, which produced a clear Socialist majority (with 202 seats out of 350) and placed the PCE at the fringe of the political system (with only four seats).

The PCE at the crossroads

During the transition to democracy and in the years that followed, the PCE refused to become an anti-system party. Instead, by insisting on the necessity of consensual policies and agreements between the main parties of the Left and the Right, it took on large responsibilities in the building of the new political system.

It is still an open question whether this strategy in itself harmed the PCE or whether the party's internal crisis prevented it from taking advantage of the role that it was playing (Carrillo has observed how, in the 1979 general election – that is, at the peak of the consensus phase

– the PCE was the only party actually to increase its previous electoral results).[9]

However, what is important in this respect is the way in which the PCE, for the sake of the process of political democratization and of the image it was trying to create (as a Eurocommunist, 'renewed' party) took steps that would subsequently weaken its situation. Or rather, it did not take the steps that would strengthen it. It is interesting how the PCE, the protagonist of the democratic opposition to Francoism, has renounced the chance of exploiting this cleavage. (This must be compared with the French or the Italian situation, where the topic of the anti-Fascist resistance has been constantly present in the Communist press, and in speeches and ceremonies). It is arguable whether the PCE has not wanted, or has not been able, to build a sub-cultural setting that might become a shelter for hard times; what is clear is that this kind of sub-cultural presence does not exist and is not likely to appear in the foreseeable future.

These shortcomings turned out to be crucial, at least at the electoral level: as surveys have shown, nearly a half of Communist voters in the pre-1982 period did not think of themselves as Communists and, when asked to place themselves on a left/right scale, chose positions close to the centre. What this clearly means is that an important part of the social support for the PCE did not come from ideologically motivated groups, but from democratic voters who still identified with the PCE on a 'fight for democracy' basis.[10]

As the new political system became established and developed, this basis for party identification became less and less relevant; voters, even the former Communist ones, became more sensitive to concrete policies offered or promised by the parties. In other words, the PCE urgently needed to adapt itself to the new situation, to re-shape its strategy, policies and image; but in this critical situation, its internal crises prevented it from taking steps in this direction.

The election of a moderate Socialist government in Spain in 1982 meant both additional difficulties and possibilities for the PCE. On the one hand, the party lost to the Socialists two-thirds of its previous vote; but on the other hand the moderate policies developed by the PSOE government (for example, wage control, restrictions in the social security and welfare programmes, closing of factories, entry into NATO) and the increase of unemployment, awakened working class opposition to government measures, and seemed to open possibilities for the PCE to regain, at least partially, its previous influence.

It was obvious that the party could only expect to recover, even partially, from its political and electoral defeat by trying to exploit the discontent generated by the Socialist government's policies. However, its internal problems would still be of paramount importance for the PCE for some time to come. A group with a clearly pro-Soviet orientation, under the leadership of Ignacio Gallego, left the PCE to create the *Partido Comunista de los Pueblos de España* (PCPE), with a special influence in Catalonia (where it is called the PCC, Catalonia Communist Party), whilst the new PCE leadership, with Gerardo Iglesias replacing Carrillo as general secretary from November 1982, made moves towards former PCE members, which included mainly the so-called *renovadores* who had been expelled from the party in the last months of 1981. This triggered a strong reaction from Santiago Carrillo, occasioning a deep crisis (which appeared in almost personal terms at the PCE's eleventh congress in December 1983) and leading eventually to the departure of Carrillo and some top CC.OO. leaders, who created the *Mesa por la Unidad de los Comunistas* (Platform for Communist Unity, MUC).[11] In February 1987 it became a party structure, under the name *Partido de los Trabajadores de España–Unidad Comunista* (Spanish Workers' Party –Communist Unity: PTE–UC.

In this difficult situation, the PCE made efforts to reshape its strategic statements (for instance, in the field of economic policies), but still its main problem was not (and is not) strategic but rather tactical: how to exploit the shortcomings of the Socialist government and thus regain social and political influence?[12]

Two lines of approach were possible, at least theoretically: either to focus on working class dissatisfaction with the economic policies followed by the government, or to try to build links with radical groups placed on the margins of the political system, promoting issues such as civil rights, peace or the protection of the environment. Roughly speaking, the rupture between Carrillo and Iglesias could be stated in these terms: while the former tended to put a stronger emphasis on an *ouvrièriste* perception, Iglesias and the new leadership have rather tried to find a common ground with certain social movements (what the PCE calls a 'convergence' policy).[13]

The two main attempts at mobilization that the PCE led against the PSOE government's policies, specifically its economic policy and the NATO issue, may serve as an example of the PCE's present situation and problems.

The economic policies of the PSOE government, tending towards improving the rate of profit in the private sector and closing state-owned industries with negative economic results, aroused resistance, sometimes quite strong, though usually limited to certain geographic areas and sectors (for example steel, ship-building and mining); but disagreement increased when the parliament approved a law to reform the Spanish welfare system (*Seguridad Social*) which, among other measures, included a reduction in the retirement pension, with even the chief UGT leader, Nicolás Redondo, opposing the project and refusing to vote for it during parliamentary debate. But the most important response came from the PCE and CC.OO., which called for a general strike in June 1985.

It may seem paradoxical that this strike (the third of its kind in Spanish history, after 1917 and 1934) was addressed precisely against a Socialist government; but the PCE's point of view was that the PSOE government was not conducting a socialist policy. Whatever the political evaluation, the strike was a quantitative success, being supported by something over 50 per cent of the Spanish work force; but it did not succeed politically. The welfare reform law was passed and the strike was soon forgotten; the PCE did not get the political benefits it had sought, not even in terms of the balance of forces within the UGT, or between the UGT and the PSOE.

The question of Spanish membership of NATO turned out to be rather more complicated. For a number of reasons, Spanish public opinion clearly opposed entry into the Atlantic alliance, which was decided by the UCD government in 1981. The PSOE encouraged these feelings, promising that, if it came to office, a referendum would be held, asking Spanish voters to vote against Spanish membership of NATO. Indeed, a large part of the electoral campaign that brought the PSOE to victory in October 1982 turned around this promise.

However, the assumption of governmental responsibilities by the PSOE changed its point of view. On the one hand, Spain participated more and more (although in a rather passive way) in several NATO committees; on the other, the calling of the referendum was deferred *sine die*, among contradictory statements of members of the government, and of the Premier himself (who even defined his point of view on this issue as one of 'conscious ambiguity').

The PCE and several pacifist groups pressed for the referendum to be held, presentnig to the parliament a petition with more than a million signatures. The referendum was finally held in March 1986. Only the PSOE supported the government position, not without some internal dissent; the centre and right opposition recommended abstention, or made no kind of electoral suggestion, while the streets were overwhelmingly dominated by the pacifist messages, asking for a vote of 'No'.

In quite a savage campaign, and with surveys predicting the victory of 'No' even a week before the referendum, the government played its last card: if its position was defeated, new elections would immediately be held, and the PSOE would include entry into NATO in its programme. The centre and right opposition had originally seen the referendum as a plebiscite on the PSOE government, but it was now the turn of the PSOE itself to take this stand.

The unexpected happened: for the first time, a government submitted to popular referendum the question of its participation in a military alliance, and received the affirmative vote of a majority of citizens (52.5 per cent voted for, 39.8 per cent against, and 6.5 per cent returned blank papers; turnout reached 59.4 per cent). For the PCE this result was discouraging, not only because of the defeat of the pacifist option, but also because the bulk of government support came basically from working class voters, as aggregate results and surveys have shown. On the other hand, the 7 million votes against NATO could not be taken as a starting point for the building of a new Left, as it was obvious that many conservative voters (most clearly in regions such as Catalonia, the Basque country or Navarra, in all of which the 'No' voters won) had taken advantage of the referendum to record a punishment vote against the government.

In other words, the two main battles in which the PCE could hope to fight the government with strong chances of success, and in which the party had put its trust so as to be able to regain a political and social presence, did not give the expected results. As the subsequent general election showed (June 1986), the PSOE kept its absolute majority whilst the PCE, though improving slightly on its previous results, remained too small a political actor to have any clear influence on Spanish politics.

This is even more important if we take into account the fact that the PCE fought the 1986 general elections as the *Izquierda Unida*, (United Left, IU), which included the PCE, the PCPE and the groups led by Tamames and Alonso Puerta (*Federación Progresista* and *Partido de Acción Socialista*, respectively), as well as other minor groups (*Partido Carlista, Partido Humanista*). It is clear, then, that the convergence sponsored by the PCE was able to link together only the PCE and the PCPE (which is certainly sensitive to the new lines taken by the Soviet leadership), and some politicians who had few followers. On the other hand, the electoral presence of Carrillo's group, although it achieved markedly lower results, turned out to be harmful for the PCE, as it divided the communist vote, preventing the IU from receiving the critical (if reduced) number of votes that was crucial for the distribution of seats (this was clearly the case in Valencia and in some other provinces).

If any conclusion can be drawn from this presentation, it is as follows. The end of the transition to democracy and the consolidation of the new political system have left the PCE unarmed, in the sense that its image and its political influence were largely based upon the role it had played under the dictatorship. The PCE seems to have understood this lesson, and is taking steps to reshape its profile and to redefine its strategy. It is not clear whether the PCE will be successful in its attempts to change and to adapt to the new situation; what is clear, however, is that change is necessary, if the party is to survive at all.

Notes

1   See E. Mujal-León, *Communism and Political Change in Spain* (Indiana University Press, Bloomington, IN, 1983) for a well-documented study of the PCE's evolution during the after transition. A shorter but insightful text is J. Solé Tura, 'El espacio político comunista en España', in *Nacional de Ciencia Política; Problemas actuales del Estado Social y Democrático de Derecho* (Secretaría de Publicaciones de la Universidad De Alicante, Alicante: 1985), pp. 151–60. For the period before 1970, an essential reference is G. Hermet, *Les communistes en Espagne* (Armand Colin, FNSP, Paris, 1971).

2   Personalized interpretations can be found in the following: M. Azcárate, *Crisis del eurocomunismo* (Argos–Vergara, Madrid, 1982); P. Errotetu and P. Vega, *Los herejes del PCE* (Planeta, Barcelona, 1982); F. Garcia Salve, *Por qué somos comunistas?* (Penthalon, Madrid, 1982); G. Moran, *Miseria y grandeza del Partido Comunista de España*, 1939–1985 (Planeta, Barcelona, 1986); and J. Semprún, *Autobiografía de Federico Sánchez* (Planeta, Barcelona, 1978).

3   For data on PCE membership, see J. J. Linz, 'A Sociological Look at Spanish Communism', in G. Schwab (ed.), *Eurocommunism: the Ideological and Political-Theoretical Foundations* (Greenwood Press, Westport, Conn., 1981), pp. 217–68.

4   See Partido Comunista de España, *Noveno Congreso del PCE. 19–23 Abril 1978* (Crítica, Barcelona, 1978).

5   See Linz, 'Sociological Look at Spanish Communism'. For Catalonia specifically, see J. Botella, *L'electorat comunista a Catalunya, 1977–1980* (unpublished PhD thesis, Universitat Autònoma de Barcelona, September 1982); E. Berntzen and P. Selle, 'Norwegian and Catalan Communism: Relativism in the Use of Models of Electoral Behaviour', *European Journal of Political Research*, vol. 13 (1985), pp. 41–51; and J. M. Molins Lopez-Rodo, 'La evolución del electorado del PSUC (1980–1984)', in *IV Congreso Nacional . . .* , pp. 143–50.

6   See Partido Comunista de España, *Segunda Conferencia del Partido Comunista de España. Manifiesto Programa del Partido Comunista de España* (n.p., 1975).

7   See, for instance, the classic work: S. Carrillo, *'Eurocomunismo' y Estado* (Grijalbo, Barcelona, 1977). An interesting attempt to trace the origins of the Eurocommunist line in the PCE back to 1956 is to be found in S. Carrillo, *Escritos sobre Eurocomunismo* (Forma, Madrid, 1977). For a qualified outsider's point of view, see F. Claudin, *Eurocomunismo y socialismo* (Siglo XXI, Madrid, 1977).

8   See the texts included in S. Carrillo, *El año de la Constitución* (Grijalbo, Barcelona: 1978), and also his later re-evaluation in S. Carrillo, *Memoria de la transición* (Grijalbo, Barcelona, 1983).

9   See Carrillo, *Memoria.*

10 See Linz, 'Sociological Look at Spanish Communism', and, for Catalonia, Botella, *L'electorat comunista*. For the period since 1982 see Molins Lopez-Rodo, 'La evolución del electorado'.
11 The documents that were debated at the PCE's ninth congress are to be found in Pilar Del Castillo Vera, 'XI Congreso del Partido Comunista de España', *Revista de Derecho Político*, 22 (1986), pp. 263–326.
12 For the PCE's present economic programme, see N. Sartorius (ed.), *Una alternativa a la crisis. Las propuestas del PCE* (Planeta, Barcelona, 1985).
13 See Carrillo, *Memoria*, for his present political analysis.

5 A Case of Orthodoxy
The Communist Party of Portugal

José Pacheco Pereira

The Portuguese Communist Party (*Partido Communista do Portugal* – PCP), founded in 1921 enjoyed five short years of legality before going underground for 48 years. When it emerged into the open in 1974, it had remained illegal longer than any other Western European party and had been clandestine throughout all the changes in the international communist movement. This is a decisive factor in understanding the recent history of the PCP.[1]

The revolution of 25 April 1974 brought considerable disruptive potential – it was at one and the same time equivalent to the post-war 'liberation' of Europe, a remake of May 1968 and a rapid process of decolonization. For an orthodox party whose leadership had revolutionary ideals and who understood men but not the country involved, this was a unique occasion. In the poorest country in Europe (with the exception of Albania), one which was economically backward and in which 50 years of mental repression and censorship had obliterated politics, and dictatorship had destroyed all moderate elite groups, there were ample opportunities for action. Against this background the PCP enjoyed a fair amount of political success but, as often occurs in history, the contemplation of this success and the belief that the situation that had given rise to it would never alter, cemented that party's policies and removed its drive and potential for change.

The origins of the success of Portuguese communism lie in the past: in its own social and party political history and in its capacity to have created a revolutionary and 'anti-fascist' country in the Europe of 1975. In this way Portuguese communism escaped the more obvious factors in the decline of European communism.

Membership

While it was underground the PCP was never a large party, with the exception of the immediate post-war period. At the same time neither was it an isolated group and, particularly after the 1940s, it wielded real political influence as the principal opposition group and the only party to maintain its organization. This position was checked during the last ten years of the dictatorship by the increasing strength of a powerful left-wing movement, but the revolutionary events of 1974 made this process inconclusive.

The PCP has never divulged the exact number of members it had on 25 April. However, all existing estimates indicate that the number was close to 2,000.[2] This number is relevant if it is remembered that, with the exception of left-wing groups, in practice there were no other party structures in Portugal at the beginning of 1974. The Socialist Party was little more than a small group of old republicans and freemasons and the only embryo of a social democratic, technocratic modern group, ranging from the right to the moderate left, was a small Lisbon club known as SEDES.

Once out in the open the PCP structure quickly absorbed those sympathizers closest to the party line, old militants and organizations that had been broken up or quashed by the repression, and a part of the legal sector, particularly the staff of unions, cooperatives and collective organizations. The first big surge in growth took place in 1974–75 (table 5.1).

The official number of 100,000 militants for May 1975, a time of revolutionary climax which also marks the beginning of the marginalization of the Socialist Party and other moderate forces, was the result of a rapid increase in the months from 28 September 1974, when the MFA (Armed Forces Movement) began its move to the left with the removal of Spinola, to the period immediately following the failure of

Table 5.1 Rise in PCE membership, 1974–83

1974 (July)	14,593
1974 (October)	30,000
1975 (May)	100,000
1976 (November)	115,000
1978 (December)	142,000
1979 (April)	164,713
1980 (June)	187,018
1983 (December)	200,753

Source: Portuguese Communist Party

the revolutionary coup on 11 March 1975. The PCP was then seen as the most powerful party, the holder of revolutionary legitimacy and a participant (in some cases the leader) in the process of revolutionizing the economic, industrial and agrarian structures.

After its zenith in 1974–5, it is noteworthy that the PCP managed during the following eight years to maintain high growth rates which, judging by official figures, would have doubled the number of PCP members from 1975 to 1983. However, this rise in membership moved too fast to enable the process of organization to keep in step. In 1976, 30.4 per cent of PCP members were 'non-activists'; by 1981, only 43.8 per cent of all members were 'activists', and 21.8 per cent had become 'non-activists'. At the tenth congress in 1983, it was said that 76.6 per cent of all members 'are more or less regularly active'.[3]

The electoral record and regional implantation

In the constituent elections of 1975, and in subsequent legislative elections, results for the PCP show a relatively balanced and stable vote, with the exception of 1985, which indicates the effect of a loss of votes to the new party, the PRD (table 5.2).

The best results in parliamentary elections were in 1979 and, even with a favourable domestic situation in 1983, the PCP did not again reach the same level. However, the party's ability to maintain a stable number of votes shows it has deep roots and a loyal electorate, factors that deserve further comment.

First, the strength of the PCP vote is particularly area-orientated, corresponding to geographic and socially defined areas, including the

Table 5.2   The PCP's electoral record in legislative elections, 1975–85

	No. of votes	*Percentage*
Constituent Assembly (1975)	711,935[a]	16.60
Legislative (1976)	786,701[b]	14.39
Interim (1979)	1,129,322[c]	18.80
Legislative (1980)	1,009,505	16.75
Legislative (1983)	1,031,609	18.07
Legislative (1985)	893,180	15.49
Legislative (1987)		12.18

[a]PCP + MDP.
[b]FEPU (PCP + MDP + FSP).
[c]APU.
Source: PCP: Electoral atlas

districts of Setúbal and the Alentejo, the district of Santarém to the north of the Alentejo and greater Lisbon – all areas in the south of the country. In these areas the vote rises to 40 – 50 per cent of overall results and in some places rises much higher. In the rest of the country the vote is approximately 10 per cent, or even lower in a number of districts in the north and the interior.

The PCP is strongly entrenched in four particular types of area:

1 Industrialized regions, particularly those of heavy industry (iron and steel, shipyards, chemicals, metal working), with several generations of workers (southern bank of the Tagus).
2 Latifundia regions, with a high percentage of rural wage earners (Alentejo, municipalities to the south of the district of Santarém).
3 Cities and dormitory towns on the outskirts of Lisbon, with a high percentage of unauthorized housing and seriously decaying urban living conditions (Amadora, Sacavem, Loures), in some cases with traditional light industry.
4 Some industrial enclaves in rural areas in the interior of the country, the main feature being local mono-industry (glass, textiles) and with a high percentage of resident wage earners (Marinha Grande, Tortozendo).

To understand the consistency of this geographic and social distribution it is not the Portugal of 1986 that should be considered but rather that of the 1930s to 1950s. All these social sectors emerged during this period, in some cases based on even older nuclei. They are a feature of a Portugal in which areas of high proletarianization represented a powerful element in regional differentiation and in which a 'rigid' proletariat was formed.

The latifundia area of the Alentejo was a region apart, where demographic, social and cultural features differed sharply from the rest of the country. There were vast numbers of rural proletarians living precariously and having only seasonal employment. Their culture was anti-clerical, egalitarian and Mediterranean in nature.

However, in the 1960s and 1970s this proletarian Portugal went through a process of collapse. Many of its traditional sectors, for example the canning industry, quickly disappeared. Other traditional sectors lost their hold as the internationalization of the Portuguese economy favoured the textile industry and new electronic component and assembly industries which frequently moved to interior regions where there was no traditional industry. Gradually, a 'flexible' proletariat emerged and the proletarianization of the country became more balanced.

In the Alentejo, emigration in the 1960s changed the surplus labour situation at the same time as mechanization was increasing and modern agricultural firms were appearing alongside latifundia. As a result, there was an improvement in local living standards and an increase in social tension.

The services sector increased considerably during this period, changing from old to new methods of commercial activity and there was also a change in emphasis from trade to administration.[4]

The revolution of 25 April 1974 and the nationalizations and agrarian reform of 1975 checked this process of development. The nationalizations not only decapitated the more dynamic capitalist sector and the only one with any financial capacity, but also, at the beginning of the oil crisis and as the colonial empire was being dismantled, it made the state responsible for dozens of industries equipped for a period of economic boom and for expanding markets. Besides the nationalizations, labour legislation that made dismissal practically impossible made any reconversion of the nationalized sector even more difficult by freezing employment in the traditional sectors.

At the same time land occupation, largely motivated by the need to ensure employment during a period of decapitalization, fixed not only resident labour in the Alentejo but also a large number of returning emigrants or those drawn back to the region by a lack of employment in Lisbon and on the southern bank of the Tagus, the traditional areas for surplus immigrant labour from the Alentejo.

The Collective Production Units invented by the PCP in 1975 on a Soviet-style model, which led local communist leaders to say that agrarian reform in the Alentejo 'went further than agrarian reform in Bulgaria', had the role of reconstructing the latifundia, retaining farming practices based on the extensive production of wheat, the economic viability of which was based on state-guaranteed prices.

All this – nationalizations and agrarian reform – considered as 'revolutionary conquests', was included in the constitution of 1976, suitably protected in the actual constitutional text by clauses that made it extremely difficult to revise.

In this context, which has not substantially changed since 1975, it is not surprising that the PCP is still seen by those benefiting from this situation as an essential instrument in political action and that this has meant a freeze in its electorate. However, there is another Portugal, not that of the family, and of the Catholic peasantry, but that of the enormous sector of the parallel or 'black' economy, and this escapes communist influence. Indeed, early studies on territorial and social distribution of 'underground activities' reveal that these elements are concentrated in the interior of the country, on the northern and central coastline and in the districts of Santarém and the Algarve.

In local elections PCP results are consistently higher than in the legislative elections. It is also in these elections that the PCP has had its best results – between 20 and 21 per cent in 1979 and 1982 (table 5.3). Among local elections the Lisbon results are important in that the PCP is the second political force.

Local PCP authorities have a good reputation for efficiency and administrative ability and all attempts to bring them down (which several PS–PSD alliances have tried) have failed.

Table 5.3 The PCP's electoral record in local elections

	1976 (%)	1979 (%)	1982 (%)	1985 (%)
Parish assembly	17.69	20.90	21.28	20.00
Municipal assembly	18.14	20.89	20.98	19.40
Town council (mayor)	17.69	20.48	20.69	20.60

Source: Electoral records

Strategy and ideology

Marginally placed for the first 40 years of its political life, the PCP was isolated from the major debates of the communist and labour movement and only under the combined influence of Alvaro Cunhal's leadership, the onset of the Sino-Soviet conflict and the struggle for the freedom of the colonies did it begin to produce any ideology of its own and have any say in international debates.

Cunhal's ideas from 1960 to 1964 are noteworthy in that they summarize what today, 25 years later, is the theory of the 'Portuguese revolution'.[5] At the same time, Cunhal's political stands, taken at a time when Khrushchev's administration was still in power and on the eve of its second wind in the twenty-second congress of the CPSU, were an implicit criticism of CPSU administration and, in particular, of the administration of the Spanish, Italian and Yugoslav parties.

Cunhal reiterates in his reports and in his book *Rumo à Vitória*, the idea of 'armed national uprising' and the exceptional conditions for the 'working class' and its 'allies' to bring about a revolution. In reply to left-wing criticism, which indicated the modesty of the idea of 'democratic, national revolution', Cunhal stated that in Portugal the bourgeoisie was weak and could not govern democratically and that consequently the objectives of 'democratic, national revolution' appeared in Portugal superimposed on those of 'social revolution'.

To make such a statement during the early years of the 1960s was to take a stand closely in line with that of the Chinese, and the implicit criticism of the Soviet position meant that some of Cunhal's articles were censored in international communist publications. But with the fall of Khrushchev in 1964, Cunhal was taken under the wing of Ponomarev and Suslov, who understandably admired his loyalty to Marxism–Leninism in difficult times and went on to value his adherence to the official Soviet line in the period since Khrushchev was in power. Cunhal's preeminence and, by extension, that of the PCP in the international communist movement, date in fact from the fall of Khrushchev.

In the months immediately following 25 April, but particularly in May–September 1974, the PCP acted as one of the major supports of transitional power. In a situation in which there was considerable national support for the military coup the PCP acted against all the more volatile factors of political instability: the party did everything possible against the surge of strikes immediately following the coup: it organized a demonstration 'against strikes', it appealed for political moderation, withdrew the expression 'proletarian dictatorship' from its programme, fought the radicalism of leftist groups and, even on colonial issues, supported Spinola's positions. However, sometime in September, and in circumstances still not clearly understood, a decision to boycott the first right-wing demonstration in favour of Spinola, scheduled for 28 September, started a new political trend known ironically in Portugal as the 'PREC', an acronym for *'processo revolutionário em curso'* (revolutionary process in action).

From September 1974 to November 1975, with the catalyst of the attempted counter-revolutionary coup of 11 March half way through this period, the PCP presented a vast panoply of ideas including comparison with the highlights of past revolutions. The 'People–Armed Forces alliance' was given a Leninist interpretation with its 'dual nature of power', or was more prosaically seen as harking back to the militarist populism of Velasco Alvarado, while Cunhal's invective against bourgeois parliamentarianism was reminiscent of Lenin's criticism of the Constituent Assembly of 1918, and the 'committees for the defence of the revolution' were typically Cuban in origin.

But viewed from a decade later what underlies all this is Cunhal's analysis of the 1960s in Portugal in which the 'bourgeoisie' could not live in bourgeois democracy because, since their power was weak, they needed a political dictatorship to govern; at the same time, the Portuguese 'working class' gained a series of 'conquests' in 1975 which weakened the bourgeoisie even more and placed the former in an unrivalled position in Europe for completing the 'revolution'.

Since 1975, or more correctly since 1964, there has been no deviation from the strategic outline defined for the PCP by Cunhal.

Conclusion

The PCP has been the major beneficiary of the archaic nature of Portuguese society; it is also an important instrument for preserving it.

The rigidity and homogeneity of the world created by Portuguese industrialization was established by the relationship between a large working sector and the PCP. They fed and sustained one another using practices that are purely those of survival. Close ties of dependence were formed which are difficult to dislodge because they were forged out of isolation. This isolation was geographic, chronological, political and organizational.

The PCP has become entrenched, as it were, in the 1940s. Its roots in the working class, its legendary traditional areas (the Alentejo, Barreiro) date from this period. In fact, from the intellectual, cultural, political and policy point of view everything dates from this period. The men who now hold power in the party and form one of the most stable and homogeneous communist party leaderships in Europe received their training during that period. PCP culture and the myths surrounding the party are still those of the resistance of the 1940s, its cultural neorealism and anti-fascism are Zhdanovist.

Through the PREC the PCP carried out a desperate struggle against the capitalist modernization that began during the Marcelo Caetano period, and fought for a return to the post-war developmental pattern. At the same time it turned against the very trends that had been cultivated within the party, as a result of the influx of a new services membership which played such an important part in the struggles from 1968 to 1973 and in the foundation of the 'Intersindical' (centralized trade union coordinating body). As a result, it lost these supports to the Socialist Party. Reinforcing its worker organization after 25 April, using a more radical language and preparing a putschist strategy, the PCP's policies prevented the party from following a more moderate and modern trend ('Eurocommunism'). Measures such as creating an urban guerrilla organization in the 1970s – the PCP was the only European communist party to have such an organization – were part of this trend.

This process was also possible to maintain after 1974 owing to an intake of followers from the party's former sectors of influence – the rural workers of the Alentejo, for example – in the 1974–5 period, providing those members of the leadership who had come out of hiding with ideal support for putting the intellectuals and the rank and file in order. The influx from these sectors, seriously weakened by emigration and by the structural changes of capitalism and rapidly losing power, became a powerful conservative pressure group which gave the party leadership the ideal instrument for hindering, through the 'conquests of the revolution' (nationalizations and agrarian reform), the development of Portuguese capitalism along the lines that were emerging.

Consequently, in a brief but intense moment of power in 1974–5 the PCP had the chance to stir up the old forces from past Portuguese industrialization precisely when they were dying, and had been since the 1960s. Not only did the PCP postpone the decline of these old forces – a decline which during the Caetano period was being forecast and was corroding the party by replacing its former worker basis by services employees and students – but it also gave them enormous crystallized power in the 'conquests of the revolution'. It was akin to the renewal of a pact dating from the 1940s and 1950s and a denial of the sectors that had emerged in the 1960s and 1970s. It was also a sign that the change in the social basis of the party in the 1960s and 1970s was not sufficient to alter the trend or to cut the party off from its traditional base, which although no longer organically important in 1974, was activated by the fall of the dictatorship and by the crisis of the expansionist model of capitalist economies in which the events of 1974–5 took place.

The 'conquests of the revolution' were the instrument of this old pact and its major acquisition, owing to the way in which they were brought about, their subsequent institutionalization in the constitution and finally to the PCP's ability to go along with what the Socialist Party had ideologically and politically committed itself to do to protect these conquests. This was the most important result the party had gained from 25 April, much more important than political freedom and the end of the colonial war. In turn, the state did not limit matters to keeping the expropriated property of former economic groups. It also inherited the most out-dated sectors of the Portuguese economy, and at the same time prevented any possibility of its structural change. The industrial world on the south bank of the Tagus was in its death throes but now, instead of dying or being transformed, it was put on a life-support machine.

The nationalizations and agrarian reform could only be viewed as a stage in the development process if the overall picture of the previous state of the Portuguese economy were that described by the PCP in its publications: agrarian feudalism in the fields of the Alentejo and incipient industrialization in the cities. This portrait of the economy, if accurate, would evidently allow the 'alternative' solution the PCP supported and still supports.

No policy of Eurocommunism could offer the worker base of the PCP what the present leadership offers and, quite the contrary, it would be viewed with suspicion, like something that was going to 'reduce' the strength of the party, and therefore reduce its major instrument for action. This being the case, any change in the PCP can only come from above.

The political circumstances of recent years – characterized by crisis in the Portuguese domestic economy and by an increase in the international conflicts between the Soviet Union and the United States gave the PCP a far greater amount of 'modernity' than could have been expected. It is the archaic nature of the party that in fact has been making it modern. It may be some time before changes in the party's environment, national and international, alter this situation.

Notes

1 For a general bibliography on Portuguese communism see 'Bibliografia sistemática sobre o PCP', *Estudos sobre o Comunismo*, 0–4, 1983–5.
2 For a discussion on membership numbers, see José Pacheco Pereira, 'Problemas da História do PCP', *O Fascismo em Portugal* (Regra do Jogo, Lisbon, 1982).
3 *X Congresso PCP* (Edições Avante, Lisbon, 1984).
4 The sources for an analysis of Portuguese class structure are in João Ferrão, *Classes Sociais e Indústria em Portugal* (Centro de Estudos Geográficos, Lisbon, 1982), 'Recomposição Social e Estruturas Regionais de Classes (1970–1981)', *Análise Social*, vol. XXI (1985), 87–9; and Isabel de Sousa Lobo, 'Estrutura Social e Produtiva e Propensão à Subterraneidade no Portugal de Hoje, *Análise Social*, vol. XXI (1985) 87–9.
5 The main theoretical texts of Cunhal were republished after 1974: *Rumo à Vitória – As Tarefas do Partido na Revolução Democrática e Nacional*: (Opinião, Oporto, 1974); and *O Radicalismo Pequeno-Burguês de Fachada Socialista* (Edições Avante, Lisbon, 1974).

6 Populism, Eurocommunism and the KKE
The Communist Party of Greece

Dimitri Kitsikis

Greece, Russia and the KKE

Despite a romantic view to the contrary, Greece is a Third World country. It was the West that created the phenomenon of the Third World, by breaking up the equilibrium of non-Western societies and by obliging them to develop in an unbalanced manner, in relation to an external centre and not in relation to their own needs. The Western model imposes itself gradually as the sole point of reference. This process inevitably ends in the complete Westernization of non-Western societies, that is, in their emancipation from the West as a result of their total integration in the model that it represents.

The Ottoman empire followed this process and Greece, being part of that empire, thus shared that fate. The territory of the young kingdom that became independent in 1832 was peopled by fighters who had admittedly shown their mettle, but whose territory was one of the least developed regions of the empire. Evidence of this was the fact that the Greek bourgeoisie remained in the great urban centres of the Ottoman areas and did not consider it to be in their interests to emigrate to the new kingdom which, henceforth, was dominated by a ruling class in Athens that was Peloponnesian in origin. The Greek war of independence that gave birth to this state had thus more a national than a social character.

Being a part of the Ottoman empire, Greece had never experienced the three revolutions that the West had produced: the Renaissance, the Reformation and the Industrial Revolution. From the beginning, the Greek state of the nineteenth century was used by the colonial West to weaken, and then to colonize, the Third World. From the start there were within the Greek state English and French lobbies that were used by the West to further its colonial expansion.

Greece and Russia have had a special relationship through the centuries for more than one reason. First, the two peoples belong to the intermediate region of the Eurasian continent, a civilization covering the vast area comprising Eastern Europe, Asia up to the Indus in the south, and all Siberia to the north.[1] Secondly, the Russian Church is the elder daughter of the Greek Orthodox Church, the ecumenical patriarch of which still has his seat in Istanbul. The Greek Church was for Moscow the source of its faith, a source that was unique, pure and untainted. Thirdly, when the Ottoman empire was in decline in the eighteenth century, the Greek aristocracy and bourgeoisie, which dominated it, turned to Moscow and called on it to assume the imperial mantle. The Ottoman bourgeoisie, ethnically Greek, placed its powerful merchant fleet under the Russian flag after 1774. Fourthly, the Greek revolution of 1821 was organized in Russia, in Odessa, by Greek merchants, and it was a general of the Russian army, himself a Greek, Prince Alexandros Ypsilantis, who launched it by crossing the Russian frontier and invading Ottoman Romania in 1821. A fifth factor is that what was termed the 'Russian party' in the new Greek state in the nineteenth century was the party supported by the people; it far outstripped the pro-English and pro-French parties, which appeared as foreign. Sixthly, despite the fact that the rise of Panslavism in the second half of the nineteenth century, coinciding with the transformation of the Athenian state into a Western Anglo-French protectorate, had weakened the foundations of the Greek population's pro-Russian sentiments, there remained a nostalgia for the time when the 'elder daughter' had not yet 'betrayed' the Greek source of its inspiration. Finally, Greek communism was to a certain degree able to exploit this deep-rooted pro-Russian sentiment, which remains alive in the peasant mind and in religious circles especially, in so far as their Westernization remains only partial.

From its foundation in 1918 until today,[2] the chief electoral traits of the Communist Party of Greece (*Kommounistiko Komma Elladas* – KKE) have remained the same: its vote has been 5.14 per cent of the electorate on average until the Second World War and 12.24 per cent afterwards, with 15 seats in the *Boulê* (the parliament) out of a total of 250–300 seats each time a system of proportional representation has been used – even in a diluted form – and each time that the party has stood under cover of a workers' electoral front (see table 6.1). From the legislative elections of 7 November 1926, which saw a proportional system being used in Greece for the first time (4.4 per cent of votes cast, ten seats out of 279) up until the elections of 2 June 1985 (9.89 of the votes cast and 12 seats out of 300), the KKE has always vehemently condemned all those that did not apply a *simple* proportional system as dishonest electoral laws. Moreover, since as a rule the political personalities who cooperated electorally with the KKE did not have any electoral support of their own and consequently were not able to contribute a substantial number of extra votes to the KKE's total, the party always obliged Communist voters, on grounds of principle, to elect also a certain number of *synergazomenoi* (collaborators) of the KKE who were not themselves members of the Communist Party.

Nevertheless, the influence of the KKE on the politics of the country is far greater than its electoral strength. This corresponds to the nature of the KKE, which today still sees itself as an active revolutionary minority, bringing in its wake a far larger section of the population than the numbers of its electorate. This judgement, moreover, is universally shared by Greek political analysts.

Table 6.1 Electoral performance of the Communist Party of Greece (KKE), 1926–85

Party[a]	Year	% of poll	No. of seats	Total seats in Boulê
KKE	1926	4.40	10	279
	1928	1.40	0	250
	1932	5.00	10	250
	1933	4.60	0	248
	1935	9.60	0	300
	1936	5.80	15	300
	1946	abstained		
Democratic Camp	1950	9.70	18	250
EDA	1951	10.60	10	258
EDA Coalition inc. EDA	1952	9.60	0	300
	1956	48.20	132	300
EDA	1958	24.40	79	300
	1961	14.60	24	300
	1963	14.30	28	300
	1964	11.80	21	300
KKE	1974	9.45	8	300
	1977	9.36	11	300
	1981	10.93	13	300
	1985	9.89	12	300

[a]For the years 1950–64 the KKE was outlawed and represented by the EDA.

An unimpressive enemy to the right of the KKE: Eurocommunism

The KKE's slogan has always been 'There is only a single communist party (*'ena einai to komma'*). Despite all the splits of the past, there has always re-emerged a single party of the name. That remains the case today.

From 1936 to 1941, the KKE was divided into three. The police of the totalitarian leader Ioannis Metaxas had placed his agents at the head of two sections – the groups known as the 'Old Central Committee' and the 'Provisional Directorate'. The third group was formed in the prisons, and above all in the fortress of Akronauplia, in the Peloponnese. Since each of the first two groups claimed to be a loyal follower of the General Secretary, Nikos Zahariades and to be the sole authentic KKE, virtually accusing each other of being a police creation and each publishing its own version of *Rizospastês* (the party daily paper), many militants turned to the prisons in order to know what line to follow.

The Second World War found the party much weakened, but in Athens on 27 September 1941, the KKE again adopted its electoral tactic of always standing as a front, though this time in order to organize resistance to the foreign occupying power. It established a 'coalition of parties' which it called *Ethniko Apeleutherôtiko Metôpo* (EAM) – 'National Liberation Front'. The EAM became the chief organization in the Resistance between 1941 and 1944. This was the KKE's finest hour, a success of which it could justifiably be proud. The attempt, much later, by Andreas Papandreou and PASOK (the Panhellenic Socialist Movement) to monopolize the glory of the 'EAM generation' was a political stratagem that did not respect the historical truth. It is true that not all the one and a half million EAM members during the occupation, out of a population at the time of 7,350,000, were communists, but the spirit of the movement certainly was. From having had only 14,000 members in 1936, the KKE found itself suddenly, at the end of 1944, with 350,000.

When in November 1947, at the height of the Civil War, the KKE was once again outlawed, the unity of the party that the Resistance had engendered was no longer in doubt, despite the many internal crises that arose over the question of what tactics to follow in the face of the class enemy and the British, and then American, intervention.

During the hard years of illegality, from 1950 to 1964, the KKE was represented inside the country, from August 1951 onwards, by the United Democratic Left (*Eniaia Dêmokratikê Aristera* – EDA). The EDA at no time questioned the control that the KKE had over it, from the latter's East European place of exile. As with the EAM, the KKE was for a long time wise enough to deny that it controlled the EDA and claimed that many of that party's leaders were not communists[3] – such as, for example, the highly respected Professor Nicolas Kitsikis, a member of the executive committee of the EDA, who was one of the most prominent leaders of that party and a parliamentary representative from 1956 to 1967.[4] The proof offered was that this erstwhile Principal of the 'Polytechnique' in Athens, and one of the greatest names of Greek science, had been a Liberal Senator before the war and an enthusiastic Venizelist. In fact, however, Kitsikis had been a member of the KKE since 1944, and, during the EDA's campaign in favour of restoring the KKE to legality, he had publicly stated at the beginning of 1967 – a little before the coup d'état – that he would be proud to stand as a candidate for the KKE at the next elections, in the event of the party's being legalized.

An extremely difficult period, which recalled that of 1936–41, began in 1968. The EDA, like all other parties, had been banned by the military regime and its leaders arrested. At that point there occurred a hitherto unprecedented event: the Communists of the EDA reproached the leaders of the KKE in exile with having lost contact with Greek realities, because ever since the defeat of 1945 they had been based *outside* the country. They were thus a 'KKE of the Exterior' that had become, over the years, dogmatic, opportunist and bureaucratic.[5]

In the period 1963–7, according to the critics, a struggle had taken place inside the EDA: on one side were the loyalists of the KKE, on the other those who accused it of directing the affairs of the EDA from afar, isolating the latter from Greek realities and hindering its full development, being themselves removed from those realities.[6] The coup d'état in Athens only precipitated the crisis. So it was that in February 1968 certain leaders of the EDA, who represented the Communists 'within' the country and who were languishing in the regime's gaols, decided to secede and to found a new party, which they named the 'KKE of the Interior'.[7] The split took place at the twelfth plenary session of the party's Central Committee. So as to distinguish themselves clearly from the orthodox centre, they styled the latter the 'KKE of the Exterior', a name insulting to the orthodox KKE and one which has no constitutional basis. For this reason at no time since 1974 has the name been recognized either by the Greek state or by the party itself.

Communism was introduced into Greece in its Soviet form and remained such until 1967. The people chosen by the KKE to lead the EDA, however, were strongly Westernized. This was the case in particular with Elias Iliou, Nicolas Kitsikis, Leonidas Kyrkos and even Mikis Theodorakis.[8] Under the colonels, the opposition took refuge in the West, and under the wing of European bodies such as the Council of Europe. The process whereby the country's political elite was Westernized was thus accelerated. The role that men such as Olof Palme,

Willy Brandt, Giscard d'Estaing, François Mitterrand and Jean-Jacques Servan-Schreiber played in the evolution of this elite is well known. Also it was during this period that the KKE-Interior developed its Euro-communism.[9] Confronted by a common enemy – the 'barbarian invasion' of the uncouth colonels – the Greek political elite, from the Right to the Left, from the group that sponsored Eleni Vlahou's conservative daily *Kathêmerinê*, or Konstantinos Karamanlis, to Andreas Papandreou or Leonidas Kyrkos – this elite established fraternal links with the European elite in a truly European spirit. This changed the nature of Greek political life from 1974 on. Only the Communists of the KKE, under their General Secretary, Harilaos Florakis, with their Soviet mentality, stood out like a dinosaur from a past age.[10]

A key element in the Eurocommunism of the KKE of the Interior was the claim that Greece should have a Western communist voice inside the European Community. In defence of this idea the party made great use among the Greek electorate of the image of a Western Europe acting as a counter-weight to American imperialism, an image that had become familiar since Karamanlis had associated Greece with the Common Market in 1961. The seven years of the colonels' anti-parliamentary regime, it was said, had been supported by the Americans. Consequently, in order to prevent any return to the pro-American dictatorship, the country would have to become a full member of the Common Market. By entering the EEC, said the KKE-Interior, the Greek Communists would be linked to 'the living and progressive workers' movement which is struggling to transform the EEC from a Europe of the monopolies into a Europe of the workers'.[11]

Linked to the KKE-Interior and then, later, to PASOK, was the EDA, which did not go out of existence in 1974 as might have been expected. Its survival, as a phantom party, is due to the personality of Elias Iliou, who died on 25 January 1985. He was a controversial political figure. For a long time an orthodox communist, he later became, in the period before 1967, the parliamentary leader of the EDA (the chairman of that party being Iannis Pasalides). On the one hand he had been strongly influenced by Togliatti's Italian communism, but on the other he had established links with foreign capital and in particular with French interests in Greece, represented by the aluminium company Péchiney. Before 1967 he had opposed the entry of Greece into the Common Market, but later he became a convinced advocate of European integration. After 1974 he acquired a solid respectability in Greek bourgeois circles, and even became a supporter of Karamanlis. In the election of November 1977 he was the chairman of the *Symmahia* (Alliance) electoral coalition of five small parties, of which the KKE-Interior was the leading force.

In 1974 the KKE took serious notice of the threat represented by the secessionists 'of the Interior', as it chose simply to call them. The KKE stood in the elections of 17 November of that year in a united coalition with the Interior and the EDA. The three parties together won 9.45 per cent of the poll and eight seats, of which the KKE kept five for itself and gave two to the KKE-Interior and one to the EDA.

However, the notion of a Greek Eurocommunism suffered a severe blow in the legislative elections of 1977. This time the two parties stood separately. The KKE on its own won as many votes as had the coalition of 1974. On the other hand the KKE-Interior demonstrated its extreme weakness. The *Symmahia* of five parties of which it formed part obtained only 2.76 per cent of the vote. Standing alone at the elections of 1981 and 1985, the KKE-Interior won respectively 1.34 per cent and 1.84 per cent of the poll, whilst the EDA, which hardly existed at the electoral level, collaborated with PASOK in the elections of 1981 and also in 1985 under its new leader, Manolis Glezos, after the death of Iliou.

Since 1977 vigorous discussions had taken place in the KKE-Interior as to whether the emblem of the hammer and sickle and the term 'communist' in the party's title should be abandoned, as a mark of the distance that it had put between itself and communist orthodoxy, and also with a view to accommodating the views of its new electoral clientele which was composed more and more of social democrats and left-wing liberals. This, furthermore, reflected the thinking of the Greek electorate which, even in everyday language, was following the government in dropping the 'Exterior' in the title of Florakis' party and calling it simply the KKE – that is, the Communist Party of Greece *tout court*.

A formidable enemy to the left of the KKE: Third World populism

Writing of the take-up of the Western ideology of fascism in the Third World, one political scientist has gone so far as to say: 'Future historians may well write of the last quarter of the twentieth century as the golden age of fascism'[12] – a view that this author has always shared.[13] Nevertheless, since the discrediting of this ideology following the defeat of the Axis powers, the terms 'fascist' and 'national socialist' have become so negative that only a few groups actually apply them to themselves out of nostalgia for inter-war totalitarianism. Those who have refurbished the ideology and have brought about its triumph in the Third World reject these terms with indignation as the supreme insult. In my view, the best term would be 'Third Worldism', since this refurbished ideology fits like a glove the objective, social and economic conditions of the Third World; but usually, however, the vaguer and more neutral term 'populism' is preferred. At all events, whatever the term employed, Greek experience has been caught in the trammels of precisely this ideology.

In the years preceding the coup d'état of 21 April 1967, populism developed in Greece in its Maoist form. Until 1955 there was scarcely any contact between Greece and China. In that year the Karamanlis government – which officially only recognized Taiwan – authorized Nicolas Kitsikis to send a high-ranking political and cultural delegation drawn from the Centre and the Left to the People's Republic of China. On the return of this delegation to Athens, Beata Kitsikis,[14] Nicolas's wife, founded in Athens the Friendship Union with New China (*Enôsis Filôn Neas Kinas*). This association played a crucial role in developing an awareness of Maoist China in Greece. Other delegations were sent out by the Union in subsequent years, at a time when there was still not the slightest diplomatic contact between the two countries, People's China only being recognized for the first time by the colonels' regime.[15]

Under cover of the Union, which officially played no political role, a Maoist movement grew up within the EDA. Under the leadership of Iannis Hotzeas and Isaak Iordanides, it broke away from the EDA in 1964, began to publish the journal *Renaissance* (*Anagennêsê*) and with the Union's help, launched a publishing house, financed by Beijing – *Historical Publications* (*Istorikes Ekdoseis*) – which published the works of Mao and other political texts in Greek.

The influence that Maoist populism had on the Greek Communists is clear from Beata Kitsikis' writings:

The influence of the Cultural Revolution on the whole planet was enormous. Basically what was involved was a Third World protest against the Western way of life which not only set off a chain-reaction against the technological West in the Third World – as in Libya and Iran – but also in the West itself, where the most striking example was the student uprising in France in 1968.[16]

Until 1967 populism in Greece, with its roots reaching back to before the Second World War, was violently anti-communist. But Maoism, despite its virtual absence of electoral impact, began to introduce people to the idea that populism was not necessarily linked to anti-communism, and could even use a Marxist language. On 19 March 1975, at the eleventh congress of the Hungarian Workers' Party, Florakis had declared: 'Among young people there are *gauchiste* groups working, of Maoist, Trotskyist and other derivations, who, thanks to revolutionary-sounding slogans and to provocation, objectively further the work of neo-fascist groups'.[17]

The military coup d'état of 21 April 1967 had marked populist features. If the regime's ideologues never succeeded in establishing an ideological state, this was because of the personal opposition of the regime's leader, Georgios Papadopoulos, and also because of the colonels' political incompetence. But in the gradual emancipation of Greek populism from its past ferocious anti-communism an important step was taken under the military regime. Until 1967, communism had been the *bête noire* of Greek parliamentarism. For the first time since the Second World War, right-wing personalities who had been the symbol of the bourgeois oligarchy, such as Georgios Rallis and Evanghelos Averoff, were persecuted and many other members of that oligarchy were imprisoned. The prisons thus held not only Communists who, before 1967, had suffered torture under the liberal parliamentary state, but now also dedicated anti-communists.

In foreign affairs the regime considerably improved its relations with communist countries, in particular with Albania, Romania and People's China, and also with Third World countries. At the same time it announced that it would no longer make a distinction between Right and Left and that, in choosing with whom it would cooperate, it would not take the political history of individuals into account. In this way the Greek Communists ceased to be regarded as a scourge. According to Evanghelos Averoff, the extremists of the regime of 21 April 1967 – nicknamed the 'Qadaffists' – had a profound anti-capitalist class sentiment, at least as clear as that of the Communists and therefore just as dangerous.[18]

American reports on the internal situation of Greece in the first half of 1974 had portrayed the regime of General Ioannides, who had succeeded Papadopoulos, as excessively nationalist. This was the period of the emergence of the 'Qaddafists' in the army and of Ioannides' speeches to the Evelpides Military Academy (the Greek 'West Point') which emphasized the need for a close collaboration between Greece and the Arabs and for a distancing from Europe. Instead of being at the tail of the European community, said Ioannides, Greece should put itself at the head of the Third World countries in the Eastern Mediterranean.

Although the colonels' populism succeeded in abolishing the monarchy in 1973, their evident incapacity for governing meant that they were not even able to benefit from the establishment of the republic to make themselves popular. So it was that when they fell, in July 1974, not a single voice was raised in their defence.

The return to Greece of Andreas Papandreou that year, and the foundation of his party – PASOK – caused the Third World populism that had just gone into eclipse with the fall of the Junta, to arise anew.[19] Despite Papandreou's radical opposition to the colonels' regime, for reasons much more of governmental style than of basic principles,[20] the continuity in the populism of both regimes, after the intervening period of right-wing liberal power in 1974–81, could be seen most prominently in the fact that a good number of 'juntists' became PASOK supporters. Moreover, the extremely populist pro-government *Aurianê*, which practises a cult of personality in favour of Papandreou, has juntists on its editorial board. As for the party of the extreme Right, the *Ethnikê Parataxis* (EP, later EPEN), which defended the imprisoned juntists, it in no way reflected the populism of 21 April. Atrophied and full of retired people, its influence was to be extremely limited.

To commemorate the first anniversary of PASOK's foundation, Papandreou announced to party members in a stadium in Athens on 6 September 1975:

The PASOK believes that the cornerstone of the democratic development of our country is the reconciliation between the people and the armed forces . . . The socialism that PASOK supports is clearly one of national liberation. And this will explain to you why there are present here this evening Palestinians, Syrians and all those who struggle to break imperialism's chains.[21]

In fact, PASOK's socialism was always presented as an integral part of its nationalism and as a socialism that had its roots deep in the Greek tradition, going back at least as far as the Byzantine empire. In 1982, as prime minister, Papandreou announced that the Byzantine state had, in fact, 'the first elements of a political system that today is called socialism'.[22]

When the KKE was clandestine and the militants of the national Resistance of the EAM–ELAS were languishing in the prisons of the parliamentary state, the Communist Party tried to present the EAM as a broad patriotic organization independent of the Communists. After 1974, Papandreou pretended to subscribe to this version of history and stated that PASOK was the descendant of the generation of the EAM. Even the rising sun and the green colour that he adopted as the emblem of his party recalled the sun and the green of the EPON, the EAM's youth organization. The KKE reacted energetically, demonstrating that what was of merit in the EAM's political activity derived first and foremost from the Communist Party that had founded the EAM. But PASOK did not stop there. Moreover, appropriating the slogans of the extreme Left, making ever more passionate speeches in favour of national dignity, of socialism, of the 'unprivileged class' and against American imperialism and international capital, PASOK attempted to draw to itself the members of the KKE, and thus weaken it.

Its tactics consisted in asking for unconditional support from the Communists on the eve of each election, without, however, accepting an electoral coalition with them. Its slogan was *'autodynamia,'* which meant basing itself on its own forces and governing without allies.[23] When the Communists turned and refused their unconditional support, PASOK accused them of playing the game of the reactionaries and of aiding the return of the Right. The municipal elections of October 1986 were a typical example of this situation. The KKE had demanded as a condition for supporting the governmental candidate in the second round of the mayoral election in Athens, that PASOK undertake to set up a system of simple proportional representation within a reasonable period. When PASOK refused, the KKE 'liberated' its members from any voting discipline in the election. As a result, the rightist candidate was elected major.

It is clear that PASOK's populism had succeeded, until October 1986, in channelling popular discontent to its own advantage, and in preventing an increase in the KKE vote above its traditional strength (to the undoubted satisfaction of the United States). But it is no less clear that PASOK had not succeeded in weakening the KKE to any great extent. In the eyes of the KKE, Papandreou is an anti-communist much more dangerous than was his father, who in 1944 was nicknamed by the Left 'Papatzes' – 'one who cheats at cards'.

An analysis of the legislative elections of 1985 which appeared in the KKE Central Committee's official journal and was entitled 'Some aspects and objectives of the anti-communism of PASOK's leadership' stated, first, that it had been demonstrated that Papandreou's aim in the elections had been to defeat not the Right, but communism; secondly, the means employed had been a dishonest electoral law, terror at the workplace and intimidation of Communist voters. After the elections a PASOK leader had praised, in front of foreign journalists, PASOK's ability to check communist influence, something that could not have been so efficiently achieved – he added – by the Right; and thirdly, PASOK's anti-communism was no different from that of the Right except that, in addressing a left-wing public it used a terminology of the Left. It was therefore a matter of unmasking Papandreou the demagogue.[24] On this last point, it is worth noting that on his return to Greece Andreas Papandreou had announced, with unconcealed exaggeration: 'Our programme in fact goes further than that of the Communist Party'.[25]

From the legislative elections of 1985 to the municipal elections of 1986: the KKE strengthened

For the first time since 1974, the KKE decided to direct its electoral campaign of 1985 as much (if not more) against PASOK as against the

Right. Its aim was to prevent Papandreou from obtaining a majority of seats in the parliament, so that he would need the support of Communist deputies in order to govern. This would force him to put into practice his radical declarations that had so far remained on paper.[26] When PASOK, against the general expectation, won a comfortable majority of seats (161 out of 300), the KKE, far more than the Right, insisted that the malpractices and the extortion that the opposition had unanimously condemned in the European elections of 1984, had again been used by Papandreou in 1985.[27]

The party retained its strength overall, but with a loss of one per cent of its vote in comparison with the legislative elections of 1981, and 1.7 per cent in comparison with the European elections of 17 June 1984. But it was more than ever the third party in a system where the Right (*Nea Dêmokratia* – ND), PASOK and the KKE itself had between them won 77 per cent of the poll in 1974 and 1977, 84 per cent in the European elections of 1981, 95 per cent in the legislative elections of 1981, 91 per cent in the European elections of 1984 and 96.5 in the legislative elections of 1985. If it had not been for the popularity of its chairman, Leonidas Kyrkos, who won its only seat in the parliament, the KKE-Interior would for its part have been completely destroyed.

The KKE's hostility towards PASOK increased further in 1986 in the municipal elections held in two rounds on 12 and 19 October, and this hostility bore fruit.[28] As the right-wing press remarked:

The great victory of *Nea Dêmokratia* in all three of the country's major municipalities – Athens, Thessaloniki, Piraeus – has overshadowed the heavy defeat of PASOK in major urban areas normally dominated by the Left. The bitter struggle between the governing party and the communist Left has been waged in the populous second constituency of Athens, the second constituency of Piraeus and the second constituency of Thessaloniki and the result has been a victory for the KKE, except for some results favouring PASOK that merely confirm the rule.[29]

We saw above that in 1936, when, with its 15 deputies in the *Boulê*, the KKE played the role of arbiter between the two great 'bourgeois' parties of the time, the party had only 14,000 members. By the time of its eleventh congress, held on 15–18 December 1982, it numbered 73,000, of which 32.8 per cent were workers, 14.5 per cent salaried employees, 18.11 per cent farmers, 9.7 per cent shopkeepers and artisans, 12.3 per cent members of the liberal professions and the intelligentsia and 22.6 per cent women. The party's electorate in 1985 broke down as follows: 12.2 per cent of the urban vote, 8.7 per cent of the semi-urban vote and 8 per cent of the rural vote.[30]

On coming to power in 1981 PASOK had reckoned on having some real support from the Soviet Union, given the experience of populist countries of the Third World where the Soviet Union had supported existing regimes even if those regimes maltreated their communists. In order to benefit from this support Papandreou made certain gestures towards the Soviet Union on the international level, approving the state of war of General Jaruzelski in Poland, and condemning Washington when the latter was accused of spying on military installations by means of flight 007 of the Korean Air Lines, which was shot down over Soviet territory. These gestures were received in the West with hostility. It is to be noted also that in February 1985 Papandreou made an official visit to Moscow, whilst until the end of 1986 he had made no visit to Washington. Nevertheless, as with the Papadopoulos regime that had used the same stratagem, Moscow judged that PASOK, like the 1967–74 regime, was too closely linked to the United States for it to merit an enthusiastic response.

On the contrary, just after the Greek municipal elections, and more exactly on 3 November 1986, a 'summit' meeting lasting three hours took place in Moscow between Florakis and Mikhail Gorbachev. This was regarded as an unprecedented event earning front page coverage in all the Greek newspapers, in some cases with enormous headlines. The Greeks interpreted the event as the expression of Moscow's approval of the KKE's tactics in Greek political life and of the importance that Gorbachev accorded the Greek party, at a time when so many other Western European communist parties were in the doldrums. Florakis returned to Athens with a precise mission: to make a great effort to develop the Soviet peace offensive in Greece, after Reykjavik. When one considers the efforts that Papandreou had made to present himself to Moscow as the champion of peace, thanks to the 'Initiative for Disarmament and Peace' of the Six (Greece, Sweden, Mexico, Argentina, India, Tanzania), the Florakis–Gorbachev summit can be represented as a slap in the face for the Greek populist leader. The propaganda services of the Greek government had made the following comment on the proposition to stop nuclear testing that the Six published in Ixtapa, Mexico, in August 1986: 'President Reagan rejected the Six's offer, exactly as he did, in practice, a year ago. Gorbachev, on the other hand, stated that he would extend the moratorium at least until next January, exactly as the Six had requested in their letter.'[31]

The future: Greek Khomeini-ism – new threat to the KKE

The Greek Orthodox Church traditionally calls the cultural space in which it moves '*ê kath'êmas Anatolê*' (our East). In the summer of

1986, I was able, through a study visit to the Holy Mountain (*Aghion Oros*), Mount Athos, in northern Greece, to witness the astonishing religious and cultural revival that has taken place, centred on the monks of Athos. Even members of the Communist Party go there in order to seek the truth and a possible solution to the problem of Greek identity in the face of Western cultural imperialism. Since the coming to power of Papandreou in 1981, cultural anti-Westernism has made giant strides in Greece. In 1985, for example, the Ministry of Education replaced the Roman version of the ikon representing Christ, which hung in the offices of the public administration, the courts and the schools, with a Byzantine ikon of the Saviour, justifying this measure with the aim of checking the Westernization of Greek society. The Ministry added that in this way it was contributing to the struggle against 'the decadent and corrupt cultural model of the West.'[32]

By contrast, the Ministry of Culture, directed by the actress Melina Mercouri, whose views are rather pro-Western, organized a series of grand ceremonies on the Acropolis on 21 June 1985 in the presence of François Mitterrand, in order to proclaim Athens 'the cultural capital of Europe'. The populist Christian Orthodox party, Christian Democracy (*Hristianike Dêmokratia*), which collaborates with PASOK, vigorously protested against these ceremonies. Its leader, Nikos Psaroudakis, a PASOK deputy, sent the following letter to Melina Mercouri on 21 June 1985, refusing to attend the ceremonies:

Madame Minister, . . . What has been Europe's response to Greece's cultural contribution? It has deformed Greece's civilization, as well as Christ's gospel! . . . Is Athens to become the capital of colonial civilization? . . . Such developments only accelerate the mechanism of our total cultural integration in the European economic community . . . Today's rejoicings echo the refrain of the leadership of the Right, whose aims they serve: 'We belong to the West', a refrain that does not correspond to the historical truth and which is not acceptable to us.[33]

The KKE reacted equally vigorously, and in the same way as Psaroudakis: 'Ever since Karamanlis tried to import "the European ideal" he has been stressing that "Europe's roots lie in Greece" . . . But the mass cultural movement of our country sees cultural integration in the EEC as a new form of ideological submission to imperialism'.[34]

Andreas Papandreou has disappointed those members of his party who hoped to see in Greece the development of a Third World populism outside the EEC. But the firm and consistent opposition of the KKE to the EEC has not been enough, all the same, to group around the Communist Party the broad anti-Western masses of the country. Yet the emergence of an 'oriental constituency' in Greece is a fact that can be statistically confirmed.[35] Who will manage to harness it? The 'treason' of Russia, Orthodoxy's eldest daughter, in favour of the Slavs, is fading in the Greek consciousness. There is no longer a sentiment in Greece against a 'Russian danger'. If a Greek Khomeini-ism should develop around the spiritual centre of Mount Athos, it might be anti-communist but it would probably not be anti-Russian. This trend could therefore be a formidable future threat to the KKE if the latter does not manage to turn it to its own advantage.

Notes

1   See the map given for the 'intermediate region' in D. Kitsikis, *L'Empire ottoman* (Presses universitaires de France, Paris, 1985), p. 16.

2   *Rizospastês*, 23 November 1986 (this is the KKE's daily paper), fifteen-page supplement: '68 hronia KKE' (68 Years of the KKE); Stavros Zorbalas, *Sêmaia tou laou: selides apo tên istoria tou Rizospastê, 1917–1936* (The People's Flag: Pages from the History of Rizospastês, 1917–1936) (Politikes kai Logotehnikes Ekdoseis, Bucharest, 1966); *To prôto synedrio tou SEKE. Praktika* (The First Congress of the Socialist Workers' Party of Greece – SEKE. Minutes) (Publications of the KKE Central Committee, Athens, 1983). (The SEKE was created on 17 November 1918; the word 'communist' was added to the party's name on 26 April 1920. It was under the name of SEKE that the KKE was created.) D. G. Kousoulas, *Revolution and Defeat: The Story of the Greek Communist Party* (Oxford University Press, London, 1976); J. O. Iatrides, *Revolt in Athens; the Greek Communist Second Round, 1944–45* (Princeton University Press, Princeton, NJ, 1972); J. C. Loulis, *The Greek Communist Party, 1940–1944* (Croom Helm, London, 1982); A. L. Zapantis, *Greek–Soviet Relations, 1917–1941* (Columbia University Press, New York, 1982); O. L. Smith, 'Marxism in Greece: the Case of the KKE', *Journal of Modern Greek Studies*, vol. 3, no. 1, May 1985, pp. 45–64; KKE, *Episêma keimena* (Official Texts), (Syghronê Epohê, Athens), 5 volumes, 1974–81; Petros Rousos, *Ê megalê tetraetia* (The Four Great Years) (Politikes kai Logotehnikes Ekdoseis, Bucharest, 1966); A. Solaro, *Storia del partito comunista greco* (Teti, Milan, 1973).

3   It is in this light that Jean Meynaud presents the EDA in his *Les forces politiques en Grèce* (Etudes de Science Politique, Montreal, 1965).

4   This was the author's father (1887–1978).

5   *Programma tou Kommounistikou Kommatos Elladas Esôterikou. Psêfistêke sto 1° (9°) Synedrio tou KKE Esôterikou, Iounes 1976* (Programme of the Communist Party of Greece of the Interior, adopted by the First (Ninth) Congress of the KKE-Interior, June 1976) (Publications of the KKE-Interior Athens, 1976), p. 145.

6   Ibid., p. 146.

7   *Apofaseis, Problêmatismoi tou KKE Esôterikou, 1969–76* (Resolutions and Questions of the KKE-Interior, 1969–76) (Publications of the KKE-Interior, Athens, 1976), 3 volumes. See also Stavros Karas, 'To Synedrio tou KKE Exôterikou kai ê tyhodiôhtikê antilêpsê sto ellêniko kommounistiko kinêma'

(The Congress of the KKE of the Exterior and the Adventurist Mentality in the Greek Communist Movement), *Kommounistikê Theôria kai Politike* (Athens), no. 23–24, August 1978, pp. 35–52 (this is the monthly journal of the KKE-Interior); P. Nefeloudis, *Stis pêges tês kakodaimonias; Ta bathytera aitia tês diaspasês tou KKE, 1918–1968* (At the Springs of Ill-fortune; the Deep Causes of the Split in the KKE, 1918–1968) (Gutenberg, Athens, 1974); 'Apofaseis tou 3^{ou} (11^{ou}) Synedriou tou KKE Esôterikou' (Decisions of the 3rd (11th) Congress of the KKE-Interior), *Kommounistikê Theôria kai Politike* (Athens), no. 44, May-June 1982, pp. 3–61; S. Karpathiotis (ed.), *Ê entaxê mas stên EOK* (Our Incorporation in the EEC) (Themelio, Athens, 1978); D. Stolidis, 'Giati leme ohi ston eurôkommounismo' (Why We Say No to Eurocommunism), *Rizospastês*, 15–19 April 1978. It should be pointed out that the present General Secretary of the KKE, Harilaos Florakis, was himself imprisoned from 1954 to 1966, and was from 1967 to 1972 in a concentration camp, and could therefore hardly be accused of being 'outside' the country.

8 I have often been reproached with giving too much attention in my works to this celebrated composer on the grounds that as an artist and not a political actor he does not deserve this space. The comment of Andreas Papandreou, annoyed by Theodorakis' criticisms of his policies, is well known: 'With Mikis I do not discuss politics.' I do not accept this point of view. Even if the political presence of the erstwhile head of the 'Lambrakis Youth' (1963–7) was secondary – which is not the case – his moral presence is of importance. And Theodorakis is, in many ways, a Westernist, despite the impression given by his statements in favour of Qaddafi (see his interview with *Ethnos* (Athens), 3 March 1982, p. 31) and despite his music, which is considered purely Greek. His ecclesiastical music in particular, composed during his youth but performed in more recent years, is strongly Catholic in its inspiration and shocks the traditionalists of the Orthodox Church.

9 The term 'Eurocommunism' is officially used by the KKE-Interior to refer to the European vocation of Greek communism.

10 More precise biographical details on Florakis can be found in 'Harilaos Florakis: Olê tê zôê sto Komma' (A Whole Life in the Party), *Politika Themata* (Athens), 19–25 March 1977, pp. 25–9. See also 'Harilaos Florakis', *To Bêma* (Athens), 13 and 15 March 1977; and 'Ta periousika stoiheia Andrea, Averoff kai Floraki' (The Incomes of Andreas, Averoff and Florakis), *Ethnos* (Athens), 16 March 1982.

11 *Programma tou . . .* (Programme of the KKE-Interior), p. 130. See also *Iounês 1984. Ekloges gia to Eurôkoinoboulio. Proshedio programmatos tou KKE Esôterikou* (June 1984. Elections for the European Parliament. Preliminary Project for the Programme of the KKE-Interior) (Publications of the KKE-Interior, Athens, 1984).

12 A. J. Jones, *Fascism in the Contemporary World: Ideology, Evolution, Resurgence* (Westview Press, Boulder, CO, 1978), p. 208.

13 In particular in my studies 'Le mouvement communiste en Grèce', *Etudes internationales*, vol. VI, no. 3, September 1975, pp. 334–54; and 'National-Socialism in Greece', *International Studies Association* (*ISA*), 17th Annual Convention, Toronto, February 1976.

14 The author's mother. (1907–86). Beata Kitsikis was passionately attracted to Russian thought and spoke excellent Russian, which she had learned during the Resistance. It was this attachment to the Russian tradition that led her to stay in the KKE until her death.

15   Beata Kitsikis, *Gnôrisa tous kokkinous frourous* (I Knew the Red Guards) (Kedros, Athens, 1982).

16   Ibid., p. 336.

17   *Ê Augê* (Athens), 5 April 1975 – the official daily of the KKE-Interior. Cf. the remark of the French neo-fascists: 'May 1968 in France was a pre-fascist revolt', *Essai de synthèse pour un neo-fascisme* (Paris: special number of *L'Elite européenne*, May 1972), p. 38.

18   D. Kitsikis, 'Le mouvement communiste en Grèce', pp. 338–9.

19   See A. Andrianopoulos, 'PASOK; Political Profile', *Epikentra* (Athens), May 1981, pp. 35–9 (English edition); and, in the same issue, J. C. Loulis 'The Political Philosophy of PASOK', pp. 40–50.

20   See the interview that Andreas Papandreou gave to the journalist Eric Rouleau, published in *Le Monde*, 25 January 1968.

21   *Ta Nea* (Athens), 8 September 1975.

22   K. Kolmer, 'To PASOK kai to Byzantio' (PASOK and Byzantium), *Epikentra* (Athens), no. 27, July–August 1982, pp. 19–21.

23   This tactic is identical with that of his father, Georgios Papandreou, who, in 1963–5, had as his slogan 'dimetôpos agônas' (struggle on two fronts).

24   Iannis Hatzigeorgiou, 'Orismenes pleures kai stohoi tou antikommounismou tês êgesias tou PASOK' (Some Aspects and Aims of the Anticommunism of the PASOK leadership), *Kommounistikê Epitheôrêsê*, new period, 11th year, no. 7–8, July–August 1985, pp. 26–31. (This is the theoretical monthly of the Central Committee of the KKE.)

25   *Le Nouvel Observateur*, 9 November 1974, p. 54. Cf. the statement of Lieutenant-Colonel Anastasios Spanos of the junta in 1974 to a Communist militant: 'We shall make Greece more red than you would have wished, but unlike you we shall keep it Greek' (D. Kitsikis, 'Le mouvement communiste', p. 339).

26   Panayote E. Dimitras, 'The Greek Parliamentary Election of 1985', *Electoral Studies*, vol. 4, no. 3, December 1985, p. 262.

27   For 1985, about 500,000 'ghost voters' were registered on the electoral lists (people who were dead or were registered at least twice). Also, voters were pressured openly with a view to stripping them of the right to return a blank ballot paper. If the voter insisted, his 'white' vote (voluntary act) was counted as being null, and was interpreted as an unintentional error. This illegal practice was repeated in the 1986 municipal elections. ('Stis dêmotikes ekloges ta leuka psêfodeltia metrêthêkan ôs akyra – In the Municipal Elections the White Papers were Counted as Null'. *Kathêmerinê*, 2 December 1986)

28   *Rizospastês*, 2 November 1986. Complete text of the resolution of the Central Committee of the KKE on the subject of the municipal elections: 'The leadership of PASOK has chosen its policy, which lies within the framework of the system of state monopoly capitalism, itself dependent on the centre of imperialism [the formula is 'exartêmenos kratikomonopôliakos kapitalismos']. That is the meaning of the statement of PASOK, through which PASOK becomes a member of the Socialist International'.

29   *Ê Kathêmerinê* (Athens), 21 October 1986 (a daily that supports the ND). It is to be noted that the KKE managed to become a pole of attraction in the municipal elections of 1986, thus reinforcing a trend that had appeared in the elections of 1985, when a certain number of deputies and erstwhile ministers of PASOK joined forces with the KKE and collaborated with it. So it was

that just after the municipal elections the KKE-Interior found itself divided into two tendencies: that of the present General Secretary of the party, Leonidas Kyrkos, who had supported the PASOK candidate in Athens, and that of the party's ex-secretary, Iannis Banias, who was supported by the majority of the party's organizations, and who rallied to the KKE, recommending that voters return a blank ballot paper. The same thing happened in the EDA. During that party's second congress, held in Athens on the 27–30 November 1986, the majority followed the party's secretary, Theodoros Katrivanos, who was the candidate of the KKE coalition (named the *Symparataxê*) for the mayoralty of Athens. But the minority followed the EDA's president, Manolis Glezos, a deputy elected on the PASOK list, who was in favour of a coalition with the KKE-Interior. This split in the EDA took place on 30 November 1986.

30 *Greek Opinion* (Athens), vol. 11, no. 5–6, May–June 1985, p. 6.

31 *Athena Magazine* (Athens), no. 8, September 1986, p. 266.

32 *Orthodoxos Typos*, 7 June 1985, p. 4. This is the journal of the Orthodox fundamentalists.

33 A photocopy of the complete text is in the author's personal papers.

34 Tea Vasiliadou, 'To ideologikopolitiko mênyma tês Athênas, politistikês prôteuousas tês Eurôpês' (The Ideological-Political Message of Athens, Cultural Capital of Europe), *Kommounistikê Epitheôrêse* (Athens), new period, 11th year, no. 7–8, July-August 1985, pp. 40 and 42. For a history of Greek anti-Westernism see D. Kitsikis, 'Ê anatolikê parataxê stên Ellada' (The Oriental Constituency in Greece), *Tote* (Athens) no. 27, August 1985, pp. 54–68. It should be noted that the KKE supported for the first time in November 1986 a campaign in favour of the establishment of Greco-Turkish friendship, which would lead to privileged relations between the two fraternal countries of the 'intermediate region'. This initiative was undertaken after a meeting that Florakis had in Cyprus, during the sixteenth congress of the Cypriot of AKEL (the Working Peoples' Progressive Party), with the General Secretary of the Communist Party of Turkey, Haydar Kutlu. The campaign owed much of its impetus to Mikis Theodorakis and was even welcomed by the Turkish prime minister, Turgut Özal! Thus an Association for Greco-Turkish Friendship and an Association for Turko-Greek Friendship were set up in Greece and Turkey respectively in November and December 1986, to the chagrin of militant Armenians and Kurds. (See K. Ali (Kurdish historian), 'Ellênotourkikê filia kai lôtofagia' (Greek-Turkish Friendship and Lotophagia), *Anti* (Athens), 2 January 1987.

35 P. E. Dimitras, 'Greece: a New Danger', *Foreign Policy* (USA), no. 58, Spring 1985, pp. 134–50.

7 Failed Attempts at Modernization
The Finnish Communist Party

Matti Hyvärinen and Jukka Paastela

Until the 1970s the Finnish Communist Party (*Suomen Kommunistinen Puolue* – SKP) was one of the largest communist parties in Western Europe. Among these parties it has shown at least five rather exceptional features: first, very close relations with the CPSU, together with some difficulty in maintaining them in the 1970s and 1980s; secondly, participation in governmental coalitions in 1966–82; thirdly, the division of the party into a majority and a minority wing since 1966, together with attempts to preserve unity by agreements between the two; fourthly, extreme *ouvrièrisme* and a weak intellectual tradition; and fifthly, a sharp decline in the SKP's electoral support and in its membership since the late 1960s.

In our view, an examination of these features shows that the problems are not, after all, local ones. They are rather the general problems of modernization of a communist party. It is very difficult to abandon the heritage of Stalinism without losing at the same time the combative enthusiasm characteristic of Bolshevism.

The internal split in the SKP

The background

The first 26 years of the SKP's life were deeply traumatic. The party was founded in Moscow in the spring of 1918 after the close of the civil war in Finland that attended that country's emancipation from Russian rule.

Until 1944 the leadership of the party remained in Moscow, whilst in Finland the party was illegal. In the newly independent Finland the civil war was termed a war of liberation against Russia, and the losers were branded as traitors. For the SKP activists, however, the Soviet Union was seen as a haven of safety, and the leaders and most of the important party workers experienced everyday life there under Stalinism. In Finland the SKP did not manage to build any important popular front movement before the Winter War against the Soviet Union, nor any important resistance movement during the Second World War. Until 1944 the experience of the party was that of an organization that was discriminated against, persecuted and isolated but at the same time it maintained an almost military centralization. In 1944 the victory of the Soviet Union, the reorientation of Finnish foreign policy and the legalization of the SKP created a difficult situation for the party. The opportunities were enormous, but the Communists had no experience of policy-making at national level.

On the initiative of the party a front organization, the Finnish People's Democratic League (SKDL) was founded in order to promote, above all, friendly relations with the Soviet Union. This organization, however, never became politically as broad as it was intended, only managing to attract to its ranks a small group of left-wing social democrats.

The SKP entered the government of national reconstruction in 1944. In the optimistic atmosphere of freedom and popular-frontism the party soon grew to be one of the 'large parties' alongside the Social Democratic Party and the Agrarian Party (later the Centre Party). But it was led by the activists of the illegal period, and the first serious generation gap soon developed inside the party. The identity of the party was based on the heroism of the civil war and of the resistance in circumstances of illegality; it was a heroism of sacrifice. This heroism, the link of friendship with the Soviet Union and Stalinist socialization merged together in the creation of the party's identity.

In 1948, after a defeat in the general elections, the SKP was ousted from government until 1966. Its position in Finnish society from 1948 to 1966 can best be described as 'withdrawal into the fortress'.[1] A separate sphere of culture was created: hobbies, cultural and sport activities, even the bringing up of children took place within this separate sphere: 'The organizations of the workers' movement were, in fact, excluded from the leadership of political and especially cultural life of the nation.'[2] There was only one important exception, one area where the importance of the SKP was great, and that was foreign policy. However, withdrawing into the fortress did not mean small electoral support: in 1958, after the general strike, the SKDL/SKP polled 23.2 per cent of the votes and became the largest group in the parliament.

Three great social changes contributed to the disintegration of this separate culture in the 1960s: exceptionally rapid industrialization and urbanization, the spread of television, and the creation of the unified school system (to replace the old system of two separate schools, 'theoretical' and 'practical'). The traditional communities of workers and small farmers were dispersed and their organizational activities lost vigour.

It was while these social changes were taking place that the SKP came to be internally divided. It seemed that there were only two alternatives for the party: one of *traditionalism*, remaining, so to speak, at the margin of society, and the other, one of *integration* in the capitalist state by participating in its policy-making processes. This second alternative became possible after a change of attitude towards communists on the part of the bourgeoisie and the Social Democrats. In a way, the SKP selected both alternatives by splitting into two wings. The 'reformists' gained a small majority at the fourteenth congress in 1966, electing Aarne Saarinen as chairman.

The party of two centres

The most important dividing factors were the attitude to be taken towards the policy of the government, the question of relations with the Soviet Union, how to interpret and apply Marxism–Leninism, and the attitude to be adopted in respect of economic struggle. We will deal with the first two questions in separate sections below. Here we deal with the ideological and strategic aspects of the division.

Ideologically the rift in the party has opposed Marxist–Leninist fundamentalism to a desire to be open to new ideas. Since the 1960s, however, no important group in the party has questioned the validity of Marxism–Leninism. The majority, to be sure, has wanted to abandon some doctrines, such as the dictatorship of the proletariat, and promised to respect democratic rights in the transition to socialism as well as a socialist order.[3] But both wings of the party have seen themselves as defending the purity of Marxism–Leninism, although this theme has been more important to the minority.

There has never been in the SKP any profound discussion about the strategy of the party, and the political options of neither majority nor minority have been the result of any conscious strategy. It can be said that the political tactics of both sides have been based on simple differences of perception of what is advantageous to the working class and to the supporters of the party. According to the majority it is more advantageous to participate in 'real policy-making' and it has supported incomes policies and compromises, whereas the minority has calculated that more advantage can be had by continuous mobilization and strikes. The majority has believed that by de-Stalinizing and democratizing the party it is possible to emerge from the fortress. The rising radical student movement at the beginning of the 1970s was a problem for the majority, whereas the minority, which stressed struggle and condemned 'rotten compromises', managed to attract young people who were in rebellion. The de-Stalinized majority, thus, was also de-Bolshevized. The only perspective of enthusiastic struggle that it offered was an internal one, against the minority.

The split of the party followed no social lines that could have been predicted. The minority won over to its side the large district organizations in industrial southern Finland, but the important district of Helsinki was majority-dominated. The majority won many district organizations in the agricultural north but others went to the minority. It is very difficult to explain the decisions of individual members of the party. The majority of those members who had joined before 1944 usually favoured the minority. An uncompromising marginal position was more natural for this generation than for the generation of the post-war period; to the latter the withdrawal into the fortress was much more a stigma.[4] It should be stressed that the choice of faction was for many members quite accidental. The cadres of the district organizations were in a decisive position: they made the choice and the large majority of the members followed them.

The minority marched out of the fifteenth congress in 1969 and founded a nationwide organization of its own. The reunification brought about in 1970 through the active support of the CPSU and by agreement between majority and minority remained formal in its nature. Unity was to be attained by open discussion and common activities. In fact what was created was a very curious model of party structure and party activity.

There were three different 'democratic centralisms' in the party. Firstly, there were formally united congresses, strongly supported by the CPSU, where a 'common policy' of the party was defined on such an abstract level that very different interpretations were possible. Secondly, there was an operational democratic centralism as it was interpreted by the majority; this was that the minority should submit to the will of the majority on political matters and on appointments of persons. A third variety of democratic centralism was that of the minority: officially 'the decisions of congress' were followed, but in fact only as they were inter- . preted by the Tiedonantaja Society (*Tiedonantaja* – 'the informant' – is the paper of the minority).[5] No organ in the party organization had the right to make any decision on theoretical, political or personal matters that could be in contradiction with the decisions of the Tiedonantaja

Society. The correct theory was already in the possession of this society.

The struggle between the two wings meant a strong emphasis on centralism on both sides, and the struggle led to 'terrible pressures towards uniformity'.[6] The original idea of the majority was that the party should be democratized. What it finally demanded at the end of the 1970s was discipline, and a return to the principles of democratic centralism. Any open discussion arising from the party's congresses was impossible. The majority did not allow it in the papers under its control. The minority understood discussion as conversion and declared that it would 'not deviate an inch in questions of principle from Marxism–Leninism'.[7]

Open discussion was impossible because there was no common press. The members of the party were divided into readers of the majority or the minority press. There were two papers for youth, students and children. None of the papers made any attempt to become a means to the formation of any new initiative or consciousness inside the party. They were all only the means for propagating a ready-made political line.

At first the split activated the party cells. The bitter struggle soon led, however, to the formation of 'pure' cells, consisting of members either of the majority or of the minority, but not a mixture of both, or to the paralysis of their activities. The rank and file got their orders from above: they were required, for instance, to protest against 'the lack of discipline' of the minority or 'the disruptive line' of the majority. Any idea of independence at the basic level of the party was alien in the war between majority and minority.

The withering away of the SKP's internal democracy was very clear in the elections of delegates to congresses. In these elections every member has the right to vote for as many candidates as are to be elected from the district organization. In practice the leaders of the district organizations elected the representatives beforehand. The names of the candidates 'recommended by the district organization' were written on one side of the ballot. On the other side were written the names of those unfortunate candidates who were not recommended by the district organization. Moreover, in the election there was usually a representative of the district organization who indicated on which 'side' one should vote. Especially in the district organizations controlled by the majority people wanting to become members of the party were asked what was her or his attitude to the division in the party. Hundreds of students, scholars and young people were accepted as members by the party cells, only to find that their papers had mysteriously disappeared in the office of the district organization.

The split has bred centralism, undemocratic procedures and Stalinist methods. Only one feature has been missing: dismissals and purges were not used during the period 1970–82.

Why is it that modernization has been so difficult, and why has the struggle inside the party remained unsolved? The two wings are almost equal in size (the seats at congresses have been divided in the proportion 55 to 45). The result of a final split will be reduction to the status of a small party. The CPSU has ardently supported unity and the minority. But only a part of the matter is thus explained. Why has unification been impossible?

We would suggest that one should seek an answer in the internal problems of the Marxist–Leninist discourse and political culture. We should like to stress here two points: first, the strength of the belief that the party cannot make any 'ideological compromises', and secondly, the fact that differences are not allowed: the 'discursive practice' in relation to the differences in thought and in policy is 'struggle against deviations'. The members are not allowed freely to create theory and strategy for their party; instead it is their duty to seek and realize the 'essence of the party'. An essential limitation on Marxist–Leninist discussion is, as Michel Foucault would put it, 'the principle of commentary'.[8] There is a hierarchical relationship between the original texts and their interpretation. The correctness of an idea can be proved only by interpreting the original texts and the basic concepts such as 'Marxism–Leninism', 'democratic centralism' and 'proletarian internationalism'. The commentary limits the opportunities of any change. A new discourse has no real identity of its own and results in repetition and more of the same.

So it is that the process of the modernization of the SKP took the form of a traditional fractional struggle, the practice of a 'struggle against deviations', and the principle of commentary of the traditional ideology – in short, strong traditionalism.

The final split

The divided party was in clear crisis at the end of the 1970s. The members were frustrated, and electoral support was declining. There were three possible courses of action. The first was to maintain formal unity in spite of wide dissatisfaction with this situation; this was the position of the minority. The second was to stop patching up agreements and to oust the minority from the leadership of the SKP; this was the position of the so-called 'axe-line'. The third was to try to make a radical reassessment of the theory, strategy and policy of the party, and thus bury the old frontiers between majority and minority; this was the position of the so-called 'third line' in 1981–2 when Jouko Kajanoja was elected party chairman. All organizations and newspapers, however, remained in the hands of one or other of the wings of the party and thus these attempts came to nothing.

The 'axe-line' was victorious at the twentieth congress in 1984. Arvo Aalto – 'the Prince' – was elected chairman and no agreements were made between the minority and the majority. As a result the minority withdrew from the Central Committee and the Political Bureau of the party. The majority founded new district organizations in the areas ruled by the minority. An extraordinary congress in 1985 declared that the minority must submit to the will of the majority before the general elections in 1987 or else be dismissed.

The minority, together with some former members of the majority, reacted by founding a new leadership: the Central Committee of SKP Organizations. At a congress of the minority organizations in 1986, Taisto Sinisalo was elected chairman of this body, with Kajanoja as the General Secretary. Further, a 'new SKDL' was launched, called the Democratic Alternative (DEVA, in its Finnish abbreviation). It was intended to be a front organization, but practically no one besides the minority and splinters from the majority joined. The only exception was a tiny remnant of the split that had taken place in the Social Democratic Party at the end of the 1950s – the Socialist Workers' Party – which neither has a seat in the parliament nor can hope to win one. There were inside the minority some hard-liners who demanded the foundation of a new, officially registered, communist party, but the minority leaders followed the wishes of the CPSU and refused to take this course. The minority still speaks about restoring the unity of the party but to all intents and purposes it now forms a totally separate party.

The division of the party was dramatic. The Central Committee of the SKP dismissed no fewer than 494 local organizations and 11,000 members on 13 June 1986. There remained in the party 805 local organizations and 20,000 members. The party lost more than a third of its effectives and after the split its membership was less than half what it had been in the 1960s.

The influence of the governmental role of the SKP on its internal life

The SKP has more experience of participation in governmental coalitions than any other communist party in a capitalist country. Immediately after the Second World War the party participated in the government of national reconstruction from 1944 to 1948, and then in the broad centre–left coalitions in 1966–71, 1975–6 and 1977–82. It can be estimated that participation in government has been one factor in the sharpening of the internal struggle of the SKP, though not a decisive one. First, the 'revisionist' development of the SKP began before the party had any idea of becoming a party of government; secondly, the decision to take that step in 1966 was made unanimously in the SKP, and only in 1975 did the minority categorically oppose entry into government and behave in the parliament as an independent opposition party; and thirdly, the decisive development towards an organizational split began in 1984 when the party was in opposition.

Participation in government was not a direct cause of the internal difficulties of the SKP. The attitude of the emerging minority from 1966 to 1970 was critical of participation, but it was not rejected in principle. In this regard the attitude of the minority was different in 1975–6 and 1977–82, when it opposed entry into the governments of those years on the grounds of their bourgeois policy. A theorist of the minority, Dr Seppo Toiviainen, wrote that Communist participation in such governments could only be either a tragedy or a farce.[9] In fact, there was a big difference between the governments of the late 1960s, with their policies of creating a more egalitarian health service and school system, and those of the late 1970s which had no important reform aims, being content to manage day-to-day affairs. The SKP majority leadership defended participation in government in the 1960s with positive arguments, that is, that the SKP involvement was beneficial to the workers, whereas in the 1977–83 period the arguments for participation were of a 'lesser evil' type or even attacked the class base of the government as such.[10]

The situation of the SKP *vis-à-vis* the government changed quite dramatically in 1983 when the SKDL's share of the vote fell from 17.9 per cent to 14 per cent. Shortly before the parliamentary elections the SKDL/SKP had returned to the opposition. The formal reason was the military budget but one can presume that the real reason was tactical. The party was trying to sharpen up its profile before the voters.

After the elections the Social Democratic Party and the Centre Party did not even consider seriously the possibility of SKP participation in government, which was a new situation in Finnish politics since 1966. One reason for this was that the Rural Party had gained an important victory in the elections (9.7 per cent of the vote and 17 seats) and showed, for the first time in its history, the signs of a willingness to take on responsibilities. In a way this petty bourgeois populist party took the place of the SKP in the government.

Arvo Aalto has affirmed that the position of the SKP with regard to possible participation in government has remained the same as earlier.[11] Although in Finland even quite small parties often participate in government and the SKP's participation is by no means excluded, the

SKDL/SKP is no longer such an important part of the coalition-forming process as it was in the 1960s and 1970s.

Soviet influence on party life

The relations between the CPSU and SKP have traditionally been very warm. In the post-war atmosphere it was natural that the SKP should stress in its propaganda the position of the CPSU as the 'exemplar that shows the way for the communist movement of the world'; in 1944–8, however, ties with the CPSU were weak and most of the SKP's international contacts were with the communist parties of the Nordic countries.[12] In the educational work of the party (study groups, ideological 'seminars', the party's residential college) mainly Soviet ideological books were used as study material until the 1970s. The party's young activists have been, moreover, educated in the Moscow international party school. So-called scientific cooperation – visits of Soviet lecturers to Finland and Soviet articles in the SKDL's press – has been extensive until recent times.[13] It has been a duty of every Communist activist to be a member of the Finland–Soviet Union Society and also active in its propaganda work.

All this should be seen against the background of the nature of Finnish society. The Finnish bourgeoisie has traditionally been hostile to the Soviet Union, although there have been important exceptions: when the business elite realized that commerce with the Soviet Union was very profitable, its attitude, roughly speaking from the 1960s, underwent a change. However, when the SKP returned to the political stage in the 1940s its natural task was to work for friendly relations between the two countries. In this regard the SKP has succeeded: all important parties support official foreign policy and the Centre Party and the Social Democratic Party have relations with the CPSU also at the party level. Ironically, these relations are today quite unproblematic, whereas those between the CPSU and SKP are very problematic indeed, due to the division within the SKP.

The CPSU has always tried to prevent an open split in the Finnish brother party. When the minority in 1969 marched out of the fifteenth congress of the SKP the representatives of the CPSU tried – in vain, to be sure – to influence the minority leaders, so as to get them to return to the congress. Afterwards the CPSU was an active factor in the negotiations between majority and minority that led to the extraordinary congress of the party in 1970, at which the division was institutionalized.[14]

Aarne Saarinen has described in an interesting way the pattern that developed at the meetings of the delegations of the CPSU and SKP in the 1970s. He writes:

On the other side of the table sat the CPSU's delegation led by a member of the Politburo and opposite them the SKP's delegation led by myself. I presented the SKP's report – a speech of the responsible leadership. After that Taisto Sinisalo, [SKP's vice-chairman 1970–82, the leader of the minority] delivered the speech of the minority, that is, that of the party opposition, which usually contained many accusations against the majority and the *Kansan Uutiset* [People's News – the organ of the SKDL and SKP] and a list of their 'mistakes' . . . After a break of a shorter or longer time, often next day, the CPSU's delegation presented their own opinions, usually in the name of the Politburo. The representatives of the CPSU expressed their irritation: there was no development toward unity in the SKP and its representatives always came to the meetings at odds. They [the representatives of the CPSU] have always expressed hope that unity will be attained on the basis of 'Marxism-Leninism' and 'proletarian internationalism'. Those communists who use these expressions frequently in various contexts are 'correct' communists.[15]

The real problem was that from the late 1960s the Socialists of the SKDL began to develop an ideological identity within that organization. For instance, the Socialist chairman of the SKDL, Ele Alenius, published a book in which he suggested that the transition to socialism should be gradual, and this attracted criticism in the Soviet Union.[16] In the 1974 discussions between the delegations of the CPSU and SKP, Mikhail Suslov expressed the fear held by Soviet leaders that the SKP would lose its influence in the SKDL. He stressed that the SKDL could not be transformed into the Marxist–Leninist vanguard of the Finnish working class because its leaders openly made statements that conflicted with Marxism–Leninism. Inside the SKDL the leading role of the SKP must be safeguarded, and moreover the organizations for women and youth should be subordinated to the direction of the SKP.[17]

In this phase of relations between the SKP and CPSU the speeches made during the negotiations were not usually published in the party press. But the minority leaders read out in particular the statements of the Soviet representatives at meetings of the party organizations and in some cases they were 'leaked' to the bourgeois press, which published them as sensational stories.[18] In 1982 this situation changed, and now the declarations of the representatives of the CPSU are published in the SKDL's press and in *Tiedonantaja*. According to Saarinen it was Soviet representative Arvid Pelshe's suggestion in 1982 that his speech be published in the SKDL's press.[19]

That year brought a serious deterioration in the relations between the CPSU and the SKP. It was the year of the SKP's extraordinary congress, which saw an attempt to unite the party. Aarne Saarinen resigned as chairman and the majority put pressure on the minority to get Taisto Sinisalo to resign also as vice-chairman; Sinisalo as vice-chairman and Saarinen as chairman had indeed become symbols of the split within the SKP. Sinisalo did not agree, but three months later a compromise was reached whereby Sinisalo was appointed chairman of the international affairs committee of the party.

Four days before the extraordinary congress, delegations of the SKP and the CPSU held further discussions in Moscow. Arvid Pelshe presented the opinion of the CPSU's Politburo, which contained seven very serious accusations against the majority in the SKP.

First, Pelshe declared that there was a lack of sincerity in the relations between the CPSU and SKP. There were 'developing tendencies' in the SKP which threatened the 'Marxist–Leninist nature' of the party and its unity. These 'developing tendencies and deeds may have far-reaching negative effects on Finnish domestic policy, on the continuing development of the friendship between the Soviet Union and Finland and on the cooperation between the peoples of both countries'. What did this statement mean, and what was its real purpose? It is difficult to interpret Pelshe's meaning and purpose in any other way than as an attempt to use as heavy an artillery as possible in order to create suspicions among the followers of the majority towards their leaders. In this Pelshe completely failed.

The other arguments were the following. Arvo Aalto, then General Secretary of the party, was charged, though not by name, with suggesting a Finnish 'historical compromise'.[20] Thirdly, there was the question of the press; Pelshe supported the publication of *Tiedonantaja*, although the paper was of course not actually named. Fourthly, there had been an attempt to substitute the SKDL for the SKP. Fifthly, opinions that one should take a 'critical stand' in relation to the Soviet Union and to 'existing socialism' had been expressed. Sixthly, there had been 'attempts to accuse the CPSU of interfering in the internal life of the SKP'. Seventhly, a 'battle' had been waged against those comrades who defended Marxism–Leninism and solidarity with the CPSU, that is, a battle against the minority.[21]

Saarinen commented at length on the relations between the SKP and CPSU in his speech to the extraordinary congress. He claimed, undoubtedly correctly, that the CPSU's statement had offended many members of the majority[22] and its effects had thus obviously been quite contrary to what had been intended. Saarinen declared that the statement did not further the unity of the party but was a starting point for 'provocational activities' on the party of the minority. Saarinen now publicly criticized the CPSU:

Much as I honour the CPSU, its wisdom generally and its great positive role in world history, I state that in some matters also it can be mistaken. There is now one such mistake in front of us. . . . We Finns do understand and take into consideration the fact that the CPSU is a great and honoured leading party of a large state. The SKP is a relatively small party of a relatively small working class. But self-esteem must not be dependent on size, since small and large have the right to identity and self-respect . . .[23]

Saarinen was clearly angry with the CPSU and at first supported the 'axe-line' of the party instead of compromising with the minority. At the beginning of Jouko Kajanoja's chairmanship (1982–84) it seemed at first sight as if there had been a turn towards unity in the party. But this was not to be.

As was pointed out above, Arvo Aalto – the leader of the 'axe-line' – was elected chairman of the party. At the twentieth congress he made a much-quoted, rather odd declaration about the attitude of the Finnish Communists toward the Soviet Union: 'We Finnish Communists are the friends of the Soviet Union even after our death.'[24]

After the split within the party the Soviet Union took spectacular action as a punishment operation against the majority: it removed the printing of the Soviet magazine *Sputnik*, which is published in many languages, from the printing house of the majority to that of the minority, which involved the former in considerable losses. There was some irony in this operation in so far as the job was too big and technically demanding for the printing house of the minority, and the work had to be farmed out to the print-shop of the leading 'bourgeois' newspaper. It should be noted, however, that this was the only punishment meted out and that not all Soviet printing work was diverted from the printing house of the majority.

There was much speculation in the spring of 1986, as the CPSU's twenty-seventh congress loomed, as to which Finnish Communists would be invited. The first Finnish party to receive an invitation letter was the Social Democratic Party, well before the congress. Only on the very eve of its opening did the SKP receive an invitation. In the delegation that attended the congress, headed by Aalto, there were representatives only of the official party. The CPSU is by no means satisfied with the situation that now exists. This does not, however, mean that the CPSU is given to declaring the SKP of the majority a gang of renegades with whom no relations are possible. The 'majority SKP' is still a factor important enough in Finnish political life for it not to be neglected. There are even signs of some normalization of relations. Every summer the CPSU invites important Finnish political leaders (except from the Coalition Party) to holiday in sanatoriums and dachas in Yalta or the Crimea. In 1984 and 1985 Aalto and his staff were not invited. But in 1986 not only Aalto but also the new General Secretary of the party,

Esko Vainionpää, who was famous (or notorious, to the minority) for having opposed the agreement between the majority and minority in 1970, spent their vacations under the Soviet sun.[25]

The Marxist–Leninist student movement

In the late 1960s and 1970s there was no radical anti-authoritarian movement outside the political parties in Finland. The New Left was only an ideological tendency among the leftist intellectuals. The mass student movement and the 'great negation'[26] coincided in Finland with the 'proletarian turn' of the student movement. The undisputed centre of the radical student movement in 1971–6 was the Socialist Student Association (SOL), which was identified with the minority of the SKP. The activity of the students involved mostly the student associations of the political parties. In Finland these, like the parties themselves and their representative movements for youth, women, education, temperance and so on, are funded mainly by the state (every party receives £22,240 for each parliamentary year, the SKDL/SKP with its 27 representatives out of a total of 200 thus receiving £600,480 in 1985).

In Finland all university students are automatically members of the student unions. In elections to the representative bodies of these unions the Left polled 40 per cent of the votes in the 1970s and the SOL about 17–18 per cent when its support was at its highest.

The SOL is a member of the SKDL just as are the SKP and the youth and women's organizations. What is important is that in the 1970s the SOL was the only member organization of the SKDL that was controlled by the minority. The SOL was deeply involved in the internal struggle of the SKP. It is illustrative that when the SOL in 1971 fell to the minority, the majority founded its own student organization which, however, remained relatively small.

It must be stressed that the generation of intellectuals that in the 1970s joined the SKP represented a novelty in the history of the party. The SKP's intellectual tradition was weak and there was no tradition of critical Marxism in Finland. The success of the SOL was, from the point of view of the 'establishment', a scandal and the subject of everyday discussion. This partly explains the fanaticism adopted by the SOL and the student movement generally.

We would maintain that the student movement did not change the SKP's political culture but, on the contrary, adopted that political culture, especially in its traditional 'Comintern' form, as practised by the minority. In a way the SOL was, in its party zeal, more royalist than the king. The SOL accepted the model of orthodoxy and 'struggle against deviations' as the starting-points of its ideological discourse. Intolerance was endemic in the debate at the beginning of the 1970s.

The SOL declared itself a 'Marxist–Leninist mass organization'. According to the rules accepted in 1975 the SOL was 'the school of Marxism–Leninism, democratic centralism, proletarian internationalism and revolutionary action'.[27] This activism was, above all, activism in student organizations, both in traditional and new 'popular front' organizations. In many cases the activists were really 'professional revolutionaries' who had no time to read their textbooks for examinations; for many this meant unreasonable personal losses. SOL's 'Struggle Programme' (written in 1973) expresses the limitless optimism as follows:

The level of organization of Finnish students is unique in the world. All university students in our country belong to the National Union of Finnish Students . . . In the fields of science the students are organized in societies of studies, faculties and guilds. . . . *This opens up overwhelming vistas for the development of the democratic student movement, for condensing its unity of action and its bonds with the masses* [emphasis added].[28]

Among communist intellectuals the attitude towards the Soviet Union was totally uncritical. Moreover the friendship with the Soviet people meant the adoption of certain cultural influences such as wearing badges, the adulation of Soviet literature and music, and so on. In all activities of the SOL ritual played a central role: the correct recitation of (often very long) slogans was considered very important, and a blue shirt was produced for the organization. In response, the majority-controlled youth organization of the SKP produced a red shirt: the result was a fanatical competition between shirts of different colours at the party's festivals and celebrations.

From the very beginning, however, there was also another, more academic, tendency inside the SOL. In 1976 the 'Society of Scholars' was founded. Although it declared itself to be a 'Marxist–Leninist mass organization', it was within this organization that the estrangement of the Marxist intellectuals from the SKP and Marxism–Leninism began. It was precisely the intellectuals who first became fed up with the struggle within the party. They tried to renew the party culture and unite the party 'over the heads of' the majority and minority wings, but unsuccessfully.

Radical students were captivated by such characteristics as militantism, enthusiasm, uncompromising Bolshevism. The students' big 'NO!' to the establishment found a channel of expression in the minority of the SKP, which alone opposed the official consensus policy. The majority, by contrast, failed completely to attract the students. The de-Stalinization of the party was of no value to the radical intellectuals. The fundamental problem of the modernization of a communist party seems to be to find a basis on which to build a radical identity after a process of de-Stalinization and de-bureaucratization. It is not enough to abandon something. An essentially new strategy and theory, and new political tactics have to be developed if the party is to offer a credible alternative to radical students and youth, who now choose the Greens, feminism or other alternative movements.

The SKP as 'a party of elderly men'

After the exchange of membership books in 1983 there were in the SKP 13 members who were 18 or 19 years old. Six per cent of members were under 30 years old, whereas 31 per cent were over 60. More than half the members were over 50. The traditionalism of the party can thus be seen also in the structure of the membership. Moreover, 69 per cent of members at that time were men.[29]

Less than 0.5 per cent of members joined before the party became legal; but, by contrast, the number of those who joined immediately after the war is still considerable, at 18 per cent. It would be no exaggeration to say that their influence on the political culture of the SKP is still decisive. In the period of the strong student movement, that is in the 1970s, 40 per cent of the present membership joined. Here we can observe the second generation gap in the SKP: on the one hand there are men of the immediate post-war period and on the other relatively young people, now 30–39 years old (24 per cent of members).

The total membership of the party is an untrustworthy measure of the party's affairs. During the internal struggle between majority and minority each has needed as many members as possible in order to achieve maximum representation at party congresses, and it can therefore be assumed that membership totals have been artificially raised. An exchange of membership books cleans up the statistics, at least partly. Therefore, the years 1964, 1973 and 1983, when membership books were exchanged, show a dramatic fall in membership (figure 7.1).

In 1964 there were 47,400 members in the party, in 1973 37,500, but in 1983 no more than 33,400 members remained. This last exchange of membership books removed about 15,000 members. One interesting question is who were, in the main, these 15,000 members who left the party? There are, unfortunately, no statistics about them. However, some trends in the SKP's membership structure, especially sudden changes in these trends, may indicate some answers to this question.

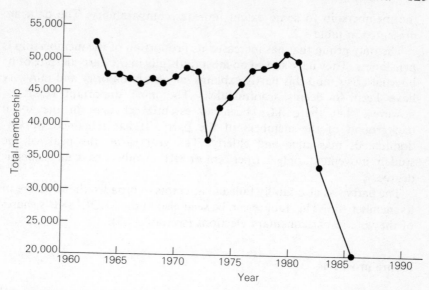

Figure 7.1 Membership of the SKP, 1963–86 (*source: Suomen Kommunistinen Puolue* – Finnish Communist Party)

One indicator is the number of members having only an elementary education (table 7.1). The percentages are not entirely comparable, because the criteria used for classifying members were changed in 1983 (see table 7.2). However, it is safe to say that the SKP has remained a party of people with a low level of education – in spite of the student movement and the rise in the general level of education in Finland. We can conclude that it was especially members with a relatively good education, and who joined the party in the 1970s, who left it in the process of the exchange of the membership books.

This observation becomes more solid when we look at the data on the social background of members. Again, the new criteria for classifying

Table 7.1 Percentage of SKP members having only an elementary education

Year	%
1973	75.0
1981	52.5
1983	77.8

Source: Unpublished report of the 1985 SKP research study (Helsinki, 1985)

the membership to some extent impedes comparability. The data are presented in table 7.2.

The only group that has increased its proportion of the membership is pensioners. They have stayed on most faithfully in the party in spite of its internal crisis, and this partly explains why both majority and minority have been so deeply traditionalist. The most important result is, however, that there have been no essential changes in the social background of the members of the party. It has remained worker-dominated, masculine and elderly. Ten years after the peak of the student movement, only 7.1 per cent of SKP members have an academic degree.

The party has also fatally failed in attempts to broaden the structure of its membership. This failure can be seen also in the SKDL/SKP's shares of the vote in parliamentary elections (see table 7.3).

Future prospects

In the 1987 general elections there were two separate Communist electoral lists. Each polled relatively well: taken together the Communists lost 0.4 per cent of the vote. But because the Finnish electoral system favours big parties, the minority (standing as the 'Democratic Alternative') lost six of its former ten seats. The majority lost one out of 17 seats. The

Table 7.2   The social composition of the SKP in 1973, 1981 and 1983

	1973 (%)	1981 (%)	1983 (%)
Workers	48.8	52.2	52.1a
Farmers	4.1	2.9	1.8
Self-employed workers	1.0	0.8	
Services	6.6	8.0	
Intellectuals	4.4	5.8	
Students	3.3	7.5	2.2
Pensioners	25.5	17.7	28.6
Housewives	6.3	5.1	
Entrepreneurs		0.9	
Higher employees		7.9	
Other wage earners		1.9	
Unknown		4.9	

a Includes 'workers' and 'lower employees' (white collar workers).
Source: As table 7.1

Table 7.3 Percentage share of the vote of the SKDL and SDP in parliamentary elections, 1945–87

Year	SKDL	SDP	DEVA (Democratic Alternative)
1945	23.5	25.1	—
1948	20.0	26.3	—
1951	21.6	26.5	—
1954	21.6	26.2	—
1958	23.2	23.2	—
1962	22.2	19.5	—
1966	21.2	27.2	—
1970	16.6	23.4	—
1972	17.0	25.8	—
1975	18.9	24.9	—
1979	17.9	23.9	—
1983	14.0	26.7	—
1987	9.4	24.3	4.2

Note the marked losses (4–5 percentage points) in 1970 and 1983. These losses coincide with situations in which the internal struggle was particularly heated.
Source: Suomen virallinen tilasto (Finnish official statistics), Helsinki, 1987

problem of each wing of the party is clearly the lack of any positive experiences to give it encouragement. The majority leadership elected in 1984 has concentrated on the internal affairs of the party: there have been no important political initiatives. The party is helplessly attached to its traditional patterns of functioning and it seems that its leaders can be only of the old *apparatchik* type.

Since the split the SKP has openly expressed a wish to restore its cooperation with the Social Democratic Party – especially in government. But the reduction in its parliamentary power has made the party less attractive as a coalition partner. The weakening of the SKP is a problem also for the Social Democrats, since it has coincided with a strengthening of the Centre and of the Right.

For the CPSU it is now more and more important to maintain relations with the SDP and with the Centre Party. The SKP has no longer any special role in the field of a Finnish *Ostpolitik* that earlier provided the basis for the party's importance in Finnish political life. The party has lost much of its identity: it is no longer a dynamic force in society. Unless some radical change in the party's circumstances occurs, which does not seem very probable, what the future offers is a small, corporatized SKP of the majority and an even smaller SKP of the minority, neither of them enjoying more than a marginal importance.

Notes

1   On the concept, see Oskar Negt and Alesander Kluge, *Öffentlichkeit und Erfahrung. Zur Organisationsanalyse von bürgerlicher und proletarischer Öffentlichkeit* (Suhrkamp, Frankfurt a/M, 1972), pp. 111–15 and 341–56.
2   Leevi Lehto and Juhani Ruotsalo, 'Kommunistinen vapautusiike', *Helsingin Sanomat*, 2 April 1983. *Soihtu*, 9/1983.
3   A document in which it was promised to honour these rights was accepted unanimously before the split, 1965. 'Marxilaisesta valtioteoriasta ja Suomen tiesta sosialismiin', *Kommunisti*, vol. 10 (1965), p. 326–7.
4   Interview with Jorma Hentilä, former Secretary General of the SKDL, 3 July 1985.
5   *Tiedonantaja* is at present published by the Committee of the SKP Organizations. Before the split it was published officially by eight minority-controlled district organizations. The executive committee of the 'Tiedonantaja Society' functioned as a Political Bureau of the minority.
6   Leevi Lehto and Juhani Ruotsalo, 'SKP:n tilanne – uhkaava katastrofi ja miten sitä vastaan on taisteltava', *Kansan Uutiset*, 17 January 1981. *Soihtu*, vol. 6/1981.
7   'Ylimääraisen edustajakokouksen päätökset 16, edusdtajakokouksen pohjaksi', *Soihtu*, vol. 1/1972, p. 77. (Originally published in *Tiedonantaja*.)
8   Michel Foucault, 'The Order of Discourse'. Inaugural lecture at the College de France, given 2 December 1970, Roger Young (ed.), in *Untying the Text*, (Routledge & Kegan Paul, London, 1981).
9   Seppo Toiviainen, *Nykyinen kriisi ja hallituskysymys* (Kuriiri, Helsinki, 1978), p. 63–4.
10 Olavi Borg and Jukka Paastela, 'Communist Participation in Governmental Coalitions: the Case of Finland', *Quaderni*, no. 26, 1983, p. 122.
11 Arvo Aalto, 'SKP historiallisten tehtäviensä mittaiseksi', in *SKP:n edustajakokous*, (SKP, Helsinki, 1984), p. 31.
12 A. F. Upton, *Communism in Scandinavia and Finland: Politics of Opportunity* (Weidenfeld and Nicolson, London, 1970).
13 Jyrki Iivonen, 'State or Party? The Dilemma of Relations between the Soviet and Finnish Communist Parties', *Journal of Communist Studies*, vol. 2, no. 1, March 1986.
14 Saarinen, *Suomalaisen kommunistin kokemuksia*, p. 120.
15 Ibid., p. 122. In 1948 the party leadership made a self-criticism of the party's 'nationalist' line. This self-criticism was not made public and the 'nationalist deviation' was revealed for researchers in 1985 when access to the archives of the SKP became free. (Kimmo Rentola, 'SKP ja kansainvälisen kommunistisen liikkeen virtaukset 1944–48', *Tiede ja edistys*, 4/1986, pp. 272–91).
16 Borg and Paastela, 'Communist Participation in Governmental Coalitions', p. 113.
17 Haikara, *Isanmaan vasen laita*, p. 412–13.
18 For example, ibid., p. 360.
19 Saarinen, *Suomalaisen kommunistin kokemuksia*, p. 132.
20 Borg and Paastela, 'Communist Participation in Governmental Coalitions', p. 115–16.

21 Saarinen, *Suomalaisen kommunistin kokemuksia*, p. 128–30.
22 Ibid., p. 134.
23 Ibid., p. 135–7.
24 Aalto, 'SKP historiallisten tehtäviensä mittaiseksi', p. 30. When Aalto declared this, the television cameras pictured the countenances of CPSU's delegates. They were astonished and confounded.
25 *Helsingin Sanomat*, 4 July 1986.
26 For example, Alain Touraine, *The Voice and Eye* (Cambridge: Cambridge University Press, 1981), p. 10–24, has used this concept about the phase of 1968 in the student movement.
27 Sosialistinen Opiskelijaliitto, *Säännöt ja periaateohjelma* (SOL, Helsinki, 1976), p. 3.
28 SOL:n Taisteluohjelma Suomen opiskelijoille (SOL, Helsinki, 1973), p. 168.
29 The source of our information about the membership of the SKP is *SKP: jäsentilasto* (the statistics of SKP's membership 1983), an unpublished party document and Jyrki Iivonen, *A Ruling and Non-ruling Communist Party in the West: the Finnish Communist Party*, University of Tampere, Department of Political Science, Occasional Papers 32/1983, pp. 16–17.

8 A New Face for Swedish Communism
The Left Party Communists

Jörgen Hermansson

In any study of the history of the Swedish Communist Party, two features stand out as of special importance. First is the fact that the foundation of the party in May 1917 preceded the October revolution in Russia. The second is the factional battle in the mid-1960s that ended in a defeat for 'the men of 1929' – a small group that had been the leaders of the party almost since 1929.

The party's original name was *Sveriges socialdemokratiska vänsterparti* (SSV, Social Democratic Left Party). It was a left-wing socialist party composed of anarchists, syndicalists, humanists and all kinds of socialists who raised objections to the centralism and militarism of the Social Democratic Party (SAP). It was not until 1929, after its third disruption (in 1921 and 1924 two minority groups had left the party and later joined the SAP), that what had now become the Swedish Communist Party fully embraced Leninism. The great majority of the party at that point disassociated themselves from the Comintern and founded a new party. But the International got its Swedish Bolsheviks, a small party unswervingly loyal to the Soviet Union and to the CPSU.[1]

Right up until the beginning of the 1960s, this party, the Communist Party of Sweden (*Sveriges kommunistiska parti*, SKP) obediently acted in accordance with the line laid down by the Kremlin. That, however, is not the subject of this paper, although it is most important as a background to the transformation of the party in the mid-1960s. Instead, the focus will be on the last two decades in the history of the Swedish Communist Party.[2]

The period of transition, 1962–7

In September 1962, the Swedish people went to the polls in local government elections. The elections were held in the shadow of the global political crises of Cuba and Berlin, and ended in a defeat for the Communists.[3] In spite of this, their chairman, Hilding Hagberg, concluded that it had been a victory for the political Left and for the working class; the Social Democrats, after all, remained in power.

This lack of self-criticism provoked a reaction among the rank and file of the SKP. Many well-known Communists called for a renewal of the party. At the next party congress, in January 1964, Hagberg was forced to resign. He was replaced by C. H. Hermansson, the editor-in-chief of the main party organ, *Ny Dag* ('new day'), and a member of the Executive Committee since 1946.

Thus, the new chairman was associated with the old regime, but he was nevertheless accepted by those who advocated change. When elected, C. H. Hermansson was a compromise between traditionalists and their critics, but very soon he became the leading spokesman for the new major faction within the party, the modernists.[4] Under the direction of Hermansson, the SKP underwent a most dramatic change all within a few years.

Most notably, the party changed its name at the twenty-first congress in the spring of 1967. The old name 'Swedish Communist Party', associated with the Comintern era, was replaced by 'Left Party Communists' (*Vänsterpartiet kommunisterna*, VPK). There was also a radical change in the composition of both the Central Committee and its executive.[5] All but two of the members of the Executive Committee elected in May 1967 by the new Central Committee had never before been members of that inner circle. Hermansson was elected for a ninth period in office, but the average member of the Executive Committee had an experience equivalent to 1.6 previous periods. This figure may be compared with the 6.6 periods that was the average for the Executive Committee elected in 1961, immediately after the nineteenth party congress. Table 8.1 illustrates how the same group had retained the top positions throughout the post-war era, but was suddenly replaced by a new generation of activists in the mid-1960s.

The renewal of the party was also manifested in other ways. The ideological orientation of the modernist faction radically differed from the old ideology of the party, which still had its advocates among the traditionalists. In tactical matters, the two factions recommended different outlooks with respect to both national and international affairs. The Swedish Communist Party had always been loyal to the

Table 8.1   Composition of Executive Committees in terms of previous experience

Congress (year and no.)	Average age of ex. comm.[a]	No. of members
1944/12	2.7	9
1946/13	3.4	9
1948/14	3.3	12
1951/15	4.3	12
1953/16	4.4	10
1955/17	5.6	11
1957/18	5.6	11
1961/19	6.6	11
1964/20	3.9	11
1967/21	1.6	7
1969/22	1.8	9
1972/23	2.7	9
1975/24	3.4	9
1978/25	3.2	9
1981/26	2.9	7
1985/27	2.1	9

[a] The 'age' of a member of the executive committee is defined as the number of earlier periods that the newly elected official had held the office.
Source: Jörgen Hermansson, *Kommunism på svenska? SKP/VPK's idéutveckling efter Komintern* (Almqvist and Wiksell, Stockholm, 1984), p. 353

Soviet Union. The defence of the centre of the international proletariat was a consequence of the Swedish party's interpretation of proletarian internationalism. In the 1950s it combined this with an almost unconditional support for the proposals of the Social Democratic Party. The purpose of this friendly pushing of the SAP was to force it gradually in a leftist direction.

The modernists reacted against both tendencies, arguing that the party ought to be independent both in domestic and international politics. They claimed that nationally it should present itself as a real alternative to the Social Democratic Party and they found support for this view in the party's small left wing. Internationally, the problems centred on the dispute between the Soviet Union and China, and here, supported by the even smaller right wing, the modernist faction advocated neutrality.

Apart from this, there was a more basic change in the ideology of the Swedish Communist Party. Since the dissolution of the Comintern in 1943, every ideological document had been characterized by some variant of a Popular Front strategy.[6] But when adopting a new party programme and a new statute in 1967, the Left Party Communists abandoned everything that resembled the classical themes of that strategy.

These two documents represented a radical break with the Comintern and the Cominform tradition.

The break can be analysed in terms of a well-known topic of dispute in the history of Marxism. This concerns the very foundation of a socialist ideology. Is it founded on ethical principles, as Bernstein once put it, or on a scientific theory (that is, Marxism) as was claimed by Kautsky? As long as the party embraced the Comintern ideology, this question did not arise, since the essential component of that ideology was a universal theory of revolution based on 'scientific' judgement. In abandoning the Comintern ideology, the Swedish Communists started to show more interest in ethical and normative commitments. They declared for the desirability of a peaceful road to socialism and adopted the idea of a democratic revolution. The catalogue of social rights that they attached to their description of socialist society was also a manifestation of this normative trend.

But the Communists continued to emphasize empirical considerations, seeing them still as more important than the moral claims. For many years, deciding whether a peaceful road to socialism was possible was conceived of as the crucial problem. Adherence to political democracy was seen as at most a matter of finding a suitable way to achieve socialism. And promises that the socialist state was going to guarantee its citizens numerous new substantial rights were still founded on the notion of the superiority of socialism. According to the Swedish Communists, the socialist mode of production would make it possible to achieve real democracy. This was not conceived of as a mere utopian promise. The Soviet Union was put forward as empirical evidence of the truth of scientific socialism. In the Popular Front ideology, the transition to socialism was described in terms of an empirical theory of revolution, and in its account of socialist society the stress was laid upon the possibility of implementing the ideals of rationality and justice, not on the ideals *per se*.

In the mid-1960s the central point of ideology shifted even further; empirical science was now clearly replaced by ethical principles. When adopting 'modernism', as the new ideology is usually called, the Communist Party committed itself to political democracy. Its ideology gained a touch of humanism; severe criticism was levelled against bureaucracy, centralism, and all kinds of injustices. In the new statute the compulsory reference to democratic centralism was removed. Instead the statute contained some paragraphs that gave the impression of an anti-centralistic and ultra-democratic party organization. According to the modernists themselves, this renewal was not an instance of revisionism. They considered themselves just as good Marxists as any of the traditional communists. And indeed, because of the discovery of the writings of the young Marx, there was at the time a change taking place in the image of Marx himself.

However, the new ideology was disputed within the party. While the traditionalists adhered to the old Popular Front ideology, the left wing wanted a return to the empirical approach of the Comintern ideology, that is to orthodox Marxism–Leninism. The right wing, on the other hand, claimed that the party ought to be still more emphatic about the problems of democracy and the ethical ideals of socialism. Although the party ideology contained more moral statements than ever before – perhaps with the exception of the left-wing socialist period preceding the Comintern era – the right wing was not satisfied.

While they were fighting the extremist groups to the left and to the right, the modernist and the traditionalist factions agreed on a ceasefire between themselves. Having lost their positions of power, the traditionalists at first rallied round the new party leaders. Thus, a broad majority supported the adoption of the new party ideology. However, this situation soon changed. Just over a year after the party congress held in May 1967, the common enemy left the party. The left wing founded a new pro-Chinese organization named the Communist League of Marxist–Leninists (*Kommunistiska förbundet marxist-leninisterna*: KFML), and the right wing, which was a less integrated group, joined the Social Democratic Party.

A new era, 1968 and beyond

Although the modernist revolution in the Swedish Communist Party marks the beginning of a new era in Swedish communism, certain aspects remain very much the same as before.

Most obviously, the Communist Party is still a small party in comparison with the big reformist SAP, whose hegemonic position in the Swedish labour movement has never been threatened. On the other hand, the Left Party Communists have been very successful in their efforts to mark out a position as the sole representative of the radical left.[7]

The Communists' vote in general elections since 1970 has been about 5 per cent of the total, that is approximately a tenth of the Socialists' vote. This is fairly well in line with the average for the Communists during the entire history of the party. As to party membership, Hermansson was able to check the decreasing trend in the early 1970s. Starting from a position just below 15,000 members, the Left Party Communists' membership rose to slightly more than 18,000 in 1981. In recent years, however, it has once again begun to fall. At the party congress in January 1985, the Central Committee reported 16,761 party members for

1 January 1984. These figures mean that the ratio between members and voters is about 0.05 for the Communist Party. This is very low in comparison with other Swedish parties. Thanks to its having a good number of collective members, the Social Democratic Party comes out with a ratio of 0.45, but the bourgeois parties also lead the Communists by a good margin.[8]

Most trade unions within the *Landsorganisationen* – the 'peak' organization for manual workers – have strong connections with the Social Democratic Party. Except for some local unions, organizing among others dock and shipyard workers, the Communists have not been able to influence the policy of any national trade union since the metal workers' strike of 1945.[9] The miners' strike in 1970 was a spontaneous action on the part of the workers; the Communist Party and other leftist organizations 'representing' the Swedish proletariat played mainly a spectator role.

As in other countries in Western Europe, there was an upsurge of leftism after 1968. This movement among youth, especially students, had a great impact on the cultural and political climate in Sweden in those years.[10] When their place in the debate is assessed, these groups for solidarity and for a restoration of Marxism–Leninism can be seen to have had an influence far exceeding their numerical strength. But this was not due to the Left Party Communists. Although it was never really threatened by 'the abysmal left',[11] the Communist Party found itself following in the slipstream of the DFFG (the Combined FNL-Groups), which was a joint organization of groups defending the liberation front in Vietnam, and of the organization behind a magazine called *Folket i Bild/Kulturfront* (People in Pictures/Cultural Front). Both of these groups were orientated towards the pro-Chinese KFML.

What, then, has changed? In what respects does the period from 1968 represent something new, that makes it reasonable to talk about a new phase in the history of Swedish communism?

A new ideology

In describing the ideological development of the Swedish Communist Party it is useful to distinguish five different periods.[12] As indicated above, a short period of left-wing socialism preceded the Leninist ideology of the Comintern period. After the dissolution of the Comintern, the Swedish Communists adopted a Popular Front ideology, essentially in accordance with international tendencies.[13] This period was not entirely homogeneous, but apart from marginal shifts arising, for example, from problems concerning the attitude to be taken towards the Social Democratic Party, it lasted until the mid-1960s. It was followed by a short period of modernism, an ideology inspired by the New Left but also resembling the left-wing socialism of the pre-Comintern period. Through the rebirth of Leninism, another change was initiated in 1968. During this last period, the VPK has elaborated a new ideology, usually labelled neo-Leninism.

The new party ideology resembles orthodox Marxism–Leninism in its choice of main themes and emphases. In the party programme adopted by the twenty-third congress in October 1972 – revised in detail by the congresses of 1981 and 1985[14] – the stress is laid on the classical themes of communism. It talks about 'proletarian internationalism', a term that was carefully avoided by the Communist Party during the modernist era. And as in the Comintern programme from 1928, the notion of the leading role of the communist party is a core element in the strategy for reaching socialism. But the leading role is viewed as an international obligation on the party, rather than as a prescription for those who seek to overthrow capitalism. The fourth paragraph in the party programme reads as follows:

Vänsterpartiet Kommunisterna is a part of the Swedish labour movement. It was developed in the struggle of the working class.

The party commits itself to take part in and to develop every movement that promotes the interests of the working people. It fights every reduction of and struggles for any increase in the democratic rights of the people; national independence; the right to elect by general and equal vote the people's representatives, who appoint and reject governments; liberty of organization, meeting and demonstration; the right to strike; freedom of opinion, speech and press.

The main task of the party is permanently to unite the workers' movement with socialism. Its basis is scientific socialism, the revolutionary theory of Marx and Lenin. It seeks to adapt this theory, develop it and amalgamate it with the struggle of the Swedish working class.

The party strives to organize in its ranks all those who want to work for a socialist Sweden. Its aim is that the struggle of the working class and the people, guided by the ideas of revolutionary socialism, shall lead to victory over capitalism and to a classless society.[15]

Although the term is not used in the statutes, the notion of democratic centralism is once again cited in the programme as the organizational principle of the party. However, as pointed out above, this attachment to orthodox Marxism–Leninism is but a matter of form. As far as the content of the statutes is concerned, it does not correspond to anything specific for a communist party. Yet the recent statutes are much more 'centralist' than any since 1967. In comparison with the modernist era, the Executive Committee and other central bodies do have far more power today. But that says more about the decentralizing thrust of the former statutes. As suggested above, they were almost ultra-democratic.

Another example of this neo-Leninist orientation is the dropping of the conception of a peaceful and parliamentary road to socialism. This was a constitutive element in both the Popular Front ideology and modernism. And had it not been for the traditionalists, who defended the thesis emanating from the documents of the world conferences of communist and workers' parties in Moscow in 1957 and 1960, any mention of the 'peaceful road' would have been altogether excluded. As a compromise the following passage was added:

It is in the interest of the working class and the majority of the people to carry out the socialist transformation of society in a peaceful way, without armed struggle or civil war. But the ruling class will defend its privileges by all means at its disposal and will not give them up by free will. The relations of force in the class struggle decide whether big business can be obliged to accept the liquidation of its political and economic power without armed resistance.[16]

The old strategic conception, according to which a popular front led by the communists will transform society in a peaceful and democratic process through parliamentary means, was replaced by a new one, resembling the strategy developed by the Comintern during the 1920s. Because of the heavy concentration of production and capital in Sweden, the VPK does not view any strategy that includes an anti-monopolistic stage preceding socialism as realistic.[17] The conclusion is that when the big bourgeoisie has been defeated capitalism itself will at the same time have been overthrown.

The power of big business can be broken only with the support of a conscious and energetic majority of the people. *Vänsterpartiet Kommunisterna* is working to develop and secure this majority through comprehensive economic, ideological and political struggle for the interests of the people. In this struggle the basis of a new political power develops that is expressed in a revolutionary government.
Such a government is a necessary instrument in the struggle of the working class to break the domination of big business, neutralize its instruments of political domination, abolish its economic power and open the road for people's power, for a socialist democracy.[18]

As in the case of classical Leninism, this strategy is founded on a conception of a one-shot attack on capitalism. However, contrary to Leninism proper, it operates within a democratic framework. And again, this indicates the relevance of 'Leninism' as well as the prefix 'neo-'.

Furthermore, since the late 1960s, the VPK has taken a great interest in Marxist theory and emphasized it as a science with universal validity.

But, unlike the Marxism–Leninism of the Comintern period, it does not promulgate general prescriptions for the claims and actions of a communist party. Marxism is used more as a conceptual scheme, and hence as a means of logically structuring the party's arguments. The Swedish Communist Party of today has designed an ideology with a national character. It includes a strategy elaborated by the Swedish Communists themselves, and more than ever before, they present a Swedish road to socialism. In addition, the vision of future socialist Sweden is an original one. It is presented with a Marxist scientific approach, but it has only a few distinctive traits in common with 'really existing socialism'. The VPK is careful to stress that its vision of the future is a Swedish brand of socialism.

Thus, the ideological development of the Swedish Communist Party since the Comintern contains a stable core. Throughout, it has accentuated the specific national conditions of Sweden. In spite of other differences, Popular Front ideology, modernism and neo-Leninism all have this point in common. The aim of the Communist Party has always been to find a formula for a national form of communism. It has consistently tried to present communism in a Swedish way.

Nevertheless, the ideological change in the late 1960s may be seen as a reaction against modernism and against the trend of including normative prescriptions in the party programmes. Once again the Swedish road to socialism became a matter of prediction rather than of prescription. In adopting its neo-Leninism, the VPK took a position almost as extreme as that of the Comintern; communism was based on Marxism, which was conceived of as a science rather than a collection of ethical principles.

The Left Party Communists did not, however, abandon the modernist attitude towards political democracy, at least not officially. Although initially neo-Leninism did not give priority to considerations of democracy, there was no shift of opinion in this regard from the modernist period. Later on, especially in the 1980s, the VPK has increasingly been engaged in safeguarding human rights and political democracy, emphasizing their crucial role in the development of socialism.

These conclusions cover the central concerns of a communist ideology, its picture of future society and its theory of revolution. There have been other, more peripheral, ideological novelties. At the beginning of the 1970s, the Communist Party suddenly changed its attitude towards the peaceful use of nuclear power. The Swedish Communist Party, as well as the pro-Soviet APK (see below, p. 144), have always been true advocates of developing the productive forces. In contrast, the VPK of today is a part of the ecology movement that opposed nuclear power in the national referendum in 1980.

Finally, there are, of course, elements of continuity in the ideological development. The writings of C. H. Hermansson, focusing on monopoly capitalism and the concentration of capital,[19] are a good example. Change, however, can be exemplified by another well-known name, that of Göran Therborn. An academic by profession, he started out in 1966 as an external critic of the VPK, representing an anti-authoritarian branch of the New Left.[20] Later on he became the most outstanding spokesman of scientific Marxism–Leninism of the Althusserian kind.[21] Louis Althusser was the source of theoretical influence when the Communist Party developed its new ideology at the beginning of the 1970s. Today, while still a defender of scientific Marxism, Therborn argues for an almost reformist strategy that pays respect to bourgeois democracy.[22] Furthermore, he is at the moment a member of the programme committee of the VPK.

A new party membership

Contrary to the ideological change in the mid-1960s, the transition from modernism to neo-Leninism was not preceded by a shift in power relations within the party.[23] Overnight, the former modernist faction deserted the young Marx in favour of Lenin. And the replacement of C. H. Hermansson by Lars Werner as party leader in 1975 constituted a succession within the same faction. Werner had been vice chairman of the party for many years, and C. H. Hermansson is today something of an *éminence grise* in the party. He is still a member of the Central Committee and up to 1985 he was a member of the parliament.

However, this does not mean that everything has been harmonious within the party since 1968. The youth association was more involved in the exegetical disputes on Marx and Lenin than was the party itself. Of course, this had some repercussions on the internal life of the party, but except for the twenty-second party congress in 1969, it was a matter of some rather innocent problems. Instead it was the traditionalist faction that constituted the real problem for the party leadership. The conflict was brought into the open when C. H. Hermansson harshly criticized the Soviet intervention in Czechoslovakia in August 1968. The former chairman Hagberg insisted on his resignation, claiming that criticism of the Soviet Union and its Communist Party was irreconcilable with Marxism–Leninism. From then on, the traditionalists formed a fraction within the party with the local Communist newspaper *Norrskensflamman* ('northern flame') as a mouthpiece. Initially, they were quite influential in the northern part of Sweden, Norrbotten, which has always been a stronghold of communism. But when the conflict reached a climax and the traditionalists founded their own party – the Labour Party Communists: APK – in 1977, it was no serious blow to the VPK. On average the traditionalists were older than party members in general, and most of them had already left the VPK before the split.

According to VPK sources, only about 3,000 of its members left the party to join the APK. Since many new members were joining the VPK at the same time, it could in fact report growth in membership for the period 1977–9.[24]

However, the split had some important implications for the composition of the party. To put it briefly, it hastened the transformation that had been going on for a long time.

Historically, the bases of the Communist Party have been the mining districts; the outbacks and some of the mill-villages in Norrbotten, Västernorrland, Gävleborg and Värmland; and the two biggest cities, Stockholm and Gothenburg. In sociological terms, the typical member of the Communist Party was clearly a proletarian. But when speaking about the bases of Communism, it is common to distinguish between two kinds of proletarians:

In schematic terms . . . the old Communist rank and file were either 'working-class aristocrats' or victims of isolation and relative deprivation.[25]

This pattern may to some extent be explained by circumstances during the split in 1917. The party district organization of Norrbotten decided collectively to leave the Social Democratic Party and join the new party.

In the mid-1930s there were about 17,000 party members and half of them lived in Norrbotten, Västernorrland and Gävleborg. The two big cities did not account for more than a fifth of the membership. Today, the geographical distribution of the party is more in accordance with that of the population as a whole. Stockholm is the district with by far the highest membership density, with a fourth of all members.

There has been a steady increase in the proportion of women in the party. It was 17 per cent in the mid-1930s, 26 per cent in 1974 and in 1985 it was approaching 40 per cent. These figures are easy to find in the regular congress reports by the Central Committee, but it is harder to give a description of the development of other sociological characteristics of the party membership.

A statistical survey of party members was made by the party itself in 1974 (see table 8.2). Although we cannot know for certain how the different categories were defined, this survey indicates that the Communist Party in 1974 could still be characterized as a working class party; at least, that was the main conclusion drawn by the party itself. The survey also shows that the average age was rather high, with about

Table 8.2 The 1974 membership survey of the VPK

Occupation	%
Workers	55
Salaried employees	11
Entrepreneurs	2
Students	4
Housewives	6
Pensioners	22
Total	100
(Number)	(12,321)
Year of entry	%
Before 1920	1
1921–30	4
1931–40	12
1941–50	27
1951–60	12
1961–70	18
1971–74	27
Total	101
(Number)	(10,337)
Union membership	%
LO (Workers)	84
TCO (Salaried employees)	13
SACO (Academics)	3
Total	100
(Number)	(6,932)

Source: *Vänsterpartiet kommunisterna*, 1974

40 per cent of members in 1974 having joined the party more than 25 years before. But as early as 1974, it was possible to see a new tendency. Since the members recruited in the 1940s were beginning to die off, the growth in membership was set fair to produce a very rapid rejuvenation of the party.

Besides this survey, there are no data on the party as a whole. To analyse the changes within the party, we have to rely on less valid data. In this case, the reports on delegates at the party congresses may be useful. A comparison of these reports gives an indication of the transformation of the entire party.

Not surprisingly, a delegate at a party congress has tended to be a man rather than a woman. The women of the Communist Party have always been under-represented at party congresses. However, in recent years their representation at congresses has been almost as large as their proportion of the party membership (table 8.3).

Table 8.3 Representation of the sexes at party congresses

Year	Men (%)	Women (%)	Total number
1953	91	9	328[a]
1961	87	13	327[a]
1967	91	9	368[a]
1969	86	12	286[a]
1972	87	13	231
1975	79	21	254
1978	71	29	322
1981	64	36	313
1985	61	39	275

[a] Includes members of the Central Committee.
Source: Reports on the delegates at party congresses in published and unpublished documents of the SKP/VPK. See Jörgen Hermansson, *Kommunism på svenska? SKP/VPK's idéutveckling efter Komintern* (Almqvist and Wiksell, Stockholm, 1984), pp. 355 ff

As everyone has suspected, the party activists of today are significantly younger than those of the 1960s. The average age of a delegate was approximately 44 years in the 1960s, today it is well below 40 (table 8.4). Furthermore, while the congresses in the 1960s were dominated by delegates who had entered the party during the growth period in the 1940s, an entire new generation of activists has gradually captured the dominating positions in the 1970s. At the 1969 congress the average 'party-age' of the delegates was about 22 years, while in 1981 it was less than nine years (table 8.4).

The figures on the trade union membership of the delegates also distinctly indicate a change in the social base of the party activists (table 8.4). In the late 1960s (1969) more than a quarter (26 per cent) of the delegates stated that they were not unionized. In 1985 this group accounted for 4 per cent. At the beginning of the 1970s, a large majority (75 per cent) of those who were unionized said that they were members of the national labour union (the LO). In 1981 the other unions, notably those of the salaried employees and the academics, accounted for a majority of the unionized membership.

To sum up, a typical member of the Communist Party is quite different today from in the 1960s. Formerly, he – male, of course, – was about 45 years old, and he had entered the party 20 years previously, that is in the mid-1940s. Furthermore, he was occupied in heavy industry, say a pulp-mill in central Sweden or a mine in the far north. Nowadays, a member is also likely to be female and she or he will be less than 40 and will have joined the party just a few years previously. He may be a worker, but it is just as likely that she may be occupied with social welfare, health care or education.

A new electorate

In 1970, Sweden changed its political system. The old two-chamber parliament was replaced by a new unicameral system. Also, a barrier

Table 8.4 Composition of party congresses in terms of age, length of membership and unionization

			Congress		
	1972	*1975*	*1978*	*1981*	*1985*
Age (yr)					
0–19	1	1	1	0	0
20–29	16	20	20	20	18
30–39	20	32	43	49	45
40–49	26	14	16	18	21
50–59	27	21	15	11	11
60–69	10	9	5	3	4
70–	1	2	1	0	0
Total (%)	101	99	101	101	99
(Number)	(215)	(250)	(322)	(313)	(275)
Year of entrance					
1917–29	3	2	1	0	0
1930–39	10	7	4	0	0
1940–49	28	22	12	4	3
1950–59	17	13	7	6	5
1960–69	28	22	14	7	9
1970–79	14	34	61	59*	66
1980–84	–	–	–	23*	17
Total (%)	100	100	99	99	100
(Number)	(212)	(250)	(322)	(313)	(275)
Union membership					
LO (Workers)	58	57	50	47	44
TCO (Salaried employees)	14	17	25	31	36
SACO/SR (Academics)	4	11	12	16	14
Other unions	1	2	2	2	1
Unorganized or no answer	23	13	9	3	4
Total (%)	100	100	98	99	99
(Number)	(231)	(254)	(322)	(313)	(275)

Figures indicated by * represent 1970–7 and 1978–81 respectively.
Source: As table 8.3

against small parties was introduced. A party had to exceed 4 per cent of the total vote if it was to get representation in parliament. Although the Communist Party only won 3.0 per cent at the general election in 1968, it succeeded in passing the barrier two years later. Since then, the Communist vote has been fairly stable at around 5 per cent.

However, this does not mean that the Communist Party has had a stable electorate. On the contrary, the core of stable Communist sympathizers is in fact rather small, and electoral studies have shown that a significant part of the Communist electorate consists of voters having the Social Democratic Party as their first preference. Their primary purpose is to back up a Social Democratic government, and they realize that the possibility of the Social Democrats defeating the bourgeois parties is dependent upon the Communists' ability to get representation in the parliament.[26]

Furthermore, in some respects there has been a dramatic change in the electoral base of the Communist Party. In his book *Kommunismen i Sverige* (Communism in Sweden), published in 1954, Sven Rydenfelt concluded that the Communist Party drew its chief electoral support from two different types of areas. There was 'industrial communism', but also 'backwoods communism'. The Communist Party had many sympathizers in the mining district of Norrbotten and in some areas dominated by heavy industry. There were also several villages in the outbacks where the Communist Party almost reached a majority. The Communists still have electoral strongholds in those areas, but, in recent years, they have also developed some new strongholds. Today, for instance, the Communist Party has built up quite a good position in the universities.[27]

The working class still constitutes a significant, though decreasing, part of the entire electorate as well as of the Communist constituency. However, the proportion of workers is larger outside than inside the Communist Party. Today, the Communists' share of the working class vote is about the same as the party's share of the total vote. It is to salaried employees, especially those working in welfare, education and culture, or students, that one must look to find a group with a notably high Communist vote (tables 8.5, 8.6).

The same phenomenon may be observed if one looks at Communist sympathizers within different educational groups. Formerly, the Communist Party attracted those with a low educational level rather than the well educated. Today, the reverse is true (table 8.7).

Apart from these changes with respect to social class and education, there is another trend in the Swedish Communist electorate. Before the modernist revolution, the Communist Party found most support among older voters. Nowadays, the correlation between age and Communist

Table 8.5 Communist vote and occupation (old classification)[a]

Electoral year	Workers (%)	Salaried employees (%)	Other groups[b] (%)	(N)
1956	72	–	28	14
1960	65	8	27	26
1964	69	12	19	67
1968	46	33	21	39
1970	51	21	28	91
1973	51	17	32	98
1976	39	22	39	103
1979	41	41	18	141
1982	30	41	29	131
1985	35	31	34	130

(N) is the number of communists in the sample.

[a] Two different classification systems are used in Swedish electoral studies. The 'old' one is based on the traditional Swedish social group classification, while a 'new' one was constructed by Olof Petersson in his 1976 electoral study (see n. 26).

[b] 'Other groups' consists of six categories: Managers and owners of large enterprises, higher salaried employees, professionals; owners of small enterprises, self-employed; farmers; shop assistants, certain employees in transport and service occupations; workers in agriculture, lumbering and fishing; students. That is to say, there are certain workers and salaried employees who are not included in the categories 'Workers' and 'Salaried employees'.

Source: Swedish national election studies, 1956–85 (See n. 26)

vote goes in the opposite direction,[28] and the Communists' share of the first time voters has radically increased since the mid-1960's (table 8.8).

I have concentrated on the social changes among Communist sympathizers. To be sure, there have been other changes too: the attitudes of the Communist electorate are not the same as before. For example, survey data from the 1973 and 1976 national elections indicate a change in attitude towards the domestic affairs of the Soviet Union. Surveys showed a significant increase in negative respondents, and in 1976 these constituted a majority of the communist sympathizers.[29] Thus, the ideological change that is to be found in the party's statements and documents corresponds to a similar trend in the opinion of the communist electorate.

Summary and conclusion

At the party congress in 1964, the party leader Hilding Hagberg was forced to resign office. Although he was replaced by a well-known personality in the party, C. H. Hermansson, this event marked the beginning of a

Table 8.6 Communist vote and occupation (new classification)

| | Electoral year | | | | | | |
	1968 (%)	1970 (%)	1973 (%)	1976 (%)	1979 (%)	1982 (%)	1985 (%)
Occupational groups							
Industrial workers	2	6	6	5	5	5	5
Other workers	1	4	6	5	5	4	5
Salaried employees, low	2	1	2	3	3	5	6
Salaried employees, middle	2	3	3	5	8	8	7
Salaried employees, high	2	3	1	3	3	4	4
Small businessmen	0	1	3	2	5	3	3
Farmers	1	1	1	1	0	0	0
Students	5	11	18	8	19	11	14
Occupational sectors							
Agriculture	1	2	1	3	1	2	2
Production	2	6	4	4	4	5	4
Trade, communications and transport	1	3	5	3	3	3	4
Welfare, education and culture	2	3	6	8	12	10	10
Administration	1	1	0	3	4	4	2
Entire electorate	1	4	4	4	5	5	5

Source: As table 8.5

Table 8.7 Communist vote in different educational groups

| | Educational level | |
Electoral year	Low	High[a]
1956	2	0
1960	2	0
1964	3	1
1968	1	2
1970	4	5
1973	4	8
1976	3	9
1979	4	10
1982	4	8
1985	4	8

[a] 'High' means at least '*studentexamen*'.
Source: As table 8.5

Table 8.8 Communist vote according to age group

Electoral year	Age			First time voters (%)
	Up to 39 (%)	40–59 (%)	60 plus (%)	
1956	1	2	1	0
1960	1	2	3	0
1964	2	3	3	0
1968	2	2	1	2
1970	5	3	2	11
1973	6	3	3	12
1976	6	2	3	9
1979	10	2	2	11
1982	8	3	2	7
1985	8	3	3	6

Source: As table 8.5

new era for Swedish communism. The replacement of a chairman does not, of course, explain everything that followed. The rise of leftism among young people after 1968 was not at all a product of the Communist Party's activity.

However, the replacement initiated a generational shift in the leadership of the party that had some very important consequences. It prevented the development of a situation such as obtains in Denmark and Norway, where left-wing socialist parties have become a political force at the expense of the Communist parties. The Swedish Communist Party was therefore the only real alternative for radical youth at the beginning of the 1970s. Furthermore, the change of leadership contributed to a gentle solution of the 'Finnish' problem. The pro-Soviet traditionalist faction gradually disappeared from the party, so that when a split occurred in 1977, they were too few to hurt the party.

The ideological development of the Swedish Communist Party since the mid-1960s may be characterized as a repeat of its earlier history. The content of modernism was very much the same as the left-wing socialism of the pre-Comintern period. The neo-Leninism of the late 1960s and the early 1970s resembles Leninism proper, though there are some very important differences. And as with orthodox Leninism, neo-Leninism has gradually been revised. Today, the Communist party once again emphasizes democracy and other ethical principles.

The development of the party's membership parallels that of its electorate. The old supporters have been replaced by a new generation of communists. In comparison with the old generation, it consists of more women, more young people, more well-educated people and fewer workers. Thus, the Swedish Communist Party has changed a good deal with respect to its ideology as well as to its membership and its electorate. In these respects, Swedish communism has a new face.

Finally one might ask what it is that still makes this party a *communist* party. Of course, the party itself claims to be one, and presumably this must be counted as evidence. But as regards the particular feature that counted as a hallmark of a communist party during the Comintern era – its principles of organization – the modern Swedish Communist Party does not have very much in common with its own past.

Today the Leninist ideas are nothing but formulae in the party's documents. The internal life of the Left Party Communists does not seem to differ very much from that of other parties. The party leaders do dominate the discussions within the party, but they do not control the debates as was always the case in the past. During the last congress the party's leadership was criticized in a manner reminiscent of the debates within the Liberal party. And as for the programme committee – one of the most important bodies for initiating and stimulating internal debate – it has come to be distanced more and more from the Central Committee and its Executive. Formerly the process of framing a new programme was carefully controlled by the party leadership. Nowadays the programme committee is mainly composed of academics without any further positions within the party.

Although there is no systematic research on this point, it may be concluded that the culture of democratic centralism that dominated the life of the party up to the beginning of the 1960s has completely broken down. The Swedish Communist Party of today represents a new type of communist party. The demand for a renewal of the party in the mid-1960s has thus been realized.

Appendix A The Swedish Communist Party in general elections, 1917–82

	Communist Party vote as a percentage of:		
Election	valid votes	socialist bloc	radical left
1917 P	8.1	20.6	100
1919 L	5.8	16.0	100
1920 P	6.4	17.7	100
1921 P	4.6	10.5	59
1922 L	4.5	11.5	71
1924 P	5.1	11.0	100
1926 L	4.1	9.5	100
1928 P	6.4	14.7	100
1930 L	1.2	2.6	30
1932 P	3.0	6.0	36
1934 L	2.8	5.7	41
1936 P	3.3	6.2	43
1938 L	3.8	6.8	67
1940 P	3.5	6.1	83
1942 L	5.9	10.5	98
1944 P	10.3	18.1	98
1946 L	11.2	20.1	100
1948 P	6.3	12.0	100
1950 L	4.9	9.2	100
1952 P	4.3	8.5	100
1954 L	4.8	9.2	100
1956 P	5.0	10.1	100
1958 P	3.4	6.9	100
1958 L	4.0	7.9	100
1960 P	4.5	8.6	100
1962 L	3.8	7.0	100
1964 P	5.2	9.9	100
1966 L	6.4	13.2	100
1968 P	3.0	5.6	100
1970 P	4.8	9.5	92
1973 P	5.3	10.7	91
1976 P	4.8	10.0	94
1979 P	5.6	11.3	93
1982 P	5.6	10.9	98
1985 P	5.4	10.6	95

The vote for the Swedish Communist Party (SSV, SKP, VPK) as a percentage of the valid votes, of the socialist bloc and of the radical left in parliamentary elections (P) and local government elections (L).
Source: Sveriges officiella statistik, Allmänna valen

Appendix B Turnover rates in the party's executive bodies

Congress		Executive committee			Central committee		
Year	No.	Re-elected[a]	Newly-elected[b]	Number	Re-elected	Newly-elected	Number
1944	12	89	11	9	64	36	25
1946	13	89	11	9	72	28	25
1948	14	100	25	12	92	23	30
1951	15	100	0	12	87	13	30
1953	16	67	20	10	80	20	30
1955	17	90	18	11	93	20	35
1957	18	73	27	11	94	27	45
1961	19	100	0	11	82	18	45
1964	20	55	45	11	76	24	45
1967	21	18	71	7	38	46	31
1969	22	57	56	9	71	37	35
1972	23	78	22	9	74	26	35
1975	24	78	22	9	69	31	35
1978	25	78	22	9	69	31	35
1981	26	56	29	7[c]	63	37	35
1985	27	67	33	9	69	31	35

[a] The share (%) of *re-elected* members is calculated from the old composition.
[b] The share (%) of *newly elected* members is calculated from the new composition.
[c] The committee was enlarged to nine members during the period.
Sources: Annual reports and minutes of the congresses and the central committee

Remarks to Appendix C p. 155

Remarks:	SAP	Social Democratic Party
	SSV	Social Democratic Left Party
	SKP(KI)	Communist Party of Sweden (section of the Comintern)
	SKP	Communist Party of Sweden
	SP	Socialist Party
	SKA	Communist Workers' League of Sweden
	VPK	Left Party Communists
	KFML	Communist League of Marxist—Leninists
	APK	Labour Party Communists
	KPML(R)	Communist Party of Marxist-Leninists

Note: Besides these parties there is a small Trotskyist party which today calls itself the 'Socialist Party'.

Appendix C A historical map of the Swedish Left

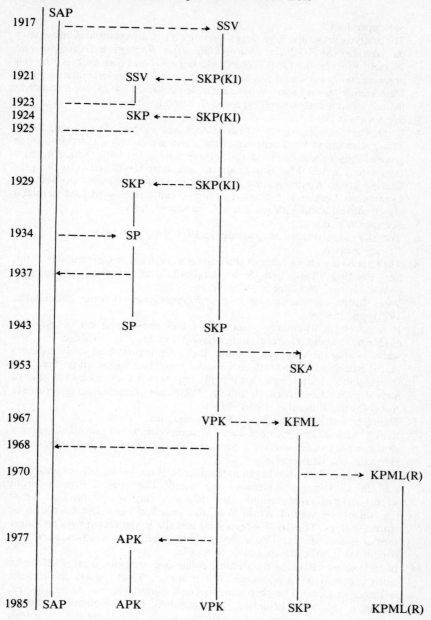

Notes

1   See appendix C.
2   The analysis presented here draws heavily on my dissertation: *Kommunism på svenska? SKP/VPK:s idéutveckling efter Komintern* (Almqvist and Wiksell, Stockholm, 1984). When I do not refer to other sources, the full argument will be found there. See 'Kommunism i Sverige–ett temanummer', *Meddelande fran arbetarrörelsens arkiv och bibliotek* 24–25, for a complete list of research and writings on Swedish communism up to 1982.
3   See appendix A.
4   C. H. Hermansson, *Vänsterns väg* (Rabén and Sjögren, Stockholm, 1965). Those who called for a renewal of the party are usually divided into three groups. Apart from the modernists there were a left wing, which urged a return to classical Marxism–Leninism and later developed into the pro-Chinese group *Kommunistika förbundet marxist–leninisterna* (KFML, the Communist League of Marxist–Leninists), and a right wing that wanted a closer collaboration with the Social Democratic Party.
5   See appendix B.
6   The SKP adopted new programmes in 1944, 1953 and 1961.
7   Cf. appendix A.
8   Their ratios are about twice or three times as high as the Communists' ratio. See Per-Erik Back and Sten Berglund, *Det svenska partiväsendet* (AWE/Gebers, Stockholm, 1978), p. 96.
9   Vater Korpi, *Arbetarklassen i välfärdskapitalismen* (Prisma, Stockholm, 1978), pp. 268–99.
10 It is uncertain whether this movement had any impact on the Swedish electorate. Swedish electoral studies have put in doubt the existence of a 'left wave' among the voters as a whole. But a representational study indicates that it had a significant influence on the politicians within all parties. And several policy studies show that it really represented a leftist trend in governmental policy (see Sören Holmberg, *Riksdagen representerar det svenska folket* (Studentlitteratur, Lund, 1974).
11 The term was introduced by C. H. Hermansson.
12 Kent Lindqvist, *Program och parti. Principprogram och partiideologi inom den kommunistska rörelsen i Sverige 1917–72* (Arkiv, Lund, 1982), and Hermansson, *Vänsterns väg.*
13 The decline of Leninism began in the middle of the 1930s, but not until 1944 was the shift in party ideology terminated. The original Popular Front strategy had involved nothing more than a defence against fascism. But at the end of the Second World War, this idea had been developed into an entire ideology. The Russian revolution and the Soviet Union were no longer seen as historically valid examples of development, but as cases marked by conditions specifically applicable to Russia.
14 In late summer 1986 the programme committee presented a proposal for an entirely new party programme. The proposal, which clearly showed the influence of Göran Therborn, contains only minor reference to the classical themes of Marxism–Leninism. Two members of the committee entered reservations concerning certain formulations, and there was vigorous discussion among party members. The twenty-eighth party congress in May 1987, however, adopted a programme that played down controversies within the party.

15 Party programme (1981), para. 4. Before 1981 the sentence in italics read: 'The party organizes the most conscious part of the working class'.

16 Party programme (1981), para. 25.

17 Cf. the strategies elaborated by the French or Finnish parties, or any strategy founded upon the usual analysis of state monopoly capitalism. Such strategies are a common feature of the pro-Soviet parties, such as the APK in Sweden.

18 Party programme (1981), para. 24.

19 In addition to *Vänsterns väg*, see his *Det monopolkapitalistiska Sverge* (Arbetarkultur, Stockholm, 1943); *Koncentration och storföretag* (Arbetarkultur, Stockholm, 1959); *Monopol och storfinans* (Arbetarkultur, Stockholm, 1962); *Monopol och storfinans – de 15 familierna* (Rabén and Sjögren, Stockholm, 1971); and *Kapitalister* (Arbetarkultur, Stockholm, 1979 and 1981).

20 Göran Therborn (ed.), *En ny vänster* (Rabén and Sjögren, Stockholm, 1966). .

21 Göran Therborn, *Vad är bra värderingar värda?* (Zenit/Cavefors, Lund, 1973), and *Frankfurtskolan. Till kritiken av den kritiska teorin* (Arkiv, Stockholm, 1976).

22 Göran Therborn, *Vad gör den härskande klasse när den härskar?* (Zenit/Raben and Sjögren, Lund/Stockholm, 1980), pp. 238–82.

23 See appendix B.

24 VPK Kongress 1981. *Verksamhetsberättelse* (VPK, Stockholm, 1981).

25 Daniel Tarschys, 'The Changing Basis of Radical Socialism in Scandinavia', in Karl H. Cerny (ed.), *Scandinavia at the Polls; Recent Political Trends in Denmark, Norway and Sweden* (American Enterprise Institute for Public Research, Washington DC, 1977).

26 The pages that follow are based on the results of the Swedish National Election Studies, 1956–85. The results from the 1976, 1979, 1982 and 1985 studies are reported in Olof Petersson, *Väljarna och valet 1976. Valundersökningar*, rapport 2. (SCB/Liber, Stockholm: 1977); Sören Holmberg, *Svenska väljare* (Liber, Stockholm, 1981) and *Väljare i förändring* (Liber, Stockholm, 1984); and Sören Holmberg and Mikael Giljam, *Väljare och val i Sverige*, (Bonniers, Stockholm, 1987). My own tables, however, have been composed directly from the original survey data with help from Sören Holmberg and Anders Westholm.

27 Olof Petersson, *Känn Ditt Land*. no. 11. *Partier och väljare Svenska turistföreningens orienteringsserie om svensk natur och kultur* (Svenska turistföreningen, Stockholm, 1981), pp. 38ff.

28 Holmberg, Väljare i förändring, p. 76.

29 Olof Petersson, *Väljarna och världspolitiken* (Norstedts, Stockholm, 1982), p. 53.

9 The End of Dutch Bolshevism?
The Communist Party of the Netherlands

Meindert Fennema

Many of the problems that have beset the Western European communist parties in the post-war period have been experienced by the Communist Party of the Netherlands (*Communistische Partij van Nederland* – CPN) with particular acuity. This is especially true, as this chapter will show, of the impact on the party of a change in its social composition. But before the crisis stemming primarily from that factor began to form in the late 1970s, it was the party's equivocal relationship with the Soviet Union that marked it out from most other Western European communist parties, and the roots of that troubled relationship reach back to an earlier post-war period.

Early post-war history

The history of the Communist Party of the Netherlands since 1945 cannot be understood in separation from the history of the trade union movement and especially the history of the 'United Federation of Unions' (EVC). The EVC had been founded directly after the liberation at the end of the Second World War with the purpose of replacing the old Catholic, Protestant and social democratic unions and thus creating unity in the trade union movement. At first this initiative was very successful, because the pre-war unions, and especially the social democratic one, had lost a good deal of credit as a result of their lenient attitude towards the German authorities during the first years of the German occupation. In contrast, the CPN had gained much confidence (and more than 10 per cent of the votes in the first post-war elections) due to its heroic role in the resistance movement. The CPN took a leading role in supporting the newborn EVC, organizationally as well as ideologically.

Both Catholic and social democratic leaders, however, saw the danger of a united, communist-orientated trade union and recreated their pre-war Catholic and social democratic unions. With the help of the government, Marshall Aid and the cold war offensive they succeeded in recapturing the lost political ground and by 1947 the EVC was left without its general support and, even worse, its heterogeneous leadership. From then on the EVC became a Communist-led union in the narrow, sectarian sense.

By 1955 this was realized by some of the Communist leaders, and in 1956 Paul de Groot launched an internal campaign to liquidate the EVC and to call for renewed unity in the trade union movement. By doing so he had to face the opposition of those who maintained a position in the EVC. But the authoritarian way in which de Groot presented the EVC issue also met with opposition from those who, while basically agreeing with his trade union policy, wanted to do away with his Stalinist practices.[1] The opposition was destroyed in a classical way; its protagonists were expelled and unmasked as agents and liquidators.

During this internal conflict the leaders of the old EVC looked for international support in the World Federation of Trade Unions, of which the EVC was still a member. This was an unusual position that the EVC shared with the French CGT and the Italian CGIL. The EVC's leadership was indeed able to get some support, which worried in particular Secretary General Paul de Groot, and made him all the more careful to monopolize the CPN's international relations. Relations with the CPSU became strained, and this came to a head in November 1960 at the Moscow world conference of communist and workers' parties, when the Sino-Soviet conflict came in the open through the interventions of Deng Xiaoping and, more bluntly, of Enver Hoxha.[2]

After a furious denunciation of Hoxha by the Spanish Dolores Ibarruri, the delegations of all parties rose to applaud her defence of the Soviet position except for the delegations of China, Albania, Indonesia and . . . the Netherlands.[3]

After 1960 the CPN consolidated its autonomous position within the international communist movement. It tried to steer a middle course between China and the Soviet Union and to arrive at a compromise between the two. During the Cuban missile crisis, for example, the CPN supported the Soviet solution of the conflict, and in return obtained Soviet approval for its neutrality policy.[4] In spite of the policy of neutrality and autonomy, the CPN, and above all the rank and file members of the party – remained ideologically tied to the Soviet Union. In 1961, for example, the CPN distributed 10,000 copies of the CPSU's programme, in which the economic prospects of the Soviet Union were said to be so promising that the stage of communism could be reached in 1981.[5] After breaking with Moscow in 1963, the CPN took a more 'anti-revisionist' position, but it never became a pro-Chinese party.

It came as no surprise, at least not to those familiar with the CPN's affairs, when the invasion of Czechoslovakia by Warsaw Pact troops in 1968 was explicitly denounced by the party in a 'Manifesto'. More surprising perhaps was the strong criticism of the policy of the French Communist Party during the events in May 1968. In the view of the CPN, students should not be considered as children of the bourgeoisie, but as potential allies of the workers, suffering from similar oppression and struggling against the same enemy.[6]

The policy of autonomy was in fact a *conditio sine qua non* for a move 'out of the fortress' into Dutch society itself. A dialogue was started with progressive Catholic and Protestant intellectuals. International commotion was created, for example, by an interview with Professor Schillebeekx,[7] and Adam Schaff's theory of 'alienation' was discussed in the party press. During the first half of the 1970s many student militants became members of the party.

From 1967 onwards the CPN can be seen as a communist party with a Maoist inclination, united internally but isolated in the international communist movement. It attracted the most activist elements in the student movement, paying a lot of attention to students' demands and their syndicalist struggle. However, whilst the party was prepared to give ideological and logistic support to the students during the 1969 occupation of the administrative centre of the University of Amsterdam, it also attempted to guide and control the student movement. The CPN was particularly ready to correct the students when they stressed the more anti-parliamentary and radical aspects of their struggle, for example referring to the writings of Anton Pannekoek, and the contemporary Johannes Agnoli and André Gorz. Such ideas, it was said, belonged to the past and were spread by the reactionary press to lead the students astray. Spokesmen on the student movement within the party up until 1972 were still the old guard or their student children.[8]

In 1972, at the party's twenty-fourth congress, the number of students among the delegates was still a mere 18, but in 1975 the figure jumped to 69. From table 9.1 it can easily be seen that between 1972 and 1975 an enormous shift took place in the social composition of the congress. The manual workers' representation declined, while the student, teachers' and academic representation jumped from 36 in 1972 to 141 in 1975. This trend continued after 1975. In 1977 the 'educational field' was repre-

Table 9.1 Social composition of CPN congresses, 1967–84

	1967	*1970*	*1972*	*1975*	*1977*	*1980*	*1984*
Total number of delegates	436	437	432	545	485	489	?a
Building workers	94	77	77	66	—	23	8
Metal workers	67	87	61	69	—	36	6
Printing trade	39	27	21	15	—	—	20
Dockers	—	6	16	—	—	—	—
Factory workers, and others	—	17	21	—	—	30	1
(Manual workers)	(200)	(214)	(196)	(150)	(130)	(89)	(35)
Office workers	35	39	43	64	31	22	7
'Service'	—	55	26	20	—	—	6
Agrarian sector	—	4	—	4	1	—	—
Teachers	—	3	9	53	37	65	35
Academic professions	8b	3	9	20	47	28	26
Students	7	16	18	69	54	27	27
Artists	7b	3	7	7	5	—	—
Civil servants	—	—	—	9	21	30	25
Shopkeepers	10	3	9	3	9	—	—
Nurses	—	—	—	11	10	27	16
Welfare workers	—	—	—	17	43	42	31
Party workers	—	—	—	9	—	—	22
Journalistsc	—	18	24	25	27	19	
Housewives	28	—	—	—	—	30	13
Without occupation	—	—	—	62	—	31	28
Unemployed	—	—	—	—	—	20	46
Miscellaneous	—	—	—	—	22	59	7
Total of delegates surveyed	295	358	341	532	437	489	324

a The number of delegates at the 1984 extraordinary congress was never recorded.
b In 1967 these categories were taken together.
c These journalists were all working for the party paper and should be considered as party workers.
Sources: Politiek en Cultuur, 1968, p. 2; 1970, p. 119; 1972, p. 334; 1975, p. 241; 1978, p. 107; *Verslag 27e.partij congres van de CPN*, 1980, p. 167. Figures for 1984 collected at the congress by D. Hellema and the author

sented by 138 delegates, somewhat fewer teachers and students, but now many university lecturers. At the same time a brand new occupational group came to the fore: in 1977 welfare workers formed nearly 10 per cent of the delegates. The pattern is clear enough: after 1970 students enter the party and by 1975 they form, together with the teachers, nearly a quarter of the delegates. By 1977 they have outnumbered the manual workers. This can also be seen from the age of congress delegates (table 9.2). Until 1972 the age composition is fairly stable: the age group between 18 and 25 contains some 55–60 delegates. By 1975, however, this number has nearly doubled to 105 and the next higher age group also nearly doubled between 1972 and 1975. Together, these two age groups form the majority of delegates after 1975.

Did this mean that by 1975 the conception of the CPN's stance had altered dramatically and moved to a more Eurocommunist position? Far from it. Rather than breaking up the Stalinist isolation in which the party found itself, the new generation of student activists was absorbed, at least for the time being, into the existing party structure and Marxist-Leninist party culture.

The international position of the CPN contributed *ex silentio* to the party's success in the first half of the 1970s. The fact that the party was not allied to Moscow made it difficult to make the 'gulag' a political issue within the party. Both pro-Soviet and anti-Soviet partisans could live in peaceful co-existence and the Soviet Union was hardly at all an issue in party debates. The primary goal of the leadership was not to have the party split along the lines of the Sino-Soviet conflict. This meant that

Table 9.2   Age distribution of delegates to party congresses

	1967	1970	1972	1975	1977	1980	1984
Number of delegates	436	437	432	545	485	489	?a
Number of women	—	67	69	90	83	113	125
Age group							
18–25	55	58	58	105	72	—d	19
26–35	—b	98	110	199	231	—d	180
36–45	—b	105	110	79	74	—d	72
46–55	—b	120	95	94	63	—d	24
56–65	47	47	51	42	63	34	21
above 65	10	7	8	8	7	11	12
(unknown)		(3)c	(17)c				(3)

a See table 9.1.
b 26–40 = 138, and 41–55 = 186.
c This number is not explained in the documents.
d 18–30 = 189, 31–40 = 171, 41–55 = 84.
Sources: As table 9.1

individual members could have their own interpretation of the conflict and judge the Soviet Union accordingly, on condition that the issue was not taken up to congress level. Nobody was obliged to defend the Soviet Union, although neither was support for the dissidents allowed. Furthermore, the intermediate position of the party left little room for Maoist or Trotskyist groups, which were so successful in France, Germany and Great Britain. Although Maoist groups had some impact between 1969 and 1972 they remained very small indeed. Only the KEN, a Maoist group, recruited some students, and in 1971 laid the basis for the very tiny 'Socialist Party'.[9]

Electoral support

After the Second World War the CPN, which had been no more than an electoral dwarf before the war, suddenly began to appeal to many voters. In the national elections of 1946 the party won more than 10 per cent of the vote (table 9.3). In 1945 the Communist paper *De Waarheid* had a circulation of more than 300,000 – the largest of any paper in the country. However, from that high point onwards the Communists slowly lost their electoral support, under circumstances that resembled those in other countries. Despite the party's opposition to the colonial war in Indonesia, for which the Labour Party in government was also responsible, the CPN did not make persistent inroads into the social democratic vote. On the contrary, in the 1948 election it lost more than 2 per cent of the vote, after which time the Communist electorate crumbled, although not as quickly as is often suggested. In 1956 the CPN still gained nearly 5 per cent of the vote, and it was not until after a ferocious internal fight, which ended by splitting the party in 1958, that electoral support fell to a mere 2.4 per cent in 1959.[10] The party only slowly recovered from this position, but the recovery was steady: in each new election the CPN regained a seat, until in the 1972 parliamentary elections it came equal fifth with the traditional Protestant CHU (Christian Historical Union) and the Radical Party (a splinter of the Catholic Party), and behind the Labour Party, the Catholic Party, the Liberal Party and the Anti-Revolutionary Party (Protestant). The Christian parties, which had lost considerable electoral support during the 1960s (from 49 per cent in 1963 to 31 per cent in 1972) were preparing a merger. Against this background, the Communists had high hopes of becoming the fourth most important party current on the political landscape, behind the socialists, the Christian democrats and the liberals. Although in the provincial elections of 1974 the CPN lost considerably (from 4.5 to 3.5 per cent), this was not taken as an adverse trend, and the

Table 9.3 Results of parties of the Left in parliamentary elections, 1946–83

Year	CPN (%)	Labour (%)	Pacifist Socialist Party (%)	Radical Party (%)	Democrats 1966 (%)
1946	10.6	28.3	—	—	—
1948	7.7	25.6	—	—	—
1952	6.2	29.0	—	—	—
1956	4.8	32.7	—	—	—
1959	2.4	30.3	1.8	—	—
1963	2.8	28.0	3.0	—	—
1967	3.6	23.5	2.9	—	4.5
1971	3.9	24.7	1.4	1.7	6.8
1972	4.5	27.4	1.5	4.8	4.2
1977	1.7	33.8	0.9	1.7	5.4
1981	2.1	28.3	2.1	2.0	11.0
1982	1.8	30.4	2.3	1.7	4.3
1986	0.6	39.3	1.2	1.3	6.7

Source: Parlement en Kiezer (Martinus Nijhoff, Leiden, 1985, p. 169)

party campaigned in the 1977 election with the ambitious slogan '*Van Agt eruit, de CPN erin*': the Catholic prime minister, Van Agt, should leave the cabinet, while the CPN should enter it. Although many members and adherents did not agree with the latter part of the slogan, very few foresaw the electoral disaster of 1977.[11]

After the 1977 elections a party struggle was launched by Paul de Groot.[12] His defeat would eventually pave the way within the party for the defeat of Stalinism and of the old leadership. This will be treated below; but first the integration of student militants into the party organization, and the relationship between the CPN and the student movement must be analysed.

Students in the party organization

Between 1972 and 1977 membership of the CPN increased by 4,357.[13] Given the declining number of workers in the party and the high turnover of membership, my estimate is that in that period some 5,000 students applied for membership. Those students who entered the party mainly on the basis of workerist sentiments, must have been rather disappointed. First, the party encouraged the students to be active in their own field, at the university. And in so far as they were encouraged to do party work, this was in the local branches that were regionally organized. The organization of party members in 'cells' based on industry or trade had long been abolished in favour of an organization based on the territorial principle. These *afdelingen* were run predominantly by pensioners and women, while the active workers were organized separately in 'enterprise groups'.

Students were asked to do organizational work for the communist daily, *De Waarheid*, by raising money, distributing the paper and campaigning for new subscriptions. The circulation of *De Waarheid* expanded in the period 1972 to 1980 from 1000 to 2000 subscriptions per year between those dates except for 1974, when it expanded only slightly, and 1977, when there was a slight decline.[14] University teachers were induced to engage in syndicalist struggle but were never approached in their capacity as intellectuals, either in the context of their university work, or as party intellectuals. The scientific bureau of the party (IPSO), headed by grand old Paul de Groot, invited in some younger intellectuals, but only those who had a formal education in natural science. Social scientists and historians were effectively barred from theoretical work.

At the regional level, in Groningen, the situation was slightly different. Under the popular leadership of Fre' Meis not only were the student leaders invited to take part in party work, but also university students and teachers were encouraged to do research work that supported the struggle of the workers and included detailed investigation of labour conditions in local industry and the possibilities for regional development. Groningen, therefore, was atypical of the general party line; it created a more stable alliance between students and workers and remained a Stalinist stronghold for a long time to come.[15]

In general, however, the party remained aloof from the theoretical discussions on Marxism that went on at the universities during the 1970s. These discussions were organized by other agencies such as the *Socialistische Uitgeverij Nijmegen* (SUN), which started as a student publishing house but soon turned professional and until the 1980s was quite successful in introducing the 'French discussion' (Althusser, and later Foucault). The SUN was attacked with Stalinist arguments. A strongly anti-intellectual climate remained dominant within the party, with the result that party intellectuals refrained from theoretical debate altogether, or separated their intellectual activity from their party activity. This being so, the party had little influence on scientific discussion and what influence it had was negative in one of two ways: it did nothing to stimulate these discussions, and it interfered negatively when its position was seen as being at stake. The party's influence has often been overestimated: it wanted to use, and in fact could only use, its organizational power to prevent declared 'enemies of the party' from getting university nominations on the ticket of representing the student movement. Such cases were rare. The party line was primarily damaging the party's potential influence within the universities.

In structural terms the political efficacy of students who became members of the party increased. The party organized its student members in 'student groups', where syndicalist strategies were discussed and tactics were developed. The united interventions of party members in the student unions were meant to increase the power of these unions (this power was, of course, contested by non-communist members) but it certainly increased the influence of the Communist members within the unions.

A related appeal of the party was its historical experience with syndicalist and socialist struggle. The CPN was regarded as a revolutionary party fighting for a better society. Even in its distorted, Stalinist form, the experience and knowledge of elder party cadres were often very useful in the struggle waged against more conservative groups within the university staff. Even in the field of theory and research itself the views of the party, which were anathema in academic discussions, formed for many students a stimulating alternative to the rigidly positivistic and apologetic social sciences.

A third factor in the appeal of the CPN to students was its heroism in the Second World War. The older members had often fought in the resistance movement and the Spanish Civil War. Many students felt they could learn from such people, admired them and were proud to have a comradely relation with such distinguished heroes, the more so because those communist militants had been, and still were, underestimated and maltreated by the rest of society.[16] A fourth attraction for the students was the CPN's hatred for social democratic hypocrisy, with which they were confronted in their struggle against professors, faculty boards and the ministry of education. Within the university some of the students' worst enemies were important members of the Labour Party, and yet the social democrats were needed to support in parliament legislation favoured by the students.

A fifth factor of communist appeal was the sense of belonging that resulted from an active membership. This existed not only at the level of ideology, in the way Raymond Aron has suggested, but also, and maybe even more so, at the social level, where students came into contact, often for the first time, with working class culture. The culture of sharing, the informal exchange and kinship networks that still existed there, contrasted sharply with the middle class culture of possessive individualism, formalism and containment in the nuclear family.

The workers

As elsewhere in Western Europe, in the Netherlands the Communist Party had its strongholds in traditional industries: in the port of Amsterdam, the shipyards, the steel and construction industries and the board factories in Groningen. In the modern industries, and especially in the large multinationals, the party's influence was very small indeed. The restructuring of industry which started in the 1960s met with resistance in backward sectors, a resistance organized by the CPN. This meant, however, that the Communist-led struggles were mainly defensive.

The CPN had to confront another difficulty, which was more specific to Dutch labour relations. After the party had liquidated its 'own' trade unions – the EVC – in 1959, communist workers were induced to join the social democratic unions. This, however, was easier said than done. First, the latter tried to prevent communist workers from joining by erecting formal and informal barriers. In fact, the only way to join these unions was to conceal one's membership of the Communist Party, but this strategy was not open to the well-known communists on the shop floor. At the same time, and partly as a result of this, many rank and file members flatly refused to join these anti-communist 'traitor unions' and continued to organize themselves along the old syndicalist lines, enrolling also non-communist workers who were outside the 'official' unions in so-called 'action committees'. Especially in Groningen and in the shipyards these 'action committees' flourished, causing many problems for the corporatist unions. In the building trade the old Communist-dominated EVC union (ABWB) even continued to exist. The leadership of the Communist Party had to steer a middle course between the official line of working within the large social democratic unions and the line of the 'action committees' which often organized the more militant and radical workers, but also, and at the same time, those communists who were not admitted into the social democratic unions. This strategic problem divided the workers within the party, and the above-mentioned 'middle road' was in fact a zig-zag course that the leadership also used, to complicate the matter further, to crush opposition within the party. In short, workers organized in 'action committees' always ran the risk of being accused of not following the party line and of being anarchistic, whereas those who held a position – always precarious – in the unions ran the risk of being scolded as 'reformists' who yielded to the trade union leadership.

An example of the first tendency was the 1966 revolt of building workers who were not organized in the official trade unions. When the latter, in collaboration with the employers, threatened to punish them financially for not being unionized (at least not in the 'proper' unions) the Communists organized a demonstration in front of the union office, in which a worker died. The rumour spread that he had been killed by a police bullet. When *De Telegraaf*, a right-wing paper, wrote that he had died of a heart attack (which was true), the workers smashed the windows of the paper's offices.[17] The CPN denounced the riots as organized by the Provos (a loosely organized urban protest movement which did indeed participate) and in secret took disciplinary measures against the party members who had led the demonstration.

In 1970 a strike broke out in the docks of Rotterdam, this time led by a Maoist group, but again directed against the policy of the social democratic union. The Maoist action committee was condemned and when the strikers reached a deadlock because the employers were unwilling to give in to their demands, the party intervened successfully by sending in the charismatic Fre' Meis, who negotiated a compromise.[18]

These examples show how the party was most successful when workers revolted against the corporatist trade union structure but at the same time did not want to attack the trade unions frontally. The party was in practice radical-reformist rather than revolutionary.

The Communists were successful in forcing the unions into a more radical stance, but did so mainly from outside. When, for example the union of metal workers, after merging with some smaller unions into the 'Industriebond NVV' radicalized under the leadership of Arie Groenevelt, this was not due to internal pressure from communist cadres, since these were still excluded and boycotted.[19] Only in the teachers' union (ABOP) and the civil servants' union (ABVA) did the party make some progress, mainly through its influence among university teachers, welfare workers and nurses.[20]

In Groningen, again, the situation was different. The position of the official unions was weak both in the agrarian sector and in the board industry. Communist-organized action committees were strong and 'hegemonic', since they organized students also and were broadly supported by the Groningen population. At the end of the 1960s they organized a number of successful strikes,[21] but could not prevent the dismantling of the board industry.

To sum up, Communist workers were at the beginning of the 1970s still predominantly active outside or at the margin of the official unions. They successfully defended the interests of non-unionized workers and attacked the system of corporatist labour relations from outside. This certainly forced the unions into a more radical position. But, on the other hand, the union leadership held the Communists in a grip: since the party line was to enter the unions, the party could not take an outright anti-union position, while the individual Communists who had entered the union were committed to maintaining the principles of democratic centralism within that union.[22] Thus, participation in action committees was a ground for expulsion from the union. The Communist position in labour relations was therefore one of structural ambivalence, which was reflected in the internal organization of the party and created discontent and frustration among active workers. Apart from this structural ambivalence, the fact that the party had its strongholds in those industries that were to be dismantled in the 1970s meant that its position in industrial centres was tendentially undermined. Together these factors contributed to a decline of the traditional base of the party – a decline that, in my view, was inevitable in the circumstances.

The party's declining industrial base and its strategic ambivalence towards the social democratic unions, however, were, in the first half of the 1970s, hidden from view by the appeal it had to radical youth. The influx of student militants strengthened the party organization and extended the circulation of *De Waarheid* by more than 1,000 new subscriptions a year.[23]

Breaking with the past

This apparent success of the CPN came abruptly to an end when in May 1977 the party's share of the vote fell from 4.5 to 1.7 per cent in the national elections. This dramatic electoral defeat was at first ascribed to the hi-jack of a train in the same month by a group of Moluccans, behind which lurked sinister reactionary forces (according to *De Waarheid* of 26 May 1977). It was obviously Paul de Groot who had inspired this analysis, as was demonstrated in a long article that he published in *De Waarheid* of 15 June.[24] Shortly afterwards de Groot's analysis shifted somewhat. In an article published in *De Waarheid* of 2 August, he argued that the electoral defeat of the party had been caused by lack of revolutionary spirit on the part of the party leadership, which had allowed the party to be taken over by students and civil servants and to lose contact with the manual workers. De Groot called for a re-Bolshevization of the party, along with the restoration of democratic centralism in its most rigid form. The party, he said, should concentrate on the organization of the unemployed. In that same article he pleaded for relations with Moscow to be restored and he launched a sharp attack on Eurocommunism. Finally, he attacked the leadership of the party for its leniency towards revisionism and its passivity in the class struggle. In secret de Groot prepared a new version of the party statutes, and during the summer he tried to organize a group of young communists to take over, just as he had done in 1958. This time, however, he overplayed his hand. The Central Committee[25] stood firm, and after a long and carefully orchestrated 'discussion' in the party, de Groot was ousted from the scientific bureau and stripped of his 'honorary membership for life' of the Central Committee.[26]

However, the victorious Central Committee accepted in practice some of the proposals made by de Groot, especially those in the field of international relations. Friendly relations with the Soviet party were restored and a successful initiative to campaign against the neutron bomb was launched. But, in spite of the enormous success of the N-bomb campaign, opposition against the pro-Soviet line grew. When, for example, the CPN's Joop Wolff visited the Czechoslovak hard-liner Vasil Bilak while 'on holiday' in Czechoslovakia,[27] this caused indignation, as did the defence of the Soviet treatment of Orlov and Sakharov (*De Waarheid*, 27 May 1978). There was an anti-Soviet group which was quite successful in organizing opposition within the party.

The feminist opposition

It was, however, the feminist opposition that was to give the final blow to the traditional party structure. It succeeded where all former opposition had failed. This was because the anti-Stalinist opposition was too divisive, while the party had a long experience of dealing with such opposition. At no time did the opposition dare to organize for fear of being accused of fractionalism, or else – as was the case in 1958 – it organized secretly, using the same methods as the party leadership. Because the latter could, in general, count on a loyal bureaucracy, its position was strong and the only possible winning strategy for any such opposition group boiled down to a palace revolution, leaving the party structures intact. The anti-Soviet opposition at the end of the 1970s had been able to curb the pro-Soviet policy, it had also been able to liberalize the internal discipline of the party, but the party bureaucracy remained intact. Hence the centralist structures lived on.

It was the women who finally confronted the party with a radically new opposition that disorganized the party bureaucracy by working from both within and without, by demanding the right to organize separately as women, and by uniting at the congress of 1982 under the banner of equal representation for men and women at party congresses and in the Central Committee.[28]

How was this possible? In the first place for the reasons mentioned above: the anti-Soviet opposition had done some useful groundwork.

The feminist movement was relatively unknown to the party militants. Feminists themselves could easily take advantage of the very acceptable slogan of equal representation, but there was something in the structure of the party that added to these factors. The party had, since 1946, its own women's organization, the *Nederlandse Vrouwenbeweging* (NVB), which included, apart from a few non-communist women, the wives of many party members. The NVB position had always been ambivalent. On the one hand, it was the only women's organization that, during the 1950s and 1960s, defended the rights and interests of working class women, but on the other hand it was a typical front organization, for many years effectively led by the Dutch Passionaria, Annie van Ommeren-Averink.

Within the party, on the other hand, the NVB was looked down upon with typical and deep-rooted male chauvinism. Women played an important role in the daily routine of the *afdelingen* but the higher echelons of the party were dominated by their husbands. The Central Committee was a man's world, and those few women who were elected acted accordingly. The female part of the new student generation refused massively to be contained in the NVB, and became active in the party itself, while being forced to neglect the feminist issue. So that for diverse reasons the feminist issue was in fact a non-issue, both in the party and in the NVB. Female party members who raised the issue in the party were referred to the NVB, while in the NVB feminist debates and demands of the recent period were qualified as elitist and bourgeois.[29] When, however, the women in the party refused to accept this Catch-22 situation, both the party and the NVB were in trouble; and when the party allowed feminists a platform, this created an ideological crisis within the NVB. The more so because the feminists, although they attacked the NVB's line, did not attack the women members of the NVB themselves but, on the contrary, tried to win them for their cause.[30]

The gulf between the women of the workers and working women appeared to be not as large as the leadership had reckoned and, more important, by 1980 the representation of workers (let alone their wives) was small (see table 9.1). Male dominance in the Communist Party (expressed, for example in the fact that female party cadres earned even less than their male colleagues) led to a challenge to the party system as such. The feminists profited from the experiences of their sisters who had struggled for equal opportunities in the Labour Party and, at the twenty-eighth party congress of the CPN, not only was a large part of the Central Committee filled with women of the 1968 generation, but also the chair of the party was taken over by a woman, while of the three remaining Communist parliamentary representatives, two were women, one of them a militant lesbian. Traditional party structures crumbled and the party culture underwent a radical change.[31] This change was the result of a coalition between feminists and young party cadres who had been only superficially Stalinized. In this coalition the feminists provided the ideological ammunition, while the party cadres provided the organizational support necessary to 'take over' the party. This time fractionalism was not as easy to attack because it disguised itself as women's platforms or even 'consciousness-raising groups'.

Besides, those female party cadres who tried to contain the feminist tendency by participating in these platforms, pleading for moderate and 'realistic' demands, were themselves carried away by the feminist issue. Furthermore, the demands were also difficult to counter because all that the feminists wanted was 'more women in the Central Committee'. After this had been accomplished at the twenty-eighth congress of November 1982, an ideological struggle was launched with the preparation of a new party programme that was to replace the old programme of 1952.

In an extremely intense and bitter discussion in the party lasting over a year a new programme was accepted that lacked nearly all the elements of the Marxist–Leninist ideology. The very notion of a party ideology was rejected in favour of the concept of a 'programme party'. As a compromise with the old guard Marxism was called 'a source of inspiration', but so was feminism.[32]

For the Bolsheviks, who were under attack, it was not easy to fight back because of the risk of being accused of male chauvinism. Besides, proponents of the pro-Soviet and syndicalist tendency, which overnight became oppositional, suffered from three weaknesses: one strategic, one political and one social. First, they could not decide whether to become an organized opposition within the party (thereby contradicting their own adherence to the principles of democratic centralism and thus conforming to the enemy who had attacked this very principle) or to leave the party and form a new communist party. In fact the pro-Soviet and syndicalist opposition split on this issue. Although the distinction between their positions was far from clear, when, at the extraordinary congress of January/February 1984, Marxism–Leninism was replaced by Marxism–feminism, it was the pro-Soviet opposition that formed a new party, while the syndicalist opposition remained in the CNP. One could even discard this distinction and simply say that the Groningen district remained in the party (because the organization there could still rule its own district with the traditional iron fist), while the opposition in Amsterdam left the party to form the Union of Dutch Communists (VNC).

The two fractions were unanimous in their attack upon *De Waarheid*, which on the whole supported the anti-Stalinist and feminist tendency since 1981 but also tried to become more independent of the party, claiming a 'journalistic independence'. When journalists of *De Waarheid* started a campaign to strengthen relations with the other radical socialist parties, the Pacifist Socialist Party and the Radical Party, and participated in a platform that called for a new political formation of the Left,[33] the syndicalist and pro-Soviet opposition openly campaigned against the party paper. Old party cadres suspended their subscription and in Groningen the distribution of *De Waarheid* was sabotaged. This brought the paper to the brink of collapse, since it was not yet properly accepted as an independent left-wing paper by the non-communist left, while it was already boycotted by the traditional militants who had carried the paper both organizationally and financially through the cold war. The Bolshevik opposition organized itself in the 'Horizontal Overlag van Communisten (HOC)' and started a journal entitled *Manifest*. The circulation of *De Waarheid* dropped from 30,000 in 1979 to less than 10,000 in 1985.[34]

The second weakness of the Bolshevik opposition was that it was caught in the political dilemma of having to defend the Soviet system (at the very moment when the Polish workers, or rather their oppressors, were smashing the last illusions about socialism in the socialist countries) or to attack the feminists in the party. These had been the two main issues in the party struggle and on both issues the Bolshevik opposition was on the defensive. In fact a group of Amsterdam workers who tried to evade this dilemma by taking a narrow syndicalist position failed, since they were squeezed between the two positions.

Thirdly, the position of the opposition was even more gloomy, because it could do nothing to prevent the decline of the traditional industries, from whose workers their support had used to come. Its social base was bound to crumble, whatever strategy and policies were chosen.

In short, the victory of the feminists and anti-Stalinists seemed inevitable, but at the same time it was a Pyrrhic victory. During the party struggle the anti-Stalinist rank and file left the party in great numbers or else became 'paper members', thus creating an interesting paradox. At the very moment when the party liberalized, the members who had always pleaded for such liberalization lost interest in it. How can this paradox be explained?

In a way one could say that a non-Bolshevik communist party is a contradiction in terms. With Bolshevik discipline came also the mobilization and enthusiasm that had been so characteristic of communist parties. In the process of de-Stalinization the party lost the radicalism that had appealed to the generation of the 1960s. As a social democratic formation the tiny CPN could not compete with the Labour Party which now absorbed the disillusioned communist militants. The process of social democratization had been a long and creeping one from 1976 onward, with the influx of students and welfare workers, and it became more intense after these groups had begun to occupy positions in the state apparatus. They provided the party not only with new expertise but also with an administrative perspective and 'sociocratic' practice, which was used in welfare work as a new, 'democratic' and individual-orientated form of social control. Appearances notwithstanding – the party's opposition to the Labour government (1973–7) was, after all, rather extravagant – the process accelerated with the influx of students and welfare workers. This structural development found its political expression when, in 1970, the Communists accepted two posts of 'elderman' on the Council of Amsterdam. In 1975, too, in Groningen and Zaandam, Communist eldermen were nominated. These positions made it possible to recruit Communists in the local state apparatus, with the result, among other things, that the expert opinion of such Communist civil servants became more influential within the party.

Again it was in the welfare departments that communists were most influential. But the process was reciprocal: sociocratic practices penetrated party life. Discipline 'from above' (democratic centralism) was slowly replaced by discipline 'from below'. Mass rallies were not as effective in consensus formation as they used to be. Discussion in small groups where 'emotions can be shown', where 'you feel free' became popular.[35] Thus the power of the sociocrats increased while at the same time the relation between party organization and parliamentary work became looser. The situation in which the party leaders decided what their representatives in parliament and in other councils had to say and to vote for was reversed and became more like the situation typical of social democratic parties. This was expressed, for example, in the refusal of the new parliamentary representatives to donate their salaries to the party, as had hitherto been the rule. For all practical purposes de-Stalinization meant not only the feminization, but also the social democratization of the CPN.

Racism and migrant labour

During the 1980s a new issue has become prominent in the CPN, one that cuts across the cleavage between 'new' and 'old' communists in an interesting way.

As in other Western European countries, migrant workers were recruited from Mediterranean countries from the beginning of the 1960s. By 1977 the number of registered foreign workers totalled 185,000. By that time, the total of Antillian and Surinam people with a Dutch passport was estimated at 134,000.[36] The CPN opposed the recruitment of foreign workers and regarded their presence, at least until 1979, as a temporary phenomenon.

These foreign workers could not, according to the party's statutes, become members of the CPN. This rule, abolished at the twenty-eighth party congress, resulted from the Stalinist idea that foreigners were always potential agents of foreign governments. Thus relations with foreign workers were in a classical communist way restricted to contacts with their respective communist parties.

In a way this reflected the initial perspective of the foreign workers themselves, who predominantly organized themselves along party lines of the country of origin. Especially with workers from countries with strong and well-established communist parties, such as those from Italy and Spain, the contacts were good and the CPN did indeed represent these workers in the Dutch political arena.

However, for those workers who did not come from countries where the communist party formed a stable political force, problems arose. They were not allowed to become members, but neither were there any other institutionalized means of communication. However, it was not only organizational constraints that hampered contact between Dutch communists and foreign workers in Holland. The emphasis on the Dutch identity of the CPN as an ideological shield against the cold war allegations that communists were a fifth column in Dutch society, effectively weakened internationalism in the party culture. In fact, the party pretended to defend Dutch interests rather than working class interests alone, and by doing so became open to chauvinist sentiments.

This is one of the reasons why the party was unable to recruit among the Antillian and Surinam leftists who did not think it a revolutionary duty to march behind the Dutch flag. The Dutch road to socialism tended therefore to become a road to socialism for Dutch workers.[37] Fortunately the CPN did not follow the French Communists in an ethnocentric and even racist policy, but its discourse remained highly ambivalent. Until the 1980s anti-racism was more often than not confined to fighting anti-semitism and recalling the glorious past of the party during the Second World War and its fight against colonialism.

As the race issue became more urgent the pressure within the CPN to do something about it mounted, and in the 1980s the struggle against racism became one of the principal goals of the new CPN. During the extraordinary congress in 1984, it was decided that 'the CPN regards the struggle against exploitation and oppression, based on class, gender and race, as its revolutionary task'.[38] And, for the first time in the history of the Dutch party, the black members united themselves at the end of 1984 in a caucus called 'the black communist'.

This new line has received some publicity because one of the Communist councillors in Amsterdam is a leading woman in the black movement and the Amsterdam municipality itself has emphasized the fight against racism. The new perspective within the party is, however, still weak.

In the preparations for the twenty-ninth congress, for example, the Central Committee still opposed the demand that foreign workers should have the right to vote in parliamentary elections. Officially it was said that there were 'legal problems', but informally it was argued that a foreign constituency may, because of loyalties to the governments of the countries of origin, jeopardize national independence.[39] At the twenty-ninth congress, in March 1985, the Central Committee was outvoted by a large majority, even though its *eminence grise*, Marcus Bakker, defended the Central Committee position. By voting a foreign delegate on to the Central Committee and demanding full voting rights for foreign workers the congress made a historic decision.[40]

This relatively new issue may well become important in the present party struggle because it cuts across the cleavage between 'new' and 'old' communists. Both tendencies pay at least lip-service to the importance of this issue (although there are disagreements on strategic matters between these tendencies), and the black communists themselves tend to adhere to neither one and take an independent position. Such cross-cutting cleavages may increase the turbulence within the party, but it may also reunite opposing factions. In the meantime, however, electoral support has dwindled to a mere 1.2 per cent. As a result, the party lost its parliamentary representation in the May 1986 elections, to its own surprise and to the distress of even its enemies.[41] The end of Bolshevism may well have implied the end of the Dutch Communist Party altogether.

Conclusion

Historical circumstances made the syndicalist and internationalist tendencies within the CPN particularly strong. Paradoxically this created a break with the Soviet Union and led to an independent but internationally isolated position in the 1960s. In turn this position made it relatively easy for the party to support the student movement and this attracted many new student members.

Contrary to what one would expect, these new members were integrated with remarkable success into the Stalinist party structure. Difficulties arose when in the economic crisis decreasing support among the working class became painfully evident in the electoral disaster of 1977. A bid for renewed Bolshevization of the party and rapprochement towards the Soviet Union failed, because the new party cadres were no longer recruited from the working class and were politically unwilling to accept Soviet guidance. The anti-Soviet opposition, however, was not able to do more than liberalize the party discipline and to force the leadership to take a more neutral stance with the Soviet Union. It was the feminist movement that won over the party cadres and delivered a final blow to the democratic centralist structures of the CPN. This meant the end of Dutch Bolshevism and, paradoxically, not only many Bolsheviks but also many anti-Stalinists left the party. In doing so, were they thereby proving that a non-Stalinist communist party is a contradiction in terms?

Notes

1 A. Koper, *Onder de banier van het stalinisme*, (Van Gennep, Amsterdam, 1984); see also F. Claudin, *The Communist Movement. From Comintern to Cominform* (Penguin Books, Harmondsworth, 1975).
2 L. Marcou, *L'internationale après Staline* (Grasset, Paris, 1979), pp. 95–117.
3 The delegation consisted of Paul de Groot, Theun de Vries, Tjalle Jager and Jaap Wolff.
4 The Soviet Union would not, in case of an armed conflict, direct its missiles on the Netherlands (declaration after Dutch delegation had visited Moscow in 1961).
5 Rob Milikowski, 'De autonome politiek van de CPN', in *Komma. Tijdschrift voor politiek en sociaal onderzoek*, vol. II, no. 2, 1979.
6 A. de Leeuw, 'De radicale studenten en het testament van Marx', in *Politiek en Cultuur*, vol. 28, no. 5, May 1968, pp. 203–15.
7 *De Waarheid*, 7 January 1966.
8 G. Schreuders, 'Buitenparlementair en anti-parlementair, in *Politiek en Cultuur*, vol. 30, no. 1, January 1970, pp. 10–18; J. Wolff, 'Studenten-beweging belangrijke factor in strijd voor socialisme', in *Politiek en Cultuur*, vol. 39, no. 3, March 1979, pp. 102–9.
9 G. Harmsen, *Nederlands Kommunisme* (SUN, Nijmegen, 1983), pp. 283–301.
10 See Koper, *Onder de banier*.
11 Even the election polls did not forecast a decline of the Communists.
12 De Groot's attack was prepared at the scientific bureau (IPSO) in collaboration with Jurrie Reiding.
13 *Documentatie bij de stellingen van het 26ste congres van de CPN, deel 3* (CPN, Amsterdam, n.d.).
14 Oral communication Gerard Pothoven.
15 Groningen always had been a somewhat separate district comparable with the Northern districts of the British Communist Party.
16 Especially those who had participated in the Spanish Civil War and those who had refused to fight the colonial war in Indonesia. The former were for a long time without passports, the latter were imprisoned together with the Dutch collaborators and war criminals.

17   See G. Harmsen/B. Reinalda, *Voor de bevrijding van de arbeid* (SUN, Nijmegen, 1975), p. 373.
18   Ibid., p. 384.
19   The radical Arie Groenevelt was strongly anti-communist.
20   Until 1973 the ABVA did not allow Communists to become members. By 1976, however, the chairman of the ABVA university group in Amsterdam was a communist.
21   *100 Jaar uitbuiting in de strokarton* (SUN, Nijmegen, n.d.).
22   Centralism has been very strong in Dutch unions, especially between 1945 and 1970. See John P. Windmuller, *Labor Relations in the Netherlands* (Cornell University Press, Ithaca, NY, 1969).
23   Oral communication from Gerard Pothoven. According to Pothoven this expansion starts in 1972 and goes on until 1979.
24   The article had been sent to *Le Monde* but not accepted.
25   Formally the CPN did not have a Central Committee but a 'partijbestuur'.
26   See *Verslag van het 26e partijcongres* (CPN, Amsterdam, n.d.).
27   *Politiek en Cultuur*, April 1979.
28   *Verslag van het 28ste partijcongres* (CPN, Amsterdam, n.d.).
29   See for an interesting analysis of the NVB, Jolande Withuis, 'Opoffering en heroiek. De NVB in de Koude Oorlog', *Socialistische-Feministische Teksten*, 8/1984, pp. 65–106.
30   A study on feminism in the CPN is in progress. See for a critical internal evaluation: *Heksentoer, Over strategie en struktuur van CPN-vrouwen* (CPN, Amsterdam, 1984).
31   The ideology of 'feminist organization', which was supposed to consist of non-oppressive discussion and decision-making, particularly made inroads in to the party culture.
32   *Partijprogram van de CPN*. CPN Brochure-handel (CPN, Amsterdam, 1984), p. 15. The theoretical basis of this programme can be found in A. Benschop, *Voor een vrijheidslievend en democratisch communisme*. Brochurehandel CPN, 1984. See also Paul Lucardie, 'De recente programmatische vernieuwing van de CPN', *Jaarboek DCPP*, 1985.
33   De 'Doorbraakgroep' was formed in 1983.
34   See *De Groene Amsterdammer*, 27 February 1985. Figures presented here are not consistent with those given by Gerard Pothoven.
35   For a critique of sociocracy, see Anneke van Baalen/Marijke Ekelschot, *Tegennatuurlijk* (De Bonte Was, Amsterdam, 1985).
36   Netherlands Scientific Council of Government Policy, *Ethnic Minorities* (The Hague, 1979).
37   M. Hisschemoller, 'Oude tradities en nieuwe obstakels', *Komma* vol. 5, no. 1, pp. 85–109.
38   See n. 32.
39   *CPN ledenkrant februari 1985*. Beschrijvingsbrief 2, 29ste Congres (CPN, Amsterdam), p. 7.
40   See *De Waarheid*, 4 March 1985.
41   See D. Hellema (ed.), *Crisis in het Nederlandse communisme* (Jan Mets, Amsterdam, 1986).

10 The Price of Delayed Adaptation
The Communist Party of Belgium

Marcel Hotterbeex

It is conventional to preface any discussion of politics in Belgium with a reference to that society's divided nature. The Communist Party of Belgium (*Parti communiste de Belgique* – PCB; the Flemish form is *Kommunistische Partij van Belgie*) has not been immune to the tensions between the French-speaking and the Flemish-speaking communities, but it has maintained its unity. In fact, the problems that beset the PCB in the present period stem less from this factor than from others that resemble the problems of other communist parties in other, less divided, societies.

Certain very general features of the PCB are worth noting before passing to a closer examination of the party's internal functioning, its place within the political system of Belgium, its stance in international affairs and its electoral record.

The Belgian workers' movement as a whole has always been noted for its pragmatism and its more or less conscious refusal to enter into great ideological discussions. The Communist Party of Belgium has duly followed that trend. For a considerable time there was a struggle within the party to make good this deficiency but, at present, the members of the PCB are little given to theorizing and, except in the preparations for a congress, scarcely any reference is made to Marxism.

A second feature of the PCB is one that it shares with all Belgian political organizations. The internal development of the political parties, and in particular that of the BCP, has been quite independent of international affairs. The latter serve as a cover or pretext for supporting or combating internal developments, but they are never the cause of those developments. The process of de-Stalinization that has shaken almost every communist party serves as an example of this. When this question first arose within the PCB, the party had already sorted out all its internal problems and de-Stalinization was merely used to justify an existing situation.

A third general factor that aids an understanding of the way in which the PCB functions is the self-discipline of the membership when the unity of the party is threatened. As the phrase goes: 'Guard the unity of the party as the apple of your eye'. There is no reason to suppose, as many unthinkingly do, that this is an imposed discipline; it is one that arises from a deeply held conviction on the part of the vast majority of the party members, even if this conviction is beginning to lose its sway. This attitude to unity explains why the PCB, seen from the outside, seems somewhat immobile. In point of fact, what is apparent to the observer is only the result of previous deliberations. A decision taken against a 40 per cent opposition will present the same outward aspect as a decision taken unanimously. This explains also why the victory of one faction over another is always very spectacular.

There is a fourth point to bear in mind – the small size and the isolation of the PCB. The diminishing size of the party has become particularly marked in recent years. It really seems as if it is about to drop below the level under which, with the best will in the world, a certain number of political actions can no longer be performed. This situation has discouraged many militants, even those of the longest standing. The party presents the classic image of a snake swallowing its own tail.

This reduction in size, moreover, has made it easier for the party to be squeezed out of many areas of political life, and has also made easier the task of those who, on the Right and on the Left, strive daily for the marginalization of the Communist Party through censorship in the media, and manipulation in political institutions. Admittedly the party must fault itself to some extent for this, but external causes have been just as much to blame.

Other factors, less specifically concerned with the PCB, ought also to be taken into account. For example, the gradual conversion of the majority of voters into an electoral clientele that expects from political parties a fair return for their vote disadvantages a party that has not exercised governmental power for 37 years and has no immediate prospect of doing so. Another important development is the growing power of persuasion in the hands of the mass media, from which the PCB is systematically excluded.

These introductory remarks are intended simply as background to the material that follows.

The internal functioning of the party

The organization of the Communist Party of Belgium is the familiar classic pyramid, with cells and sections at the base, then a federation level, and finally a central level comprising the Central Committee and the Political Bureau.

The basic level is like a trellis: a lot of holes, with a certain number of strong points. The cells and sections are particularly active in the three provinces of Brabant, Hainaut, Liège and in the regions of Ghent and Antwerp. However, the degree to which basic organizations are active or exist at all is extremely variable – though this is not peculiar to the PCB. At present, all political organizations in the country are passing through a crisis of implantation and membership. What makes this particularly hard for the Communist Party is its small size, which magnifies the problem of implantation.

The federal level is subject to the same problems but at times is called on to play a special role. This is particularly the case with the smaller federations, where it sometimes happens that, faced with the apparent absence of basic level organizations, the federal level substitutes itself for them to guarantee the party's continuity.

The Central Committee is usually presented as the governing body of the party, but as in any structure of this nature, this image departs a good way from the reality. The Central Committee exercises pressure, sometimes strong, on the Political Bureau, but it is clearly the latter that determines the day-to-day policy of the party. Moreover, over the past ten years and more there has been a noticeable immobility in the leading bodies of the PCB. For example, the chairman, Van Geyt, has held that office without interruption since 1972. The only innovation that has taken place from the organizational point of view has been the creation of 'federal' structures.

Unlike all the other conventional political parties in Belgium, the PCB still remains today a single national party and not two parties representing the two communities, one Flemish and one francophone. The furthest the party has gone has been to introduce into its organization structures that reproduce, more or less, the structural reforms that have been made within Belgium as a whole to accommodate the conflicting interests of the two linguistic communities. Although the moves had been planned for many years, it was 1971 that saw the real development in the party of separate structures for the French-speaking Walloons, for the Flemish and for Brussels – structures, that is, that represent both regions and communities. It took a long time to create these structures and the party congress of 1982 brought further adjustments. Not only is the old reflex for a unitary form still very

strong, but the existence of profound divergences within the francophone wing led the leadership to delay these new arrangements for as
long as possible.

The experience of the PCB in relation to the formation and activity of
fractions is worth recording. The term 'fraction' is chiefly used in
communist parties when the leadership wants to get rid of adversaries or
an opposition without embarking upon too wide-ranging a campaign of
justification. If, however, one looks beyond this simple level of in-
fighting within the party, the term can be seen to have a rather precise
meaning, with two components. For a fraction to exist there must be, at
one and the same time, basic divergences on important parts of the
political programme, and secondly, a distinct organization separate from
that of the party, often accompanied by an independent press and by a
political life that parallels that of the party (and is often carried on to the
detriment of the party).

It is this second condition that has never been met in the case of the
PCB. There have been many divergences, but there has never been an
organization within the party enjoying a discipline distinct from that of
the party. Members of the PCB who have disagreed profoundly with the
policies espoused by the party leadership have chosen between three
courses of action. Most of them have expressed their disagreement within
the party's organizations whilst respecting, in the main, the party's
norms ('in the main' here means 'at least to the same extent as the leadership'). A much smaller number have elected to express their disagreement by forming structures outside the party. Such was the case with
René Noël who, at the beginning and at the end of the Democratic and
Popular Unity episode (on which more will be said below), found himself
in disagreement with the party. A further very small number have
preferred to leave the party, some of them to join other political formations (for example the Socialist Party, or the Rassemblement Wallon);
others have remained aloof from all political parties.

There are differences, they are often very profound, but they are
accommodated within the party's structures. However, this simple statement should not mislead. What we are dealing with is first and foremost
a matter of the play of personalities and the exercise of power. Louis van
Geyt's accession to the chairmanship of the party was accompanied by
the installation in positions of power of a group of leaders made up for
the most part of intellectuals, people in public service and a few workers
who held jobs as party or trade union officials. It was the exercise and
the retention of power that welded this group together. It was composed
chiefly of people from Brussels and Hainaut with some from Liège
whose real home was Brussels. This group found itself in direct conflict
with those who, in the party's parlance, are known as 'the Liègeois' –that

is to say leaders who originate from the province of Liège. This conflict between regional groups has considerably perturbed the life of the party, but the ideological quarrels that have accompanied the conflict do not in themselves explain what is at the root of these disputes.

It was shown above that the evolution of the PCB has been the product of internal factors. There is no direct link, therefore, between the present international economic crisis and the crisis within the PCB. On the other hand, there have been indirect consequences, and the most important of these, in my view, are the following.

First, the national economic crisis poses problems of such a magnitude that the BCP (nor is it alone in this) experiences ever greater difficulty in proposing credible solutions. Secondly, the running-down of the industrial base in Wallonia has had the effect of sharply reducing the milieux in which the PCB can engage in activity and recruitment – in the steel producing areas, for example. Thirdly, a generalized impoverishment and social repression have created a climate of withdrawal and resignation of a kind that has not been favourable to political militancy, particularly a militancy so demanding as that of the PCB. And finally, the unbridled growth of political patronage discriminates against those parties that do not exercise governmental power and have no hope of doing so.

Turning now to changes in the social composition of the party, there are no reliable statistics that would enable one to draw a full picture of the party's evolution. It is, however, possible to discern a certain number of clear trends.

The proportion of women in the party's leading organs remains minimal. There are none in the Political Bureau, there is one in the Walloon Federal Bureau, there are none in the federal secretariats, and only 15 per cent of the Central Committee are women. In the working class federations, the number of workers who are members of the party is constantly diminishing. It can be seen from unpublished surveys on the legislative elections of 1977, 1978 and 1980 that the social composition of the PCB was as follows, in order of diminishing size: the largest group comprised intellectuals, then came public employees, then workers and then, far behind, the other social categories. In the 1981 elections the PCB suffered serious defeats in the working class cantons. It is clear that the most important change in the social composition of the party is the dwindling of its working class base.

The problem of the relationship between the intelligentsia and workers within the party has today lost its salience, and one has to look hard to find traces of it. However, its disappearance has to be attributed to two quite distinct causes. The first is the development, in the provinces of Hainaut and Liège for the most part, of a truly shared working relationship between worker and intellectual militants. This relationship has been strongly reinforced by the numerous strikes and trade union actions of the past ten years. The two groups have their particularities but, in the main, they have fought together and a real mutual understanding has developed between them. The second cause (best illustrated, for example, in Brussels) is simply the very much reduced number of workers in the party. In this case, no conflict is really possible, given the virtual non-existence of one of the potential antagonists.

Relations with other parties and pressure groups

The attitude of the Communist Party of Belgium towards the Socialist Party has always oscillated. At times the BCP acknowledges that the greater part of the working class will rally politically to the banner of the Socialist Party and that the latter follows basically left-wing policies. At other times an awareness comes to the fore that when the 'socialist leaders' are in power they 'make pacts with the class enemy' and 'betray the working class and the interests of the people in general'. A study of the way in which the PCB has alternated between these two views would constitute a good part of its history.

When, in 1969, the Socialist president Léo Collard launched his celebrated appeal for a 'progressive union' he aroused great hopes. At last a clear vision of unity was being offered to the Left as a whole, coupled with a respect for the particular identity of each political organization. Very soon the level of disappointment was as high as that of hopes had been, and no one could any longer doubt that the 'progressive union' was being transformed into a vague offer of integration into the Socialist Party.

It was then that an initiative arising in the Mons region made a timely appearance and suggested another tactic for the PCB to follow. This was the experiment associated with the name of René Noël, the Communist mayor of Cuesmes – a little commune in the region of Mons. Talking advantage of the merging of communes that was happening at the time, Noël presented a list called the 'Democratic and Progressive Union' in the local elections. This list included Communists, Christian trade unionists and independent socialists. In political terms, the aim of this list was to get a grip on the Socialists and force them to honour their promise of bringing about a 'progressive union'. This list met with instant success, and Léo Collard, who was mayor of Mons, thereupon put together a majority on the local council.

But now that the Socialists and the DPU enjoyed a joint majority, Léo Collard – the man who had been responsible for the appeal for a 'progressive union' – managed to assert the domination of the Catholic Party within this new majority. This example illustrates well the limits that the Socialist Party sets on a union of the left. The electoral success was a shock for the Communist Party, and above all for its national leadership, which had given hardly any support to René Noël. Very swiftly the question spilled over from the Mons region and affected the party as a whole – this was the renowned question of alliances. In general terms the initiative received a positive welcome, for electoral success was to everyone's liking. But serious problems surfaced when the national leadership made a sharp turn and set out to elevate the ideas behind the DPU into a new credo.

The principal impediments to the successful establishment of the DPU were, first, the process of consolidation that took place within that organization; at the outset it did not wish to be a new political party, but it found that, objectively, it could not avoid becoming one. Secondly, the alliances with other political formations, some of which were well-established, whilst others were created for the new circumstances (the GPTC – the Political Group of Christian Workers; the MAS – the Movement for Socialist Action) created problems, since all of these had in common an anti-communism of a more or less explicit kind. A third impediment was the very sectarian nature of the PCB's hostility to the Socialist Party. Finally, there were real divergences when it came to analysis of the electoral situation, and particularly in assessments of the real influence of René Noël's political stance and personality.

However, with the encouragement of the national leadership, the DPU was brought into being in the provinces of Hainaut, Namur, Brabant and in Flanders, and presented electoral lists in alliance with the BCP. The results were everywhere disappointing for the CBP (with or without the DPU). Since the DPU's chief *raison d'être* had been to achieve electoral success, the outcome was as might be expected, and, except in Mons, the DPU is now little more than a memory.

Nevertheless, at the level of electoral politics, there are still some traces left of the DPU. Whilst up to that point the small parties (such as the Trotskyists) had been firmly excluded from the PCB's electoral alliances, there are still now one or two alliances of this type to be found. At present, the effect of this experiment on relations with the Socialist Party has been nil. There are in fact no relations worthy of that name between the Socialist Party and the PCB, except in specific places and at specific times – as on issues of peace and disarmament.

The party's relationship with the trade unions and with student movements has been affected by the structure of Belgian trade unions. These are divided into numerous branches, but there are two umbrella organizations: the socialist FGTB and the Catholic CSC. The Communist Party has always maintained that its members should belong to trade unions. Originally, it required that they should belong to the FGTB exclusively. Nowadays, however, whilst membership of the FGTB is preferred, affiliation to the CSC is tolerated. The party makes available to the trade union movement a proportionately large number of militants. These are numerous at grass-roots level, but thin out as one proceeds up the trade union hierarchy; there is no Communist in the national leadership of the FGTB – nor, be it said, is this accidental.

In its political activity, for example at parliamentary level, the PCB acts as a channel for, and supports, trade union demands. This is true also at local level, for example in commune councils.

The trade union movement poses a number of problems for the PCB. The party must decide what relations to maintain with the trade unions when the trade union leadership, in the eyes of the party, acts against the interests of the population. Secondly, a way has to be found of reconciling in an organic way the experience and policies of 'politicians' and 'syndicalists'. The first problem closely resembles that posed by relations with the Socialist Party and is often parallel with it. The second illustrates the effects of a kind of 'membership specialization', which, if the party neglects its ideological work, leads swiftly to mutual incomprehension. These two problems have up to now never found a general solution and are dealt with in piecemeal fashion as they arise.

Links with the student movement are maintained specifically through the UNEC (the National Union of Communist Students), which enjoys a certain autonomy in this domain. The party's cells sometimes play a role in the universities, but the national leadership has no constant policy in this area.

The feminist movement in Belgium does not have a truly independent form. Only a few isolated and not very significant initiatives at the mass level have had an enduring existence. Women's demands are made, in a permanent manner, by the party's women's organizations, by the trade unions and by professional organizations. To this end the BCP has a Women's Commission that organizes and coordinates activity in this sphere. The situation has not moved forward in the period under review.

The Ecologists present an obvious problem for the PCB, first of all because in electoral terms the Ecologists are in the process of replacing the PCB on the political map of Belgium. Secondly, the Ecologists' programme and political activity, at least at first sight, fall outside the normal realm of politics. The day after the European elections of 1984, Communist Party chairman Van Geyt categorized the Ecologists as progressives. It should be noted that if there are hardly any relations between the Communist and Ecology parties, this is due in no small part to the policy of the Ecologists in maintaining their distance from the Communists.

The party's ideological position on international affairs

A good part of the present leadership of the Communist Party of Belgium is made up of old-style 'Stalinists' who have been embittered by the various 'revelations' concerning the socialist countries and above all by their own failures, the responsibility for which they are anxious to pass on to others. Among the younger leaders, on the other hand, quite a wide range of tendencies can be discerned, having as a common denominator a wish to disassociate themselves from the socialist countries and their experiences.

For the PCB all international questions, including the most central ones such as the problem of peace, are coloured by the image the party has of the socialist countries. In order to understand how the PCB reaches a standpoint on any international matter, consider the following process. First, a problem arises that concerns the socialist countries. A first policy position is adopted at the level of the Political Bureau or the Central Committee. This usually involves a statement condemning, in cautious terms, 'restrictions on political liberties', but one that takes into account the susceptibilities of any internal opposition. No further initiatives are taken at the official level, but members of the leadership, either as individuals or within other organizations, take part in or themselves embark upon various initiatives. These initiatives provoke reactions from internal opposition groups. The situation develops and at times the divergences between the initiatives give rise to problems and questions that are neither decided nor even confronted. The result is that the whole question comes to be enveloped in the utmost uncertainty.

The issue of Eurocommunism is a clear example of this state of uncertainty in which the PCB drifts. In the words of the chairman of the party himself, the PCB is not Eurocommunist; but neither does he condemn Eurocommunism. Yet, when you look in detail at the various positions that are held within the PCB, you discover that virtually all the elements that constitute Eurocommunism are to be found in the party. The way in which the problem of pacifist organizations has been dealt with is another aspect of the evolution of the PCB. Up until 1980, these organizations defended a line on peace that was close to that of the World Peace Council. Members of the Communist Party who were members of these groups supported this point of view. But since then there has been a very noticeable shift. Party members close to the national leadership have come to regard both superpowers as responsible for the arms race, and not only the USA; and they have joined with others in a move to withdraw from the World Peace Council. Communist militants who do not wish to support this new orientation are at present the object of systematic harassment and insults.

The electoral record of the Communist Party

In electoral constituencies where the DPU has not stood for election, the electoral record of the PCB presents no problems of analysis, since the whole series of elections can be studied. This is the case with the province of Liège and its various subdivisions.

On the other hand, where the DPU has stood, the category 'Communist Party alone' in the electoral record does cause certain problems. The series of elections before the DPU stood can be taken as a base – that is, those between 1950 and 1971 – in which case 1978 becomes a starting point for a distinct later series, or a single case. Or else a theoretical series of nine elections can be constituted, comprising those from 1950 to 1971, plus those of 1978 and 1981, in which case the elections of 1974 and 1977 have to be ignored. In our view there is no good reason for preferring one base to the other; each contributes to an interpretation of the record. The series prior to the DPU (1950–71) allows one to examine the electoral performance of the PCB before the DPU lists were presented, and also to relate these DPU lists to the way in which the Communist Party's electorate developed. On the other hand, the theoretical series of nine elections offers an opportunity to compare overall the performance of the 'Communist Party alone' lists and those of the DPU.

I shall follow convention and allow that election results for the Kingdom and Wallonia give a balanced picture for the various competitors, whether it be the PCB, the PCB and the DPU together, or the DPU, since the performance of each of these lists was more or less even.

In elections in the Kingdom, the evolution of the Communist vote can be described in two phases. The first runs from 1950 to 1958 inclusive, and sees a steady fall from 4.74 per cent to 1.89 per cent, the latter figure being the lowest since the Second World War. Figures from 1961 follow a sinus curve, with a maximum of 4.54 per cent in 1965 and a minimum of 1.18 per cent in 1985. The average of this second period is 3.24 per cent. It is very close to the overall average for 1950–78, which is 3.34 per cent, and it corresponds closely enough to the results of 1961, 1971, 1974 and 1978 (with a variation of under 10 per cent on average).

For Wallonia, the evolution of the vote is substantially the same as that in the Kingdom. It falls from 7.91 per cent in 1950 to 4.55 per cent in

1958. Thereafter, it varies between 9.70 per cent in 1965 and 4.24 in 1981. The average of this second phase is 6.28 per cent. This average is also very close to the overall average, which is 6.33 per cent. The sub-series 1971–8 is also worth looking at. It shows an average of 5.74 per cent with a typical variation of only 4 per cent of the average, which is rather remarkable for the PCB, whose vote has tended to fluctuate considerably. This sub-series is interesting, since it indicates a tendency towards a stabilization of the electoral record, which is not continued after 1981. At the level of the Kingdom, this sub-series gives an average of 3.07. It should be noted also that in the Kingdom no result in the second phase reaches the results of 1950, whilst in Wallonia the results for 1965 exceed those of 1950 by 23 per cent.

In the electoral district of Liège province the electoral record of the Communist Party follows, in general, a similar curve. The fall from 1950 to 1958 is from 8.60 per cent to 5.27 per cent. However, this last result, which is the lowest in the period from 1950 to 1978, is very nearly reached in 1971 and 1974. The period of wide variation from 1961 to 1978 shows an average of 6.79 per cent (with a typical variation of 27 per cent of the average) and the sub-period 1971–8 gives an average of 5.53 per cent, with a typical variation of 5 per cent of the average. The year 1981 produced the worst result of all, with 4.10 per cent. The overall average practically coincides with the average of the second period. The electoral record fluctuates wildly, with a lurch from a loss of 32 per cent of the electorate to a gain of 58 per cent.

The figures for the province of Hainaut are higher than those for Liège, and follow a higher curve, but for the main part the variations are of the same order. The period from 1961 to 1978 shows an average of 9.08 per cent. This average was never to be reached again after 1971, whilst the 1981 result is two-thirds of this average.

There is no correlation between the votes for the Socialist Party and the Communist Party in the electoral districts of the Kingdom, Wallonia, Liège (province), Liège (*arrondissement*), Liège (canton), Liège (city communes).

In sum, the vote for the PCB's lists follows a falling curve from 1950 to 1958 (this last election being in many places the worst result for the whole period 1950–78), then it peaks in 1965, with another fall towards a stable period from 1971 to 1978. The year 1981 marks a new electoral setback, with an absolute minimum recorded in many regions.

Geographically, the PCB shows interesting electoral results in the provinces of Hainaut and Liège, as well as in the Brussels region. In Flanders, the results are of interest in Ghent and Antwerp, at approximately 3 per cent in 1981.

Table 10.1 Electoral record of the Communist Party of Belgium, 1950–81: Chamber of Deputies

Electoral district		1950 (%)	1954 (%)	1958 (%)	1961 (%)	1965 (%)	1968 (%)	1971 (%)	1974[a,b] (%)	1977[a] (%)	1978 (%)	1981 (%)	1985 (%)
Hainaut (Province)	PC	9.61	8.53	6.14	8.93	11.23	9.37	9.14	—	—	8.70	6.31	3.64
	UDP								8.70	7.50			—
Liège (Province)	PC	8.60	7.66	5.27	6.18	10.23	7.52	5.31	5.30	5.80	5.70	4.10	2.62
Kingdom	PC	4.74	3.57	1.89	3.08	4.54	3.29	3.08	3.22	2.72	3.25	2.31	1.18
Brussels (Conurbation)	PC	5.49	3.72	2.73	3.56	4.12	2.40	2.81	4.00	2.45	2.80	2.10	1.95
Wallonia	PC	7.91	6.77	4.55	6.48	9.70	7.02	5.92	5.85	5.38	5.82	4.24	3.20

a For 1974 and 1977, the figures for the Communist Party also contain those for the DPU.
b Source: J. Beaufays, 'Analyse des résultats des élections législatives belges du 10 mars 1974', in *Annales de la Faculté de Droit de Liège*, 1974, super-numerary number (Conference of francophone political scientists), pp. 167–204; and *Atlas électoral du CADOP* (University of Liège)

Conclusions

The Communist Party of Belgium seems, then, from 1968 to 1984, to have suffered an internal crisis and not to have been able to separate out all the different aspects of that crisis. On the ideological plane its evolution has been like that of most Western European communist parties; it has kept its distance, more or less clearly, from the experience of the socialist countries and has taken refuge in a rather narrow nationalism. But this position is especially difficult to maintain in the case of Belgium because this nationalism is strongly contested within the party, the PCB itself having only partially adapted to the country's regional and community reforms.

From the point of view of size, electoral returns and the quality of its theory, the Belgian Communist Party is constantly diminishing, and seems to be slipping deeper and deeper into a pervasive gloom. The party's decline in the country's day-to-day life can be judged by the fact that it no longer even serves it enemies as a bogey. In fact, anti-communism in Belgium is rather an international matter; on the internal level it only operates in local or personal terms (at which two levels it does still retain a persistent vigour).

Unless there is some revival of the party's fortunes – a revival of which, it must be said, there are few visible signs – the Belgian Communist Party appears to be condemned to feature on the political map of Belgium as no more than a marginal formation.

11 A Red Herring in a West European Sea?
The Communist Party of West Germany

Paul Lucardie

This chapter deals with the West German Communist Party (*Deutsche Kommunistische Partei*, DKP) founded in 1968 as a successor to the Communist Party of Germany (*Kommunistische Partei Deutschlands*, KPD), which was banned in 1956. It does not deal with other successors of the KPD, such as the East German Socialist Unity Party (*Sozialistische Einheitspartei Deutschlands*, SED) or the West Berlin Socialist Unity Party. Yet a few comments on the history of the KPD are needed in order to explain the origins of the DKP. This historical survey of KPD and DKP will be followed by a description of the party's culture and organization and its relations with other parties and movements.

The predecessor of the DKP: the KPD (1918–68)

Whereas the DKP is one of the smallest communist parties in Western Europe, its predecessor was at one time the largest, in terms of members and votes. The history of the KPD was marked by three traumatic events: the 'abortive revolution' of 1918/19, the Nazi 'counter-revolution' of 1933 and the division of Germany in 1945–9.

The KPD was founded by small groups at the fringe of the Social Democratic party (SPD) at the end of the revolutionary year 1918. Common opposition to the pro-war policy and to the growing reformism of the SPD united these groups. Ideologically they were far from united; some leaned towards a libertarian or ultra-leftist communism, others towards 'orthodox' Marxist socialism. When the clash came in 1920, the latter prevailed. Through a merger with the left wing of the Independent Social Democratic Party – which had split from the SPD because of the war policy – the KPD developed into a mass party. The revolutionary fervour subsided, but not the massive resentment against the 'treason' of the Social Democrats who had repressed the revolutionary action with the help of right-wing military forces. The Communist party articulated this resentment. Until 1933 it fought both the social and the political system of the Weimar republic, even if it took part in elections and in local or provincial governments.[1]

Whereas the SPD embraced parliamentary democracy in general and the Weimar Republic in particular, the KPD maintained a critical attitude towards both. The gap between SPD and KPD became even wider when the latter was 'Bolshevized' and 'Stalinized' in the late 1920s. They clashed not only in parliament and in the workplace – Communists set up factory cells as well as Red Trade Unions – but also in the streets, where Communist militia men battled with Social Democrats. The rise of National Socialism did not stop them; at times the Communists even cooperated with the Nazis against the Social Democrats.[2] More often the Communists fought the Nazis, too. Street battles between Communist Red Front Fighters and SA Storm Troopers took hundreds of lives. The polarization of German politics may have benefited the KPD – though not as much as it benefited the NSDAP (National Socialist Party). The rapidly growing mass of unemployed workers often turned to the KPD instead of the SPD. In 1928 the SPD won 30 per cent of the popular vote, the KPD little more than 10 per cent. At the elections of November 1932 they came very close: 20 per cent and 17 per cent respectively. However, the Nazis were the real winners, with 33 per cent of the vote and a few months later they came to power and destroyed both the SPD and KPD. The Communists suffered probably more than any other party: about half of the 300,000 party members were imprisoned, tortured and sent to concentration camps; about 10,000 were killed. A few leaders managed to escape to the Soviet Union or to Western countries.[3]

When the Nazi regime collapsed in 1945, these leaders returned to Germany to rebuild and renew the KPD. In East Germany, which was occupied by Soviet forces, Communists and Social Democrats merged – under some pressure – into a new Socialist Unity Party (*Sozialistische Einheitspartei Deutschlands*, SED) in April 1946. Initially it claimed to pursue a 'German road to socialism' rather than the Soviet road, but in the cold war it sided unambiguously with the Soviet Union.[4] In West Germany, which was occupied by American, British and French forces, the Social Democrats refused to merge with the Communists. In vain the Communist party tried to broaden its base, proposing to change its name into 'Socialist People's Party' – the authorities only allowed the name

'Communist Party of Germany' (KPD). Its isolation increased during the cold war, when it took a strong pro-Soviet position and expelled any 'neutralist' or 'Titoist' elements from its ranks.[5]

Naturally the KPD opposed the foundation of the Federal Republic, which consolidated the division of Germany into a pro-Soviet and Communist-led eastern state and a pro-American and 'bourgeois' western state. In a Platform for National Reunification the KPD called for 'the overthrow of the Adenauer regime'.[6]

This platform, adopted by the executive committee of the party in 1952, provided the constitutional court of the Federal Republic with important evidence to ban the KPD in August 1956, by request of the government led by Adenauer.[7] Yet the KPD did not engage in revolutionary action, apart from organizing a mass petition against rearmament. Its close cooperation with the East German SED, however, and its loyalty towards the Soviet Union had made it rather unpopular in West Germany. At the first elections for the *Bundestag* (the federal parliament) in 1949 it won 5.7 per cent of the popular vote, but at the second elections in 1953 it received only 2.2 per cent. Membership went down from about 300,000 in 1946 to 185,000 in 1950 and 70,000 in 1956.[8] In March 1956 the party began to modify its 'revolutionary' course – inspired by de-Stalinization in the Soviet Union – but failed to impress the court. The KPD was considered a threat to the free democratic order of the Federal Republic. Many leaders received prison sentences of two or three years. In fact, legal repression had started already in 1951 with the dissolution of the communist youth organization Free German Youth. Between 1951 and 1966 more than 6,000 Communists were tried for treason or subversion of the state ('*Staatsgefährdung*').[9]

The prohibition and persecution of the KPD may have served to prove West German loyalty to the Western alliance and to legitimize the political system of the Federal Republic in general and the hegemony of the Christian Democratic party in particular.[10] It did not contribute to the popularity of the Communists: membership in the illegal KPD fell to about 7,000 by 1967, according to intelligence reports.[11] Communist participation in electoral alliances and in the German Peace Union did not result in electoral gains – unlike, for example, in Greece, where the Communist Party was banned after the Civil War and participated in a fairly successful alliance between 1951 and 1967.[12]

As in 1933, most KPD leaders fled abroad in 1956. In 1957 and 1963 the party held its congresses in the German Democratic Republic. In 1963 it adopted a new platform, advocating a peaceful transition to socialism in West Germany, 'on the basis of the constitution' but 'inspired by the example of the German Democratic Republic'.[13] The West German party members devoted their energy mainly to propaganda for the GDR and for re-legalization of the KPD. The ban has never been lifted; but in 1968 the Federal Government made it clear that it would not prevent the foundation of a new communist party. Perhaps it cherished the hope that a new communist party would divide or at least channel the 'Extra-parliamentary Opposition' (ApO) which had come into being in the 1960s.[14]

The Extra-parliamentary Opposition was a loose coalition of trade unionists, left-wing Social Democrats, liberal intellectuals and radical student groups. The most active forces were the Socialist German Student League (*Sozialistische Deutsche Studentenbund*, SDS) and the Campaign for Democracy and Disarmament. The latter had been founded in 1960 by pacifists and leftists who objected to German rearmament and to nuclear arms in particular. Communists played an important part in it.[15] The SDS had started in 1946 as a social democratic student organization, but refused to follow the SPD on its revisionist road to 'Bad Godesberg'. While the SPD began to promote a more loyal student organization – the *Sozialdemokratische Hochschulbund* (SHB) – the SDS rediscovered Marx. A majority interpreted Marx in the light of the Frankfurt School (Horkheimer, Adorno, Marcuse), but a minority turned to traditional Marxism. In 1968 the leaders of the minority were expelled from the SDS. Early in 1969 they founded the Association of Marxist Students, later to be called the Marxist Student League – '*Spartakus*'.[16] The SDS did not benefit from this purge. It disintegrated into a bewildering variety of conflicting ideological factions, women's groups and faculty cells; it dissolved itself officially in March 1970. Some of its members retained a libertarian neo-Marxist perspective, others tried to organize new Marxist–Leninist or Maoist workers' parties – often imitating the old KPD, even in their name: '*Kommunistische Partei Deutschlands/Marxisten–Leninisten*', '*Kommunistische Partei Deutschlands/Aufbauorganisation*' ('constructing organization') and the like.[17]

With the SDS the Extra-parliamentary Opposition collapsed as well. It had failed to achieve its first objective: to prevent the Emergency Laws proposed by a coalition of Christian Democrats and Social Democrats from being enacted. In May 1968 these laws passed parliament.[18] Fragments and ideas from the movement survived, however, in the left wing of the SPD and in independent groups such as the Socialist Bureau. In the 1970s and early 1980s they would contribute to a new opposition movement, the *Bürger-Initiativen* or 'civic action groups' against pollution, nuclear power, nuclear arms and other issues. Quite a different fragment ended up in the new German Communist Party, which was founded at the end of 1968.

The DKP from 1968 to 1987: ideology and strategy

The new German Communist party (DKP) could be considered the heir of both the old KPD and of the traditionalist wing of the Extraparliamentary Opposition and the SDS in particular. The old KPD had by 1968 shrunk to a cadre of about 6,000, mostly older industrial workers; the Extra-parliamentary Opposition could count on tens of thousands of young intellectuals, students and some workers.[19] One might have expected ideological conflicts between the two groups within the party, but they seem to have been few and far between. Initially some young members objected to the party discipline.[20] There were also debates over the Soviet intervention in Czechoslovakia.[21] On the whole, the leadership of the party was left firmly in the hands of former KPD cadres. At the first party congress at Essen in 1969 Kurt Bachmann was elected chairman. Born in 1909, he trained as a leather worker and had joined the KPD in 1932. He spent most of the war years in a concentration camp and many post-war years in East Germany. Herbert Mies became vice-chairman; born in 1929, he is an electro-technical worker, who joined the KPD in 1945 and led the Free German Youth office until 1956, studied economics in Moscow and went to East Germany in 1959. In 1973 he was to succeed Bachmann as chairman of the party.[22]

Loyalty to the Soviet Union and to Leninist principles was asserted even at the press conference at Frankfurt in September 1968, when the founding committee announced the establishment of the party.[23] It was confirmed at the first party congress. Factory groups (*Betriebsgruppen*) were given high priority – especially after the disappointing experience with the elections of 1969 when an alliance of the DKP with other small leftist groups polled only 0.6 per cent of the popular vote. The spontaneous strike wave of September 1969 seemed to confirm the validity of Marxist–Leninist principles: the working class did still resist capitalism. Between 1969 and 1971 factory groups were established in about 400 (mostly industrial) firms. They enjoyed the same rights within the party as local groups (*Wohngebietsgruppen*). In giving some priority to factory groups, the DKP revived a KPD tradition; but the KPD had still 1,400 factory cells in 1956, whereas the DKP never managed many more than 500. Quite likely their number could not grow much further, owing to the economic recession and repressive measures of employers – as well as to the rigidity of the party leadership, who alienated some popular shop stewards at times.[24]

The ideological continuity between KPD and DKP seems as striking as the organizational continuity. The first DKP congress adopted a rather moderate Declaration of Principles, emphasizing the need for peace, democratic rights and education against the manipulation by monopoly capital. It called for 'unity of action' of all socialist and anti-monopolist forces. This seemed different from the older KPD programme; but not from a new programme drafted by the illegal KPD in 1968.[25] Quite likely by 1968 the KPD leadership had discussed and accepted the theory of state monopoly capitalism, developed by theorists in Eastern Europe as well as in Western communist parties in the 1960s. Thus the anti-monopolist Declaration of Principles of 1969 should not be interpreted as an ideological sop to former supporters of the Extra-parliamentary Opposition.

At a second congress at Düsseldorf in 1971 the DKP elaborated its principles and strategy in a manifesto. State monopoly capitalism was defined as the integration of monopoly capital and state power. Through active intervention in the economy the state ensures monopoly capital a safe profit, at the expense of the working class, the farmers, the intelligentsia, artisans and shopkeepers, and even the small capitalists. All strata of the population are gradually 'proletarianized' and made dependent on monopoly capital. Hence all strata should unite in a democratic struggle against the monopolies, to defend their social and democratic rights. The working class has to lead this anti-monopolist coalition, because it still constitutes the main productive force in society – it produces surplus value – as well as being the best organized and most militant political force. To play a leading role, however, the working class should unite in action. Especially Social Democrat and Communist workers should cooperate, in spite of the resistance from right-wing leaders of the Social Democratic Party. The DKP does not claim leadership within this unity of action; it does claim, however, to represent the 'total interest' (*Gesamtinteresse*) of the working class, in the present and also projected into the future; and to include the most progressive and most class-conscious workers within its ranks, because it bases itself on the theory of Marx, Engels and Lenin and because it belongs to the world-wide communist movement.[26]

Though the DKP still referred to the 'growing importance of the socialist example of the GDR', it did not argue for the reunification of Germany – unlike the KPD before 1968. It gave priority to peaceful co-existence and mutual recognition between the two German states.[27] The anti-monopolist coalition strategy did not help the DKP to improve its electoral performance. At the federal elections of 1972 it received only 0.3 per cent of the popular vote. However, it had waged only a half-hearted campaign, in order not to prevent the SPD from beating the Christian Democrats. In this it was successful: the SPD won five more seats than its rival. Yet in 1976, the DKP campaigned more actively without increasing its share of the electorate. In state elections it did somewhat better. In the early 1970s it won about 3 per cent of the vote in the Saar and Bremen, 2 per cent in Hamburg and 1 per cent in Hesse and North Rhine/Westphalia; by 1976 it won 2 per cent in Bremen and Hamburg, 1 per cent in Hesse and the Saar, 0.5 per cent in North Rhine/Westphalia.[28]

At a congress at Mannheim in 1978 the party adopted a new programme, yet without changing its strategy. In view of the economic recession and the growing reactionary tendencies in West German society it called for a turn (*Wende*) towards social and democratic progress. For this purpose it invited not only Social Democrat workers, but even their (right-wing) leaders to unite in action with the Communists. In alliance with other democratic forces the workers could reduce the power of the monopolist financial oligarchy that controlled the state. By expanding the freedom and democratic rights of the people, they would lead the way to socialism. The decisive role of the Communist Party is stated clearly:

The working class can fulfil its leading role in conquering the power of the monopolies and in realizing socialism the more effectively, the more the revolutionary party succeeds in exercising decisive political influence.[29]

Of course, this revolutionary party is the Communist Party. But the DKP recognized the need for a variety of parties and tendencies, even in a socialist society. More expressly than before it expected a coalition government to lead the transition to socialism. It also defined socialism more explicitly in the 1978 programme. Major monopolies would be nationalized. Production would be planned and controlled democratically; workers should take part in the decision-making process. The state apparatus of army, police, judiciary, administration and mass media should become more democratic and free from neo-Nazi and militarist elements.[30]

The example of the German Democratic Republic received less attention in the programme of 1978.Even so that programme did not show any Eurocommunist tendencies: it still acknowledged the inspiration from 'real socialism' and stressed the close fraternal relations with the SED and the CPSU. Eurocommunism was discussed only indirectly. In 1977 chairman Mies had condemned it as a ploy of the bourgeoisie to divide the communist movement. The DKP continued to reject 'any attempt to revise the doctrine of Marx, Engels and Lenin', he warned.[31] In a similar dogmatic vein the party rejected the idea of 'critical solidarity' with the Soviet Union: only 'principled solidarity' seemed acceptable.[32] Hence it did not express any sympathy for critics of 'real socialism' such as Biermann and Bahro, who were exiled from the

German Democratic Republic in the late 1970s. The DKP disapproved also of the Solidarity movement in Poland, because it opposed 'real socialism' and in particular the centralization of the means of production in the hands of the state.[33]

The party lent active support to most civic actions against pollution, nuclear power and nuclear arms. It did not welcome the ecological parties that emerged around 1980, because these might split the ecological movement and hence serve the interest of monopoly capital – as well as draw (protest) voters away from the DKP. The DKP also disagreed with the dogmatic rejection of nuclear energy by the Greens (*Die Grünen*) and criticized their naive analysis of society.[34] Nevertheless the Communists declared their willingness to cooperate with the Greens, at a DKP congress in 1981. Cooperation could involve not only common actions against nuclear arms and other issues, but even electoral alliances. Common actions were not unusual; for example, the Communists were very active in the peace movement against new nuclear missiles, side by side with the Greens.[35] According to some observers, they were the driving force behind the Krefeld Appeal, a mass petition against the Pershing II and cruise missiles.[36]

At the party congresses of 1984 and 1986 the DKP showed even more willingness to cooperate with Greens and other democratic forces. An electoral alliance was set up under the name *Friedensliste* (Peace List), which included Communists as well as pacifists (members of the German Peace Union) and the Democratic Socialists (a small group which broke away from the SPD in 1982). At the elections for the European Parliament in 1984 the Peace List won 1.3 per cent of the vote – the DKP by itself in 1979 only 0.4 per cent. At elections for the *Landtage* (state assemblies) the Peace List also did better than the DKP alone.[37] Efforts to involve *Die Grünen* in the alliance failed. In order not to split the Left vote at the federal elections of 1987, the Peace List presented only candidates for the so-called first vote and advised its supporters to give their second vote to either SPD or *Grünen* candidates. Thus it collected 0.5 per cent of the (first) votes.[38] However, many members objected to this strategy – and were allowed, for the first time in the party's history, to voice their opposition in the party journal. They felt that the party had resigned itself to its electoral irrelevance, and they were probably right.

At the same time the DKP lent more emphasis than ever to extra-parliamentary action, especially in the anti-nuclear peace movement and in the labour movement – for instance, the trade union campaign for reduction of working hours without loss of pay. The party devoted also more attention to foreign immigrant workers, a large group in Germany. Its main publications were now to be translated into Turkish, Greek and Italian, the 1986 party congress was addressed by a member from Turkey and in 1987 a Turkish woman headed the party list in state elections in Hamburg.[39]

These actions possibly contributed to the growth of the party organization. Whereas the party lost voters, it won members.

The organization of the party: leaders and members

Though the term 'democratic centralism' has been avoided by West German Communists since 1956, it could still apply to the organization of the DKP. In 1969 the party adopted a constitution that has not been changed drastically since. It specifies the rights and duties of party members in the Leninist tradition: the right to criticize leaders and other members, the duty to take part in a primary party group and to represent the party in social life, to carry out decisions taken by the party and to assess one's own activities critically.[40]

Preferably a new member should join a factory group (*Betriebsgruppe*) rather than a local group (*Wohngebietsgruppe*). Yet by 1986 there were more than 1,000 local groups and at most 500 factory groups. College groups (*Hochschulgruppen*) had been set up at about 80 colleges and universities in the Federal Republic.[41] Both factory groups and local groups can direct proposals to the party congress. Actually most proposals seem to come from the next higher echelon, however, the local organization at the level of village or urban district (*Orts-* or *Stadtteilorganisation*).[42] These local organizations are joined together in county organizations (*Kreisorganisation*). Against the will of the party leadership the first party congress decided in 1969 to give these county organizations the right to elect delegates to the national party congress. In 1973 the leaders had their way, however; congress delegates were to be elected by the 12 district organizations (*Bezirks-* or *Landesorganisation*) which correspond roughly to the 11 states (*Länder*) of the Federal Republic.[43] The decisions of a party congress bind all party members. The congress elects the national executive committee (*Vorstand*) of 91 members, which in turn elects a presidium of 17 members. At any organizational level, executive committees are responsible to the membership, but their decisions bind all lower echelons.

Fractions or tendencies are not allowed. The DKP claims to be a 'community of like-minded people' which does not tolerate 'destructive or harmful criticism' from any member.[44] Outsiders have reported a few incidents which indicate at least fragmented opposition in certain areas. For instance, an active local organization in Hesse opposed the Dusseldorf Manifesto of 1971; in 1973 it broke away from the party and existed for a while as an independent League of German Communists (*Bund Deutscher Kommunisten*).[45]

Leaders are usually elected unanimously, without alternative candidates, 'because of complete agreement between party leaders and members on all political questions'.[46] The DKP is proud of the working class background of its leaders, which contrasts with the middle class background of the SPD leaders. Yet the DKP leaders have come a long way; as Heimann points out, they have often been party officials since the 1950s.[47]

Most congress delegates seem to share the working class background of their leaders. Of the 994 delegates at the first congress in 1969 763 (that is, 77 per cent) claimed to be blue or white collar workers ('*Arbeiter*' or '*Angestellte*'); so did 639 of the 879 delegates (73 per cent) at the eighth party congress in 1986. Students, scientists and other members of the intelligentsia made up a minority of 15 per cent in 1969 and only 6 per cent in 1986 (See table 11.1). The number of women increased gradually from 17 per cent in 1969 to 43 per cent in 1986 (see table 11.2). In 1969 about half the delegates were under 40; in 1986 almost three-quarters. About one-fifth had been a member of the KPD before joining the DKP in 1968.[48]

Blue and white collar workers seem to prevail among rank and file members as well, but their number has declined slightly among recent recruits; of the latter, 29 per cent were blue collar workers, 22 per cent white collar '*Angestellte*'. About 40 per cent of the membership are women – more than in the major German parties; the same proportion are under 30 years of age.[49]

Table 11.1 Social class background of DKP congress delegates

	1969	1971	1978	1981	1984	1986
Blue and white collar working class	763	533	632	659	578	639
Cultural, scientific and technical intelligentsia	101	85	62	87	58	55
Students	45	86	67		52	
Farmers, small business	18	6	21	20	—	185
Housewives, pensioners	58	71	32	46	39	
Unemployed, other	9	—	—	—	51	
Total	994	781	814	812	778	879

Source: Congress reports in *Unsere Zeit*

Table 11.2   Age of DKP congress delegates

Age (yr)	1969	1984	1986
20 or less	47	14	17
21–30	218	266	605
31–40	294	276	
41–50	276	90	202
51–60	159	92	
61 or more		40	12
Total	994	778	836

Source: Congress reports in *Unsere Zeit*

Party membership rose rapidly in the early 1970s, more slowly in the late 1970s and early 1980s: from 22,000 in 1969 to 39,000 in 1973, 46,500 in 1978, 50,000 in 1984 and – owing to a competitive membership drive – 58,000 by 1986.[50] As the Communist electorate dwindled to 66,000 voters (at the federal elections of 1983), the party reached an extraordinarily high membership ratio of 75 per cent or even 88 per cent (by 1986). Given repressive measures such as the banning of DKP members from the public service (*Berufsverbote*) on the one hand and the secrecy of the ballot on the other hand, one might have expected a low membership ratio. However, the DKP can probably rely on the support of a very loyal core of workers and intellectuals who join the party with all family members; but not on a wider and more fluid category of sympathizers who would vote but not join the party. Moreover, more and more party members may even vote for other parties – the SPD, or *Die Grünen* – in order not to waste their vote. Only at local elections can the DKP still count on a loyal electorate in certain areas. Electoral decline does not seem to discourage party members. Staritz has attributed this to their 'diaspora spirit': like the ancient Jews they put up with suffering and isolation by maintaining solidarity and cherishing their dream of a Promised Land.[51]

Dedication of the membership may explain the wealth of the party. By 1984 it claimed to have received 9 million DM in membership fees and 8 million DM in donations and profits from sales of publications, festivals and so on. But more money may have come from the German Democratic Republic, in particular through companies engaged in trade between East and West Germany. West German intelligence mentions donations in the order of 50 or 60 million DM.[52] Apart from contributions in cash, the East German regime also provides benefits such as training courses for party workers, children's holiday camps and Marxist literature.

Relations with other organizations

Like most other communist parties, the DKP can rely on a network of auxiliary and peripheral organizations, such as a Soviet friendship society, women's groups, cultural organizations, a children's group (Young Pioneers) and a publishing house. The most important of these seem to be the Socialist German Workers' Youth and the Marxist Student League (*Marxistische Studentenbund*, MSB) 'Spartakus'. The former was founded in 1968, a few months before the DKP itself, and had about 15,000 members in 1985. It has been very active in representing the interests of young workers and conscripted soldiers.[53] Both the Workers' Youth and the Marxist Student League – of about 6,000 members – have been more successful than the DKP in finding serious coalition partners. Thus the MSB cooperates closely with the Socialist College League SHB (*Sozialistische Hochschulbund*). In the 1970s the two together usually won about 25 per cent of the seats on students' councils; by 1980, about 15 per cent.[54]

Ironically, the SHB had been founded in 1961 by students who wanted to remain loyal to the SPD and broke for that purpose with the radical SDS. In the late 1960s the SHB had become radical too, and cooperated with the SDS. In 1970 it split into two factions, one favouring an alliance with the Communists, the other preferring an even more radical 'anti-revisionist' line. The latter faction broke away in 1972. Though the SPD cut all ties with the SHB – and forced it to change its name from 'Social Democratic' to 'Socialist' College League, SHB members still play an active part in the youth organization of the SPD (JUSO).[55]

In spite of the mediation attempted by SHB members, cooperation between Communists and Social Democrats has remained incidental and exceptional in West Germany. The SPD has mollified its negative attitude since the late 1940s, but still threatens to expel members who cooperate with Communists.[56] The German Confederation of Trade Unions, dominated by Social Democrats, has become slightly more tolerant. Though refusing to cooperate with the DKP, the trade unions tend to accept Communist members quietly. The Communists have been very careful not to oppose decisions taken by trade union leaders. Unlike the KPD before 1956 or most Maoist groups after 1970, the DKP does not advocate separate Communist lists at elections for works councils (*Betriebsräte*) but lends support to the official lists of the Confederation trade unions. Through these lists DKP members won about 600 out of 200,000 works council seats in the 1970s. Owing to their dedication and discipline they probably acquired some influence in certain unions, such as the Printers and Paper Workers, Teachers and Scientists, Trade Banking and Insurance and Steel Workers – indeed, in 1973 union leaders accused the Communists of organizing wildcat strikes in the mines and in the steel industry. The real extent of their influence seems a controversial issue among (non-Communist) West German scholars.[57] Throughout the 1970s the DKP had to compete with Maoist groups for the support of industrial workers. Whereas some Maoist groups set up their own 'Red Trade Unions' – as the KPD had done between 1929 and 1933 – others infiltrated the unions of the Confederation in order to develop fractions within them. When they were expelled by the unions, the Communists approved.[58]

Though both the DKP and the Maoist groups referred to the doctrine of Marx, Engels and Lenin, they disagreed strongly about the strategic implications of the theory and about the different forms of application. Whereas the DKP defended the Soviet Union and East Germany, the Maoists denounced these countries as 'social imperialist' if not 'social fascist' powers more dangerous to socialism than NATO and US imperialism. The Maoists identified 'real socialism' with Albania and China – at least until Mao's death. Around 1980 Maoism disintegrated; some Maoists joined the ecological parties, others tried to steer an independent course or to stick to Albania.[59] The DKP tried to ignore the Maoists at first, then to isolate and discredit them. It attributed their presence to the absence of a strong and legal Communist party in the 1960s and to the prevailing anti-Soviet feelings in West Germany.[60]

In the 1970s the DKP also combated New Left groups of anarchist or independent socialist persuasion. Since 1981 it seems willing to cooperate with at least socialists and ecologists, within the peace movement and the anti-nuclear power movement, particularly, but also with squatters, feminists and gay liberation groups. For instance, in 1981 Communists took part in a congress of squatters in Munster.[61] In 1975 Communist and Socialist feminists set up the *Demokratische Fraueninitiative* (Democratic Women's Initiative) to fight for free abortion, jobs for women and peace. By 1986 it numbered about 140 local branches.[62] A similar affinity exists between the DKP and the *Demokratische Lesben- und Schwulen Initiative* (Democratic Initiative of Lesbian and Gay People).[63]

DKP congresses are attended usually by delegates from these groups, as well as from the Association of Victims of the Nazi Regime, the German Peace Society and Association of Conscientious Objectors, the German Peace Union and the Committee for Peace and Disarmament. Some authors consider these organizations 'transmission belts' or front organizations of the Communist party.[64] Indeed Communists may play an active and even pivotal role in these organizations; but they have to cooperate with pacifists and other leftists who disagree with them on many issues, such as the role of the Soviet Union. Naturally, the

Communists try to avoid discussion of these divisive issues with arguments about the need for unity and broad popular alliances.[65] They have been fairly successful, especially in the campaign against the deployment of new nuclear missiles (Pershing II) on German soil that started in 1980 with a meeting at Krefeld. Between 1980 and 1983 millions of people signed the Krefeld Appeal and hundreds of thousands participated in demonstrations.[66] Communists have also cooperated with ecologists in civic action groups (*Bürger-Initiativen*) against pollution and nuclear power. But here it proved equally difficult to avoid controversial issues, such as the existence of nuclear power stations in the Soviet Union, which the DKP defended – because the Soviets used them presumably safely and peacefully, rather than for military or capitalist purposes. The accident at Chernobyl in 1986 led to lively debate but not to a change of mind within the party.[67]

Die Grünen, the ecological party, has always refused close cooperation or electoral alliances with the Communists. Only small groups of pacifists from the German Peace Union, Democratic Socialists (a splinter from the SPD with about 2,000 members) and a few independent leftists proved willing to join the Peace List alliance in 1984 and 1985. Some Social Democrats were prepared to talk to Communists, but these contacts seem to have been incidental – and rather sensitive in view of the sharp reactions to be expected from SPD leaders and right-wing opponents.[68]

Conclusion

The German Communist Party (DKP) could claim the heritage of both the large KPD of 1918–56 and of the Extra-parliamentary Opposition (ApO) of the 1960s. Yet it failed to put either heritage to productive use. On the one hand, the working class base of the KPD had shifted to the SPD and did not return to the DKB – the workers apparently wanted 'unity of action', as the DKP advocated, but without Communists. Whatever the SPD leaders did to alienate the working class, it was not enough to make it vote for the DKP. On the other hand, the new middle class of scientists, students, artists, teachers and the like that had supported the ApO in the late 1960s did not turn to the DKP but (in the late 1970s and early 1980s) to the Greens.

In both cases the identification of the DKP with the German Democratic Republic and the Soviet Union may have tarnished its image. In the 1920s and 1930s the KPD also identified with the Soviet Union, but could still picture it as a distant paradise. During the Second World War the Soviet Union came too close, however, to appear in such a light. The real heir of the KPD became the SED, the ruling party of the East German Democratic Republic. Though it may have tried to help its nephews in the West German KPD and DKP, it did them no favours by suppressing the workers' rebellion of June 1953, by building the Berlin wall and exiling or imprisoning dissidents such as Bahro, Biermann, Harich and Havemann.

It seems likely that the DKP will maintain its ties with the East German rulers. Perhaps it could have severed them in 1968, but not now. If it were to turn to Eurocommunism in the 1980s, it would probably gain very little in terms of votes or influence, given the competition with the Greens; but it would lose its main source of legitimation and moral – if not also financial – support. Hence it is reasonable to suppose that it will remain a more or less marginal but orthodox Marxist–Leninist party. As the Federal Republic has defined its identity in anti-communist terms, it may never tolerate a significant communist party that identifies with the 'Enemy behind the Wall'. It can tolerate quite easily a small red herring trying to swim against the stream. It may use the DKP to discredit and distract other, potentially more dangerous, opposition forces by accusing them of being infiltrated and manipulated by Communists.

Thus many factors contribute to the Communist Party's resistance to change: the anti-communist tradition of the Federal Republic, the isolation of the party, its political culture – the 'diaspora spirit' – and its close-knit organization, its leadership orientated towards East Germany and the Soviet Union; and even its ideology, which justifies coalitions with all kinds of groups provided they are 'guided' by the DKP in the long run.

Notes

I would like to thank Professor Wolfgang Rudzio, Mr R. Weijdeveld, Dr M. Hyvärinen and the staff of the library at the University of Oldenburg for their help and suggestions. Of course, they bear no responsibility for the contents of this chapter.

1   Ossip K. Flechtheim, *Die KPD in der Weimarer Republik* (Europäische Verlagsanstalt, Frankfurt am Main, 1969); see also Ben Fowkes, *Communism in Germany under the Weimar Republic* (Macmillan, London, 1984).
2   Flechtheim, *Die KPD*, pp. 263–88; see also Hermann Weber, *Die Wandlung des deutschen Kommunismus* (Europäische Verlagsanstalt, Frankfurt am Main, 1969), I, pp. 54–62, 85–97, 232–238 *et passim*.
3   *Geschichte der deutschen Arbeiterbewegung*, 5 (Dietz, Berlin, 1966) p. 436 especially; see also Hermann Weber (ed.), *Völker hört die Signale: der deutsche Kommunismus 1916–1966* (DTV, Munich, 1967) pp. 61–3, 68–71, 106–10, 119–30, 166–83, 212–14.

4 *Völker hört die Signale*, pp. 293–5; Hans Kluth, *Die KPD in der Bundesrepublik 1945–1956* (Westdeutscher Verlag, Cologne/Opladen, 1959) pp. 29–37.

5 Kluth, *Die KPD*, pp. 33–4; Kurt Müller, vice-chairman of the party and member of the Bundestag, was expelled and kidnapped to East Germany after he had defended a 'Titoist position'; in 1955 he returned to West Germany, having spent five years in prison for 'espionage'.

6 According to the German text: 'Wenn die Bevölkerung Westdeutschlands leben will, muss sie das Adenauer-Regime stürzen . . . Nur der unversöhnliche und revolutionäre Kampf aller deutschen Patrioten kann und wird zum Sturz des Adenauer-Regimes und damit zur Beseitigung der entscheidenden Stütze der Herrschaft der amerikanischen Imperialisten in Westdeutschland führen', in *Völker hört die Signale*, p. 301; see also Kluth, *Die KPD*, pp. 36–49.

7 *Das Verbot der KPD. KPD Prozess Dokumentarwerk* (Müller, Karlsruhe, 1956); see also Kluth, *Die KPD*, pp. 113–17.

8 Kluth, *Die KPD*, pp. 36, 129.

9 Alexander von Brünneck, *Politische Justiz gegen Kommunisten in der Bundesrepublik Deutschland 1949–1968* (Suhrkamp, Frankfurt am Main, 1978), pp. 110–12, 278 *et alibi*.

10 Ibid., pp. 334–50; see also Christian Bockemühl, '25 Jahre nach dem KPD-Verbot: Historische und aktuelle Überlegungun', in *Aus Politik und Zeitgeschichte*, 46/1981, pp. 3–12.

11 Otto Schönfeldt, 'KPD-Verbot – ein fortwirkendes Übel', in Max Schäfer (ed.), *Die DKP: Gründung, Entwicklung, Bedeutung* (Verlag Marxistische Blätter, Frankfurt am Main, 1978), pp. 111–44; see also Richard Loss, 'The Communist Party of Germany (KPD) 1956–1968' in *Survey*, vol. 19, no. 4, 1973, pp. 66–85.

12 See Vincent McHale, 'Greece', in Vincent McHale and Sharon Skowronski (eds), *Political Parties of Europe* (Westport, Conn.: Greenwood Press, 1983), pp. 328–63; in the last elections before the Second World War the Greek Communist Party had won 15 out of 300 seats in parliament, whereas the United Democratic Left in which it participated after 1951 won 18 (out of 300) seats in 1956, 24 in 1961 and 28 in 1963; whereas the German Peace Union in which the German Communists participated received merely 1.9 per cent of the vote in 1961 and 1.3 per cent in 1965.

13 *Völker hört die Signale*, pp. 272–3; Von Brünneck, *Politische Justiz*, pp. 43–4.

14 Von Brünneck, *Politische Justiz*, pp. 42–5; see also Schönfeldt, *KPD-Verbot*.

15 For the history of the Campaign see Karl A. Otto, *Vom Ostermarsch zur ApO. Geschichte der ausserparlamentarischen Opposition in der Bundesrepublik, 1960–1970* (Campus, Frankfurt am Main, 1977).

16 Tilman Fichter and Siegward Lönnendonker, *Kleine Geschichte des SDS* (Rotbuch, Berlin, 1977), especially pp. 129–35, 157–8; see also Johannes Henrich von Heiseler, 'SDS und Organisationstheorie', in M. Schäfer (ed.), *Die DKP*, pp. 145–56.

17 Fichter and Lönnendonker, *Kleine Geschichte des SDS*, pp. 140–3; see also Tilman Fichter and Siegward Lönnendonker, 'Von der Neuen Linken zur Krise des Linksradikalismus' in *Die Linke im Rechtsstaat*, vol. 2 (Rotbuch, Berlin, 1979), pp. 100–32; Gerd Langguth, *Die Protestbewegung in der Bundesrepublik 1968–1976* (Wissenschaft und Politik, Cologne, 1976).

18   The Emergency Laws (*Notstandsgesetze*) had been drafted already in 1960 by a Christian Democratic minister and were proposed by the Grand Coalition of Christian Democrats and Social Democrats between 1966 and 1969. In the eyes of the (emerging) Extra-parliamentary Opposition they became the symbol of 'creeping fascism'; after all, the introduction of emergency laws (or rather, their application) had also ushered in the Nazis in the early 1930s, it was argued. The sudden rise of a neo-Nazi party around 1966 seemed to confirm the worst fears of the opposition. See K. Shell, 'Extraparliamentary Opposition in Postwar Germany' in *Comparative Politics* vol. 2, no. 4, 1970, pp. 653–80.

19   Ulrich Probst, *The Communist Parties in the Federal Republic of Germany* (Haag/Herchen, Frankfurt am Main, 1981), p. 20; but his statement 'Undoubtedly the student university groups of the GCP form the backbone of the party', (p. 22) seems somewhat exaggerated; cf. Kurt Bachmann, 'Die Konstituierung der Deutschen Kommunistischen Partei', in Schäfer (ed.), *Die DKP*, pp. 167–92, especially pp. 179, 191.

20   Kurt Fritsch, 'Die DKP – eine Gemeinschaft von Gleichgesinnten', in Schäfer (ed.), *Die DKP*, pp. 265–83, especially p. 269.

21   Ossip Flechtheim (ed.), *Dokumente zur parteipolitischen Entwicklung in Deutschland seit 1945*, VII (Wendler, Berlin, 1969), pp. 575–8; see also Dietrich Staritz, 'Der "Eurokommunismus" und die DKP', in *Die Linke im Rechtsstaat* vol. 2 (Rotbuch, Berlin, 1979), pp. 133–54, especially 142.

22   Siegfried Heimann, 'Die Deutsche Kommunistische Partei', in Richard Stöss (ed.), *Parteienhandbuch*, vol. I (Westdeutscher Verlag, Opladen, 1983), pp. 901–81; see also Schäfer (ed.), *Die DKP*, pp. 324–7.

23   'Erklärung zur Neukonstituierung einer kommunistischen Partei vom 25.9.1968', in *Die DKP*, pp. 284–91.

24   Ulf Wolter, 'Dissens in der DKP', *Kritik*, vol. 6, no. 18, 1978, pp. 4–46; Heimann, *Die Deutsche Kommunistische Partei*, p. 935; H. J. Horchem, 'Infiltration von Betrieben und Gewerkschaften durch Kommunisten', in *Beiträge zur Konfliktforschung*, no. 3, 1980, pp. 87–101; Rolf Ebbighausen and Peter Kirchhoff, 'Zur Betriebsgruppenstrategie der DKP', *Politische Vierteljahresschrift*, vol. 13, no. 1, 1972, pp. 106–29.

25   'Grundsatzerklärung der Deutschen Kommunistischen Partei, beschlossen auf dem Essener Parteitag vom 12./13. April 1969', in Flechtheim, *Dokumente* IX, pp. 209–219; 'Entwurf: Programm der Kommunistischen Partei Deutschlands', *ibid*, VII, pp. 523–58.

26   *Protokoll des Düsseldorfer Parteitages der DKP* (Blinkfuer, Hamburg, 1971), pp. 305–49; see also Rolf Ebbighausen and Peter Kirchhoff, 'Die DKP im Parteiensystem der Bundesrepublik' in J. Dittberner and R. Ebbighausen (eds), *Parteiensystem in der Legitimationskrise* (Westdeutscher Verlag, Opladen, 1973), pp. 427–66.

27   *Protokoll*, pp. 321–2, 325–6, 334–6.

28   Heimann, *Die Deutsche Kommunistische Partei*, p. 959; by 1980 the picture looked even darker: 1 per cent in Bremen and in Hamburg, 0.5 per cent in the Saar and even less in Hesse and North Rhine/Westphalia.

29   My translation from the German text: 'Die Arbeiterklasse kann ihre führende Rolle bei der Überwindung der Monopolmacht, bei der Errichtung und Gestaltung des Sozialismus um so wirkungsvoller wahrnehmen, je mehr es der revolutionären Partei gelingt, entscheidenden politischen Einfluss auszuüben', in *Programm der DKP* (DKP, Düsseldorf, 1979), p. 65.

30 Ibid. pp. 66–7.
31 Herbert Mies, 'Die deutsche Bourgeoisie und der "Eurokommunismus"', *Unsere Zeit*, 2 February 1977; for a reaction see Ilse Spittmann, 'Die DKP und der Eurokommunismus', *Deutschland Archiv*, vol. 10, no. 4, 1977, pp. 346–7; see also Staritz, 'Der "Eurokommunismus"', pp. 138–39.
32 K. H. Schröder, 'Das internationalistische Antlitz der DKP', in Schäfer (ed.), *Die DKP*, pp. 247–64.
33 Gerd Deumlich, 'Polen und der Klassenstandpunkt', *Marxistische Blätter*, vol. 20, no. 2, 1982, pp. 85–92.
34 Willi Gerns, 'Grüne und bunte Listen. Schaden für die Umweltschutzbewegung?', *Marxistische Blätter*, vol. 17, no. 1, 1979, pp. 26–35; Opinion after the Ecologist successes was more positive – for instance: H. Thüer, 'Gelbe Sonnenblume und rote Nelke', *Marxistische Blätter*, vol. 21, no. 3, 1983, pp. 17–22.
35 Jan Wienecke, 'Nach dem 6. Parteitag der DKP', *Marxistische Blätter*, vol. 19, no. 4, 1981, pp. 86–91; *Unsere Zeit*, 1 June 1981; cf. Heimann, *Die Deutsche Kommunistische Partei*, p. 914.
36 Eric Waldman, 'The DKP', in Richard F. Staar (ed.), *Yearbook on International Communist Affairs* (Hoover Institution Press, Stanford, CA, 1985), pp. 475–80.
37 Compare the results of the DKP alone in Bremen (1979: 0.8 per cent) and North Rhine/Westphalia (1980: 0.3 per cent) with those of the alliances in Bremen (1983: 1.4 per cent) and North Rhine/Westphalia (1985: 0.7 per cent); whereas the DKP did not increase its electorate when it presented its own lists in the Saar (1980: 0.5 per cent, 1985: 0.3 per cent), Lower Saxony (1983: 0.3 per cent, 1986: 0.0 per cent) or Hesse (1983: 0.3 per cent, 1987: 0.3 per cent). (All figures from *Unsere Zeit*.)
38 *Unsere Zeit*, 27 January 1987 (German voters have two votes, one for the direct constituency election and a second one for the party list; but the final allocation of seats depends only on the size of the list vote. See Gordon Smith, *Democracy in Western Germany* (Heinemann, London, 1979), p. 130.
39 *Unsere Zeit*, 7 April 1987; 7 May 1986; 10 May 1986.
40 Flechtheim, *Dokumente* IX, p. 220.
41 René Ahlberg, 'Differenzen und Konflikte zwischen den kommunistischen Parteien der Bundesrepublik Deutschland', *Beiträge zur Konfliktforschung*, no. 3, 1979, pp. 67–83.
42 Gerd Walter, *Theoretischer Anspruch und politische Praxis der DKP. Eine Analyse am Beispiel der Betriebsarbeit* (Anton Hain, Meisenheim am Glan, 1973), p. 17.
43 Flechtheim, *Dokumente* IX, p. 221; see also Fritsch, 'Die DKP – eine Gemeinschaft . . .', pp. 269–70; two states, Bavaria and North Rhine/Westphalia, are divided into two districts (*Bezirke*) each; the DKP has no members in West Berlin, which has its own Communist party, the SEW (*Sozialistische Einheitspartei Westberlins*, Socialist Unity Party of West Berlin).
44 Fritsch, 'Die DKP – eine Gemeinschaft . . .', p. 280.
45 Heimann, *Die Deutsche Kommunistische Partei*, pp. 953–955; Staritz, 'Der "Eurokommunismus"', pp. 148–9.
46 *Unsere Zeit*, 10 January 1984; but cf. Wolter, 'Dissers in der DKP', pp. 8–13.
47 Heimann, p. 973; see also above, p. 196.

210   Paul Lucardie

48   Unfortunately guest delegates were included in this number; *Unsere Zeit*, 17 April 1969, cited by Walter, *Theoretischer Anspruch*, p. 26; Jan Wienecke, 'Die DKP: Partei des Friedens, der Arbeit und des Sozialismus', *Marxistische Blätter*, vol. 22, no. 2, 1984, pp. 89–93; *Unsere Zeit*, 10 January 1984.

49   The figures are quoted by party chairman Mies in his report to the eighth party congress (*Unsere Zeit*, 3 May 1986); according to him, over 60 per cent of DKP members were '*Arbeiter und Angestellte*'. See also Wolfgang Rudzio, *Das politische System der Bundesrepublik Deutschland* (UTB Leske Budrich, Opladen, 1983), p. 157: no more than 25 per cent of SPD or CDU members are women.

50   The figures are presented by the DKP in its congress reports, published in *Unsere Zeit*, but they do not deviate much from the estimations of the West German *Verfassungsschutz* (internal intelligence agency), see Rudzio, *Das politische System*, p. 156.

51   Staritz, 'Der "Eurokommunismus"', p. 146.

52   *Verfassungsschutzbericht 1985* (Bonn, 1986), but cf. *Unsere Zeit*, 6 May 1986.

53   Waldman, 'The DKP', p. 475. Heimann, *Die Deutsche Kommunistische Partei*, pp. 969–70; Helmut Bilstein et al., *Organisierter Kommunismus in der Bundesrepublik Deutschland* (UTB Leske Budrich, Opladen, 1977), pp. 41–50; see also: H. J. Rautenberg, 'Soldateninitiativen der siebziger Jahre, *Beiträge zur Konfliktforschung*, no. 1, 1980, pp. 71–96.

54   Horst Mewes, 'The German New Left', *New German Critique*, vol. 1, no. 1, 1973, pp. 22–41, especially p. 24; Ossip Flechtheim et al., *Der Marsch der DKP durch die Institutionen* (Fischer, Frankfurt am Main, 1980) p. 270: students began to switch to ecological and 'Alternative Left' groups around 1980.

55   Langguth, *Die Protestbewegung*, pp. 309–16.

56   Heimann, *Die Deutsche Kommunistische Partei*, p. 938.

57   Ibid., pp. 935–7; Horchem, 'Infiltration von Betrieben', pp. 87–101; Walter, *Theoretischer Anspruch*, p. 27; Ossip Flechtheim et al., *Der Marsch der DKP*, pp. 23–43; Joachim Bergmann, Otto Jacobi, Walther Müller-Jentsch, *Gewerkschaften in der Bundesrepublik* (Europäische Verlagsanstalt, Frankfurt am Main, 1975), p. 331.

58   Langguth, *Die Protestbewegung*, pp. 85–87; see also Horchem, 'Infiltration von Betrieben', pp. 87–101.

59   Langguth, *Die Protestbewegung*, pp. 102–211; Ahlberg, 'Differenzen und Konflikte' pp. 67–83; Bilstein et al., *Organisierter Kommunismus*, pp. 75–114.

60   Fritsch, 'Die DKP – eine Gemeinschaft . . .', p. 269; *Protokoll*, pp. 354–55; H. Otto, 'Bankrott der maoistischen Gruppierungen', *Marxistische Blätter*, vol. 20, no. 4, 1982, pp. 97–103.

61   Eric Waldman, 'The DKP', in Richard Staar and Robert Wesson (eds), *Yearbook on International Communist Affairs* (Hoover Institution Press, Stanford, CA, 1982), pp. 282–9.

62   Florence Hervé, 'Demokratische Fraueninitiative', *Marxistische Blätter*, vol. 20, no. 4, 1982, pp. 48–53; cf Karl-Werner Brand, Detlef Büsser, Dieter Rucht, *Aufbruch in eine andere Gesellschaft. Neue soziale Bewegungen in der Bundesrepublik* (Campus, Frankfurt/New York, 1984), pp. 127–44; see also: Frigga Haug, 'The Women's Movement in West Germany', *New Left Review*, no. 155, 1986, pp. 50–74.

63 At least in 1984 the group sent delegates to the DKP congress and declared that only the DKP opposed discrimination of homosexuals on principle: *Unsere Zeit*, 11 January, 1984.

64 Waldman, 'The DKP', (1985) pp. 475–80; Fritz Vilmar et al., *Was heisst hier kommunistische Unterwanderung?* (Ullstein, Frankfurt am Main, 1981), *passim*.

65 Willi Gerns, 'Ideologische Fragen im Friedenskampf', *Marxistische Blätter*, vol. 20, no. 2, 1982, pp. 13–18; Willi Gerns, 'Grundsätze kommunistischer Bündnispolitik in demokratischen Bewegungen', *Marxistische Blätter*, vol. 20, no. 3, 1982, pp. 92–100.

66 Brand et al., *Aufbruch in eine andere Gesellschaft*, pp. 215–25; cf Fritz Vilmar et al., *Was heisst hier . . .*, pp. 141–52; Fritz Krause, 'Vier Jahre Kampf gegen NATO-Raketen', *Marxistische Blätter*, vol. 21, no. 4, 1983, pp. 30–8.

67 Jörg Heimbrecht, 'DKP und Bürgerinitiativen', *Marxistische Blätter*, vol. 18, no. 4, 1980, pp. 49–55; Willi Gerns, 'Grüne und bunte Listen', *Marxistische Blätter*, vol. 17, no. 1, 1979, pp. 26–35; *Unsere Zeit*, 6 May, 1986.

68 See Wolfgang Gehrcke, 'Herausforderungen an linke Politik im Vorwahljahr', *Marxistische Blätter*, vol. 24, no. 3, 1986, pp. 46–53; *Unsere Zeit*, 7 May 1986; on the Peace List at the European elections see *Europe Votes 2* (compiled and edited by T. T. Mackie and F. W. S. Craig, Parliamentary Research Services, Chichester, 1985), pp. 86, 93–4, 104–5.

12 Democratic Centralism in a Federalist Environment
The Swiss Party of Labour

Anton Fischer

The pre-war Communist Party of Switzerland, having been banned in 1940, was allowed back into legality when the defeat of fascism was assured, at which point it adopted not only a new name but also a new form.[1] The new *Partei der Arbeit/Parti du Travail* (henceforth PdA) was joined by many left-wing socialists and held its foundation congress on 14/15 October 1944. It immediately met with a success such as the old KPS had never seen and won 5.1 per cent of the votes in the first post-war national elections. As the electoral success in the cantonal elections proved even greater,[2] the new organization seemed set to become a mass party.

The cold war, however, drove the communists back to their pre-war isolation. The anti-communist hysteria (especially fierce in Switzerland) reached its climax after the Soviet intervention in Hungary in 1956 and administered the party a blow from which it has not to the present day been able to recover. As the Swiss German areas suffered most in this process, French Switzerland became the new stronghold of the party. Self-criticism after 1956 led to a widening discussion that culminated in the new programme of 1959. This programme may be considered as a statement of a Eurocommunist position *avant la lettre*. It was an attempt to give the concept of a national road to socialism a concrete content in that it accepted the existing democratic forms and institutions in the state and the economy as a useful starting point for the building of socialism. The party's strategy should be to concentrate all social forces against the power of capital (*Volkssammlungspolitik*).

In the 1960s anti-communism began to lose its firm hold and a new spirit of social criticism started to appear that eventually created a new interest in the party. Young people were attracted to it and introduced a new style of political activity that eventually led to conflicts with the old party core. In French Switzerland the party even succeeded in establishing itself as an eligible opposition and gained a position in cantonal and communal councils.[3] The national elections of 1967 brought an increase of one-third of the previous vote. In Geneva every fifth vote was communist.[4] On the eve of 1968 the party thus had some reason for optimism.

The year 1967 had started with a wave of demonstrations, calling for autonomous youth centres, which ended in increasingly violent clashes with the police. The party welcomed this awakening of youth and deplored the repression the bourgeois state had shown, but it had very ambivalent feelings towards its own youth organization (the *Junge Sektion*), which had taken a prominent part in the struggle. By now it had become clear that the party's youth had left the theoretical orbit of scientific socialism and democratic centralism and had become a part of the new anti-authoritarian movement with its new heroes: Mao, Ho Chi Minh, Che Guevara and Marcuse. The clash became inevitable when in August 1968 Warsaw Pact troops crushed Dubček's 'socialism with a human face', an experiment that had been welcomed by the party. The intervention came as a shock, and the party did not hesitate to condemn it. The ninth party congress in November was dominated by this issue so that the discussion of the new party programme had to wait until 1971.

For the *Junge Sektion* the party's critique of the armed intervention did not go far enough. For them the Soviet Union could no longer be considered a revolutionary power, and the intervention was simply the latest proof of its oppressive nature. But their criticism of the Soviet Union was extended also to their own party. Its definition of socialism, it was said, was still identical to the Soviet model.

The party concentrated, according to its critics, too much on parliamentary work and neglected agitation outside, and had, by doing so, lost an opportunity to cooperate with the new youth movement. But the 1971 congress warded off the attack of the New Left and confirmed the official line. Secretary General Vincent rebuked the critics: they had fallen back on the idealism of utopian socialism, and were opposed to Marx and Marxism. He quoted one of Lenin's famous attacks on the intellectuals as idle boasters. Subsequently, many young people left the party.[5]

The years from 1970 onward saw the rise and fall of a plethora of new political groups calling themselves communist parties and of a whole New Left press (surviving to a small extent today). One of these organizations, after a smooth start in 1969 as the *Progressive Organisationen Basel*, constituted itself a national party in 1971 and went on to win three times as many votes as the PdA in the national elections of 1983. At first it wanted to be nothing more than an improved version of the PdA; but later it came to see the task of the day as being to reconstruct the true Leninist party, apparently the best insurance against the pitfalls of revisionism. Later it discovered Eurocommunism and propagated a version of the Swiss *compromesso storico*, finally ending as a kind of service organization for new social movements that had completely dropped the notion of Marxism.

A whole generation felt that society needed a fundamental change. This new consciousness entered also the traditional organizations of the working class movement – the trade unions and the social democratic party. Both gained what the PdA had until that point quite clearly lacked: new cadres full of new ideas. The founding congress for a new communist youth organization had to wait until 1974 (the old one having not survived the clash of 1968). Only in the mid 1970s did the party see another chance to attract young newcomers willing to pull their weight.

After this short progressive interlude, the consequences of the economic crisis of 1974/5 altered the political landscape of Switzerland fundamentally. Even before that the party had been faced with a difficult problem: the awakening of a diffuse xenophobic sentiment among the population, especially in working class areas of the big cities – the traditional territory of the PdA. Fear of social insecurity did not lead workers towards the party as their natural defender but drove them to the newly rising Right, and to the *National Aktion*, which had won a resounding victory in the national elections of 1971 (more than seven per cent of the votes, and 11 seats in the parliament). The policy of rallying the broad masses of the people had met with a brutal defeat. This however, had no effect on the new programme of 1971, nor on the tenth congress in 1974. For both socialism was the objective demand of the time. The material requirements for achieving it were already present. Economic growth was an absolute need. All that had to be done was to put it at the service of the people, removing it from capitalist control.[6]

There was still an unshakeable faith in the endless development of the productive forces and of technical progress. Thus, the party missed once more a central issue: its unconditional support for nuclear energy increased its isolation at a time when popular resistance to nuclear plants was rising to the scale of a mass movement. The congress simply confirmed the party's previously existing policy on the issue.

An *apertura a sinistra* and the abandoning of the old claim to be the only true anti-capitalistic force (which the congress had solemnly confirmed four years earlier) marked the eleventh congress held in Geneva 1978. The new party leader, Armand Magnin, who had replaced the old warrior Vincent, took the new realities into account when he delivered the report of the Central Committee. People alarmed by ecological problems were no longer to be considered victims of political manoeuvres aimed at splitting the working class movement (as Vincent and many party members had held before). The party should open itself, said Magnin, to the new social movements that were struggling for more limited aims than was the party.

This opening to new tendencies may be seen in the way in which one of the fashionable ideas of the day found its way into the congress manifesto. The demand for self-management (*Selbsverwaltung*) became the order of the day – a notion that had started its career in the alternative scene where it had served as a practical model for small cooperative enterprises. It was no longer to be the state that had to control everything, but the workers themselves through factory commissions (*Betriebskommissionen*).

But the *apertura* remained a very ambiguous one, as can be seen from the congress manifesto's treatment of the issue of nuclear energy. The manifesto starts by presenting the grave perils and unsolved problems, and ends with a soft conditional 'Yes'. Nor did the opening to the new movements affect the body of the party, as events would soon show. It was not honoured by the voters either: the elections of 1979 saw a decline in the party's electorate, from 2.4 to 2.1 per cent, which resulted in the loss of another parliamentary seat.

The Soviet military intervention in Afghanistan triggered a new grave crisis. The Central Committee published a declaration in which an unambiguous condemnation was avoided. Thirty leading militants of Lausanne (among them Central Committee member Anne Cathérine Menétrey) published an open letter in which they claimed that if the party programme and the fight for self-management were to be taken seriously, a sharply critical view should be adopted of the so-called socialism of the Soviet Union, which consisted of nothing more than a policy of emergency and coercive reactions on the part of a state machinery.[7] This critique was met with a rebuff within the party and all the members of the group resigned their membership.

However, the Political Bureau of the party went on to formulate later in 1981 a critical declaration on the state of war in Poland that was less ambiguous than in the case of the intervention in Afghanistan.

The national conference of 1982 adopted new statutes that had to take into account the programme changes of 1979. There is now no longer any explicit reference to Marxism–Leninism (as there was in the statutes of 1971), but the party still relies on scientific socialism as expounded by Marx and Engels and further developed by Lenin and other theorists of the revolutionary movement. In the same year a crisis broke out in the cantonal party of Zürich which followed a course similar to that of the 1980 crisis in Lausanne and ended with the whole group leaving the party and publishing a farewell manifesto.

In his report to the twelfth party congress (held in May 1983) Magnin acknowledged that difficulties existed. Many only paid lip service to the new programme, he declared. But the main problem was, according to Magnin, a broad anti-communist campaign that the party could not counter effectively because of its modest means. The congress met in the shadow of growing political tension and of the imminent arrival of the new Pershing II missiles and it left the impression of a party thrown back on its defences. The national elections of 1983 proved a disaster. The party lost all its seats in parliament except one, and obtained only 0.9 per cent of the vote. Most alarming of all was the fact that the party's strongholds in French-speaking Switzerland began to break down. In Vaud the vote fell from 9.3 to 4.1 per cent, in Neuchâtel from 7.7 to 4.2 per cent, in Geneva from 19.9 to 9.5 per cent. The small Trotskyist *Sozialistische Arbeiterpartei* (the former *Ligue Marxiste Révolutionaire*) nearly equalled the communist vote, whereas the *Progressive Organisationen* (hitherto considered opportunist by the PdA) totalled 2.7 per cent of the votes, which allowed them to send three members to parliament, where they kindly accepted the only remaining Communist, Magnin, into their parliamentary group. Regional elections have since confirmed this downward trend.[8]

Organization

In theory, and according to its statutes, the organizing principle of the party is democratic centralism – but this is no traditional democratic centralism.[9] First, the *Partei der Arbeit* is very small and cannot afford a big party apparatus with many paid functionaries, which is one of the main prerequisites for a strong national leadership. Secondly, the political reality of Switzerland does not favour orthodox democratic centralism because of the country's federalist structure, based on linguistic and cultural diversity. Whereas the centre of political and economic power lies in German-speaking Switzerland, the party has its strongholds in the French-speaking areas and a head office in Geneva.

All this makes control and coordination of party work in the different cantonal parties a very difficult task. In party congress reports complaints are often heard that the national leadership is not efficient and that Central Committee meetings are not held frequently enough. Only in 1983 could Secretary General Magnin report that the statutory frequency had been attained.[10] The Political Bureau, which is supposed to meet every month, rarely does so. This problem, which affects even the top of the party, is illustrated by the constant attempts to reorganize the office of the general secretary.[11] With this 'lack of structure at the national level' (Magnin) democratic centralism remains an illusion. Local conflicts can develop without much intervention from the central leadership, and local nonconformist politics and electoral alliances go largely unchecked.

The party's supreme organ according to the statutes is the party congress (*Parteitag*), scheduled to meet every fourth year. Every cantonal party selects its delegates according to its own procedure. In the party of the canton of Zurich, for example, there is a preselection by the local party leadership that aims to present a list representing the different currents. The candidates for the Central Committee (60 members) are then proposed to the congress by the cantonal leaderships and usually voted in without much discussion.

The party organization is a territorial one and follows the historical regions of Switzerland. There are no cantonal parties in the small rural and conservative cantons. Organization according to enterprises (*Betriebsgruppen*) – dear to the heart of every communist party – is provided for by the statutes, but the party has never managed to establish more than a single one (typically in Geneva) – a sad indication of the fundamental weakness of Swiss communism. The party's influence in the trade unions is small, too, even after the cold war ostracism. There are no communists among the national union leadership, only in local ones. Nevertheless, most of the party members are in trade unions, and 115 out of 150 delegates to the eleventh congress of 1978 were members of a trade union, 47 of them being trade union cadres.[12]

The small size of party membership and the high average age are responsible for a phenomenon that can be described as the 'life cycle of new militants'. This starts when a relatively small number of militants is able to take over a local leadership after a relatively short period of time in the party (especially in German-speaking Switzerland). Many party sections are Sleeping Beauties in this respect. When they are kissed back to life, the old and inactive members welcome the activity of the young newcomers – at least at first. But no sooner do the new militants embark on a policy critical of the old communist ideas, than resistance grows and the new leaders feel obstructed by a passive majority that is no longer able to carry out a policy of its own, but is still strong enough to block a policy of which it disapproves. So the frustrated newcomers leave the local leadership again after two or three years and often bid farewell to the party as well.

This life cycle can be observed best in militants in the cantonal party of Zürich. Young people approach the party as students with an interest in Marxism, are contacted by one of the party's youth or cultural organizations, enter the party after a short period of external association with it, are often elected to local leadership positions after two or three years, but then after another two or three years leave – sometimes the leading board only, sometimes the party as well. Some do it quietly, some publish a fervent farewell manifesto.[13] The life cycle of the average new activist seems thus to have a duration of six to eight years. A whole group forming a generation can go simultaneously through the different stages. From the outside, only the last stage is discernible, when a whole group leaves the party. This is what happened in Lausanne in 1980 and in Zürich in 1983. The life cycles of different individuals can overlap as well, as there are always some newcomers inspired with the faith that it should be possible to give the party new life and strength – a faith that others have by then lost. So the party has always been able to replace the disappointed resigners with enthusiastic freshmen. In the 1980s this cyclical process seems to have come to a halt, as the party has now lost its attraction to potential new members.

Party membership

The party has never published official figures on membership. The editor of the party paper *Vorwärts*, Karl Odermatt, made a private guess in 1978 of 5,000 members.[14] Insiders think this number was much too high, even for that date. Since 1978 membership has certainly diminished, and the groups that have made a great commotion about leaving the party are nothing but the superficial signs of a more silent movement out of it.

The age structure of the membership still shows the effects of the cold war. There is no middle generation in the party; in the 1950s and early 1960s hardly any new members could be won over. Therefore there are the older members, who hibernated during the cold war years and have had personal experience of the heroic days of persecution, and the younger ones who have not passed through this testing experience. These very different backgrounds make political unity hard to attain and lurk behind many party conflicts even though the two generations cannot be simply identified with the two main factions in the party – conservatives and reformers.

The new members – those, that is, who entered after 1968 – are for the most part no longer blue collar workers but employees in the service sector, such as teachers, students, welfare workers, academics and self-employed professional people such as doctors and lawyers. Between 1960 and 1981 the share of industrial workers among the Swiss working population fell from 46.5 to 39.5 per cent, whereas figures for the tertiary sector rose from 38.9 to 53.4 per cent of all occupied party members.[15] This tendency is related, of course, to a decline in the working class that has occurred in most European countries. Another factor has been present, however, that has been less generally shared, but which is a prominent feature of Swiss society – the high proportion of foreign workers in the Swiss economy. The Swiss proletariat consists more and more of foreign workers mainly from southern countries who remain organized in the parties of their home nations (the Italian and Spanish Communist Parties and the Spanish Socialist Party). So it comes about that the Swiss branch of the *Partito comunista italiano* may be bigger than that of the domestic communist party.

As there is no official statistical information available on the social composition of the party, I am forced to resort to figures that relate only to the situation of the cantonal party of Zürich and are drawn from internal reports (table 12.1).[16]

Any interpretation of these figures has to take into account that the total size of the Zürich party was about 250 members, living at that time mainly in the city of Zürich.[17] Industrial workers are no more than a small and declining minority. The statistics also confirm the observation that the party has grown too old: the 1980 report lists 44.6 per cent of members as 56 years and older. In 1978 this figure had been 50 per cent. Approximately one-third of the members in the canton of Zürich are women. It is, however, difficult to assess how these figures correspond to the national figures. Three-quarters of the communist votes come from the four French-speaking cantons.[18] The breakdown of delegates to the national congress of 1978 may serve as an indication: out of a total of 150 delegates, 86 came from French-speaking Switzerland and 50 from German-speaking areas.[19]

Table 12.1 Social composition of the cantonal party of Zürich, 1978–80

	1978 (%)	1980 (%)
Workers	17.0	15.4
Employees	28.0	35.1
Students	10.0	11.5
Housewives	10.0	6.7
Self-employed	9.0	2.9
Pensioners	26.0	28.4

Financing the party is, and has always been, a severe and intractable problem. According to the party statutes (article 29) finance comes from three sources: members' subscriptions, a proportion of the emoluments of national councillors, and fund raising and donations. The second source can really be ignored as there is only one communist left in parliament. Fund raising in the canton of Zurich totalled 10,130 SFR in 1976 and 12,622 SFR in 1977.[20] One of the main sources of funds is an annual flea market in the *Volkhaus* of Zürich. *Vorwärts* reports all the small donations: 'A.F. in Z. gave 20 SFR,' 'K.O. in B. gave 50 SFR', and so on. Generally one gets the impression that the party's finances are collected in dribs and drabs by indefatigable idealists. The shortage of means can also be discerned in the insufficient amount of paid advertising and use of bill-boards during electoral battles. Nevertheless the old rumour that the Swiss party enjoys financial support from the Soviet Union refuses to die. A former Soviet diplomat refreshed this old story some time ago by stating in a book that the PdA receives 300,000 SFR from the Soviet Union every year.[21]

The party has to rely on its own resources to fund its press, which consists of a weekly in each of the three main languages (*Voix Ouvrière, Vorwärts* and *Il Lavoratore*). It is a real miracle that these still exist, since finance is extremely difficult and usually income from sales has to be supplemented from fund raising in the same laborious way as party activity in general has to be financed.

Conclusions

For the PdA hibernation has become a political strategy, and the survival of the party apparatus an end in itself. This has meant a closing of the ranks, greater ideological uniformity and less tolerance of divergent opinions. The result is a vicious circle: the greater intolerance grows, the less attraction the party has for potential recruits. After a phase of ideological opening in the 1970s, the party seems to be on the way back to the ghetto, and a certain bunker mentality, with its defensive reflex against anything coming from outside, is making a reappearance. This renders a correct assessment of new social tendencies and movements difficult: understanding the signs of the times has never been the strong point of the party. It has never been able to take the steps necessary to prevent itself slipping down into insignificance. It adopts no countermeasures, but clings desperately to the old formulas.

This fateful helplessness cannot be understood without taking into account the party's weakness on theoretical matters. It has never developed a critical analysis of the political and economic situation of

Swiss capitalism but has always been satisfied with the general statement that the crisis and contradictions of capitalism have worsened once more and therefore the need for socialism on the part of the broad masses has risen. The party observed the theoretical discussion that was going on in its French and Italian sister parties but kept out of the debate on Eurocommunism by resorting to the formal argument that it had acknowledged the necessity of a national road to socialism long ago.

This is true in so far as the dictatorship of the proletariat has never been in the party's programme and the building of socialism has been assumed ever since the 1959 programme to have its starting point in the existing democratic institutions. But the party ignored the increasing loss of faith in these institutions, especially among the workers, that was evident from a growing tendency to stay away from votes and elections. The party did not realize either that new forms of expression of radical political opinion were developing outside the traditional democratic institutions. It remained hide-bound by these institutions and therefore could not be regarded as anything but conservative by the new radical forces.

The party has held unshakeably to two articles of faith: the revolutionary vocation of the proletariat, and the revolutionary role of the Soviet Union. These guarantee the party's identity: to renounce them would be to renounce that identity. And the party seems to prefer a loss of influence to the loss of its identity. It is a choice for which a high price has to be paid: the renunciation of all political radicalism.

The potential for radical politics in Switzerland is admittedly a limited one[22] but the party never succeeded in organizing it to a significant degree. Today radical opposition is articulated more and more by less compactly organized forces that form temporarily around single issues – the so-called new social movements. Party members often take part in these movements, but without their party deriving much benefit from this involvement.

Swiss society does not easily tolerate radical dissidence and such dissenters are subjected to heavy repression.[23] The traditional labour movement has never been able to give much protection to them, and this has proved to be a serious obstacle in the development of a radical opposition. Today this situation has changed a little in so far as there has risen a new counter-culture acting as a kind of social shelter for radicalism. Together with the appearance of new life-styles and initiatives aimed at promoting an alternative society there seems to emerge also a new quality of political activity. With its spontaneity and creativity it differs completely from the severe attitude of the PdA, whose self-image is more one of a band of unselfish militants entirely at the service of the working class, full of dogged seriousness in the face of a grave historical task where personal interests do not matter at all.

Would any alternative strategy have yielded better results, given that the social base is lacking for a mass communist party? For historical reasons – there was no anti-fascist resistance movement as in France and Italy – the party never had the opportunity to demonstrate its national credentials. A union of the Left never really had a chance, since the party could not muster sufficient votes to be of significant support to the Social Democrats in forming a government. Conceivably the party could have acted as a kind of radical conscience within the labour movement, providing a radical influence on the trade unions and reminding the 'reformist' Social Democrats of their responsibilities.

But in any case, nobody could take the party's call for more democracy in Switzerland seriously as long as it supported a political system outside Switzerland – such as the Soviet one – where the process of decision-making is so heavily monopolized. The party itself has had occasion to acknowledge this.[24] It never succeeded in overcoming its pro-Sovietism, which is nothing but the reverse side of anti-communism, one holy cow to be set against another holy cow – because the enemies of communism find everything bad, I have to find everything about it good.[25] This 'double holy cow syndrome' makes it easy for every opponent to discredit the party and is responsible, too, for most inner-party conflicts. It is also responsible for the fact that the party could not draw new strength from the rising radicalism of 1968 and afterwards. The fundamental opponents of the Swiss political and economic system had to go elsewhere; and so the question must arise whether the PdA has in fact missed its last chance of renewal.

Notes

1 Officially the outlawing of the party came to an end only on 25 February 1945, by a decision of the government. See C. Gruber, *Die Politischen Parteien der Schweiz im Zweiten Weltkrieg* (Europa Verlag, Vienna, Frankfurt, Zürich, 1966), pp. 221ff and U. Rauber (ed.), *Zur Geschichte der Kommunistischen Bewegung der Schweiz* (Zürich, 1981), p.167.

2 Geneva 36 per cent; Basle 23.8 per cent; Vaud 19.4 per cent; Neuchâtel 13.6 per cent; Zürich 6.6 per cent.

3 Geneva: from 14.0 per cent in 1961 to 16.0 per cent in 1965; Neuchâtel: from 5.2 per cent in 1961 to 8.7 per cent in 1965; Vaud: 5.1 per cent in 1962 to 8.1 per cent in 1966.

4 Geneva 20.2 per cent; Vaud 14.3 per cent and Neuchâtel 19.0 per cent.

5 *Bericht von Jean Vincent an den 9. Parteitag (1968)*, pp. 29ff.

6 *Bericht von Jean Vincent an den 10. Parteitag (1974)*, pp. 25ff.

7 'Materialen zu den Austritten in der PdA Waadt', in *Widerspruch* (Zürich) 1981, no.1.

8   In the municipal elections in Zürich in 1986 the PdA of Zürich did not even participate.
9   Party statutes, 1982, Article 3.
10 *Bericht von Armand Magnin an den 12. Parteitag (1983)*, p. 22.
11 Ibid., p. 39.
12 'Bericht der Mandatsprüfungskommission, 11. Parteitag' (unpublished).
13 For examples of the latter, compare the cases of Lausanne in 1980 (see note 7) and Zürich in 1983: 'Abschied von der PdA', in *Vorwärts*, 4 August 1983.
14 K. Odermatt, in *Sozialismus in der Schweiz?* (Basle, 1979), p. 121.
15 *Bericht von Armand Magnin an den 12. Parteitag* (1983), p. 13.
16 *Rechenschaftsbericht des Parteivorstandes an den 22. Parteitag*, Canton Zürich, 1978, p. 13; and 'Rechenschaftsbericht für den 23. Kantonalen Parteitag 1980', p. 29 (unpublished).
17 Private communication.
18 In the national elections of 1971, 71 per cent of the votes came from Geneva, Vaud and Neuchâtel, although these cantons account for only some 20 per cent of the national population.
19 'Bericht der Mandatsprüfungskommission, 11. Parteitag' (unpublished).
20 *Rechenschaftsbericht für den 22. Parteitag* (see n. 16).
21 N. Polianski, *MID. Douze ans dans le service diplomatique du Kremlin* (Paris, 1984), p. 178ff.
22 Compare the assessment offered by H. Kriesi, *Bewegung in der Schweizer Politik* (Campus Verlag, Frankfurt/New York, 1985), p. 37ff.
23 Ibid., p. 413ff.
24 Cf. 'Erklärung des Politischen Büros, Die Lage in Polen' (20 December 1981), in *12 Parteitag*, p. 73.
25 B. Rabehl, 'Die Stalinismusdiskussion des internationalen Kommunismus', in R. Medwedew (ed.) *Entstalinisierung*, (Suhrkamp, Frankfurt, 1977), p. 322ff.

13 The British Road to Eurocommunism
The Communist Party of Great Britain

John Callaghan

A new programme

In 1947 Harry Pollitt wrote that it 'is possible to see how the people will move towards Socialism without further revolution, without the dictatorship of the proletariat.'[1] In this way the General Secretary of the Communist Party of Great Britain (CPGB) calmly dropped a central tenet of Leninism. There was no major debate to reappraise the party's history and theoretical legacy, yet by 1951, when the CPGB adopted a new programme entitled *The British Road to Socialism*, it was possible to assert that only 'the enemies of Communism accuse it of aiming to introduce Soviet Power in Britain and abolish Parliament.' This was simply a 'slanderous misrepresentation' of Communist Party policy.[2]

A rationale was discovered for the new orientation but this should not be confused with a genuine attempt to situate the party's 'democratic' programme in relation to the Leninist origins of the organization. It was merely asserted that the balance of forces internationally had swung against capitalism with the defeat of European and Japanese fascism. The socialist bloc had emerged greatly strengthened. Together with the rising colonial revolution, these anti-capitalist forces made peaceful democratic change to socialism possible in countries such as Britain. In these advanced capitalist societies, it was argued, the growth of state monopoly capitalism had created the objective basis for very broad anti-monopoly alliances of 'the people'. Small businessmen and small farmers, intellectuals and white collar workers, students and housewives as well as the wage-earners, all had good reason to come together against a system run by an exploitative minority that was as irrational and destructive of genuine enterprise and diversity as it was greedy and authoritarian.[3]

Undoubtedly Communists were receptive to these arguments because of the success of Popular Frontism. Even in Britain the Popular Front policy was associated with the growth of the party and the spread of its influence far and wide. A new legitimacy and credibility and even the electoral successes of 1945–6 in local and central government were associated with Popular Frontism. Such pragmatic considerations weighed heavily in the balance and we certainly need not suppose that the party leaders had been converted to a new vision of the intrinsic value of democracy, say, or a new relationship with the Soviet Union. Even as Pollitt adumbrated the democratic road in 1947 he reminded his readers that 'since 8 November 1917 . . . the Soviet Union has never once formulated a policy that was not in the interests of the common peoples of the whole world.'[4] And in the year that he stepped down from the general secretaryship, the party's support for the Soviet invasion of Hungary made one dissident observe that the CPGB's belief in democracy was as weak as Labour's commitment to socialism.[5]

If the required anti-monopoly alliance was to have any prospect it was essential for the CPGB to find a working relationship with the Labour Left. The Party saw this need from the outset and accordingly stressed 'Left unity' as the key for its own growth as well as for the advance of British socialism. In fact the party shrank, and it has continued to lose members in nearly every one of the past twenty years. Membership today (1987) stands at a mere 9,000, and this of course reflects the party's lack of success in forging a stable, mutually beneficial relationship with the Labour Left. At the height of the cold war this was simply impossible. The party itself was too obviously Stalinist and subservient to the Soviet Union. New drafts of the *British Road to Socialism* appeared in 1958 and 1968, but even by the latter date there was still no evidence of a major rethinking on the theoretical and historical issues ignored in 1951. The party had not yet come to terms with the Stalinist past though it is not too much to say that conflicts within the party since 1968 have largely been about this issue.

If the party was able to join with most other Western European communist parties in the denunciation of the Warsaw Pact's invasion of Czechoslovakia in 1968, this was testimony to the impact of changes generated on the outside. Communist monolithism had been chipped away in the 1940s and 1950s. Popular Frontism was followed by the discovery of national roads to socialism. The authority of Moscow was challenged first by Tito, later in the people's democracies – where working class revolts were repressed by the Kremlin – and eventually by Mao. In 1963 a small group of Maoists led by Michael McCreery left the CPGB to form the Committee to Defeat Revisionism for Communist Unity.[6]

More important were the continued relationships between party intellectuals and the dissidents of 1956. Those of the latter who kept faith with socialism remained on amicable terms and in dialogue with party members. In this way a common concern to escape the confines of the mechanical Marxism associated with Leninism and Stalinism was strengthened. Individual party members became acquainted with the work of Gramsci, while the party 'machine minders' were probably more impressed by the electoral gains of the Italian Communist Party (PCI). For Western Europe's biggest communist party was also a leader in doctrinal innovation. As early as 1944 Togliatti had renounced the one-party state as a model for Italian socialism and in 1956 he had invented the formula of 'polycentrism' with its implied denial of Moscow's leading role. In every post-war decade the PCI's share of the vote increased. But this growth was especially rapid between 1972 and 1976 when as much electoral ground was won as between 1946 and 1972. The period from the late 1960s was also a time of the PCI's most innovative and daring doctrinal changes, including acceptance of NATO and the need for a 'historic compromise' with the Christian Democrats. At a time, then, when increasing numbers of Communists were discovering Gramsci and beginning to regard the special relationship with Moscow as a dead weight, the most successful Western party was the one most critical of the Soviet system and of the Leninist legacy.

The 'discovery' of Gramsci is particularly important in understanding the evolution of the CPGB since 1968. In the first place the party was in possession of a programme that was never properly theorized but which had been put together for pragmatic reasons. Yet this programme committed the organization to a long revolution based on the broadest possible alliance of all those groups and classes objectively at odds with monopoly capital.

Much of this programme could not be justified on Leninist grounds. The party had dropped the dictatorship of the proletariat, was no longer bent on smashing the state, had discovered the virtues of Parliament, and was avowedly dependent on some sort of partnership with reformists. But where Lenin had analysed bourgeois democracy as a mere sham concealing the rule of finance capital and the coercive state institutions, Gramsci had argued that the bourgeois hegemony was constituted in civil society or the realm of 'private' associations. In so doing he stressed all those facets of class rule especially germane to Western democracies which Lenin had ignored – cultural forms, the generation of consent, the role of ideology and so on.

It can be argued, moreover, that since the rule of the bourgeoisie rests on foundations of this sort which penetrate deep into the values and consciousness of the populace, the Western states are most unlikely to succumb to an insurrectionary strategy predicated on political instability arising from economic collapse. If such a 'war of manoeuvre' is to be rejected in favour of a 'war of position', by means of which the communist party establishes its supremacy through the exercise of moral and intellectual leadership in the civil society, what is this other than a strategy of building broad alliances around the real interests and aspirations of innumerable and diverse social groups and classes?

New social movements

In this way Gramsci and the party's programme were re-made for each other. But this was not just a question of finding retrospective justification for the *British Road*. For 1968 was the year of the new social movements – the women's movement, the growth of the race issue, the environmental campaigns, the new emphasis on democracy, community and participation – what all these fragments had in common, apart from being growth points for the development of radical politics, was their exclusion from the discourse and organizations of the traditional Left. But their common stress on cultural, ideological and democratic issues underlined the relevance of a Marxist approach that could avoid economic reductionism and accommodate the tolerant pluralism that alliance with these groups demanded. This further pointed to the usefulness of Gramsci.

Moreover, if the Marxist groups were to exploit the new radical movements – and not one of them had better things to do – it was obvious that some sort of adaptation was required. Issues were given attention where they had once been ignored; journals were launched to accommodate socialist feminism; organizational changes were made to promote greater representation of the relevant social groups; the International Marxist Group and the International Socialists even for a time allowed separate women's caucuses within their own organizations, although in both cases they were eliminated soon after the experiment began. But, as the latter case illustrates, while the Left made changes all the better to devour the new social movements, the transmission of ideas and values was a two-way process. Feminists in particular proved more than equal to the challenge and Leninist dogma took a battering before the onslaughts of 'patriarchy', prefigurative politics, the politics of the personal, positive discrimination, the demand for an 'autonomous' women's movement and the rest. Thus contact with the new social movements served to increase the distance from Leninism already travelled by the modernizers within the CPGB.

The Trotskyists, on the other hand, travelled in the opposite direction after 1968 and thus lost the initiative which they had briefly held in that year. The International Socialists abandoned their federal organizational forms in favour of democratic centralism. The May events had evidently persuaded their leaders that only a Leninist party could advance the socialist cause and they accordingly turned to 'organization at the point of production' so as to build a workers' party. Henceforward this group, re-named the Socialist Workers' Party in January 1977, became increasingly sectarian in its attempts to build the vanguard. The International Marxist Group emerged from the Labour Party in 1968/9 determined to grow in the student and feminist movements and ready to champion an array of guerilla movements and national liberation wars. Within a few years it had accumulated more front organizations than members and was also declaring itself the embodiment of Leninist principles.

Finally, the Socialist Labour League – always an intolerant Trotskyist sect – became the Workers' Revolutionary Party in 1973. Like the Militant entrists in the Labour Party, whose star began to rise from the same time, the WRP was loudly disdainful of the women's movement, of the peace movement and of student politics. Neither of them showed the faintest interest in environmental issues or community politics but focused exclusively on the industrial working class and the preoccupations of its mass organizations.[7] Naturally none of these organizations was prepared to concede any ideological ground to the new social movements. Even the best of them treated sex inequality, for example, as a functional requirement of capitalism and so proved incapable of learning anything from the women's movement.[8]

The Communist Party, on the other hand, proved far more receptive to the new ideas and issues. Among students the party eventually made dramatic headway by concentrating its efforts in the National Union of Students (NUS). This seemed most unfavourable soil – the NUS constitution debarred politics from the conference agenda. But while the Trotskyists created separate organizations – such as the Revolutionary Socialist Student Federation, whose constitution improbably requested the abolition of 'bourgeois ideology' from the curriculum of schools and universities – the CPGB fought for a change of NUS rules. When the change came, the party, working through a Broad Left with Labour students, was able to turn the NUS presidency and many of its vice-presidencies into CPGB-dominated positions for most of the 1970s and into the 1980s.

By the mid-1970s the party's ideological offensive among students – greatly aided by the vogue for Gramsci and Althusser among leftist intellectuals – was spearheaded by an annual Communist University of London. The success of this enterprise was helped enormously by the fact that the party had, since the 1930s, always possessed a disproportionate number of intellectuals and well-known academics. The party was also able to draw on a long Marxist intellectual tradition that the Trotskyists were disposed to ignore as Stalinist. The tables had thus been turned on the Trotskyists,who could get no further than Lenin and Trotsky in the search for an authoritative Marxist analysis. Where once this tradition had seemed comparatively open and tolerant of ideas, it now appeared intellectually barren and practically authoritarian.

Industrial politics

In Britain student militancy was very soon eclipsed by the strike wave that eventually engulfed the Heath government in 1974. A significant number of these strikes were overtly political – especially from 1969 when the first legislative proposals to curb shop stewards' power were presented in Barbara Castle's White Paper *In Place of Strife*. But the overwhelming number of industrial disputes were economic in character, and one leading Communist later referred to the experience as a new syndicalism, though one devoid of the vision and strategy of the original article.[9] The party's rivals on the far Left threw themselves wholeheartedly behind the rising industrial militancy and set themselves ambitious plans to create proletarian vanguard parties organized mainly in factory branches and capable of leading a national movement of the trade union rank and file.

Not only did these projects come to nought and the groups concerned prove incapable of surpassing Communist Party membership and industrial influence, but the experience further underlined the sectarian character and doctrinal rigidity of the Trotskyists. In particular, most of these organizations trumpeted their dislike for the issues which preoccupied the 'trendy middle class' while backing every pay demand as evidence of a growing socialist consciousness among the industrial workers. Unlike the Communist Party, moreover, the Trotskyist groups were too puny actually to lead any of the major disputes of the period.

Communist industrial strength was still evident in the early 1970s, though not at all as pervasive as Harold Wilson had implied in the previous decade, when he raised the communist bogey in order to discredit the seamen's strike in 1966: Bert Ramelson, the CPGB's industrial organizer, was on that occasion ludicrously dubbed 'the most powerful man in Britain'. Ramelson still held this party position during the lifetime of the Heath government when industrial militancy was at its height. It was then that the CPGB revived the Liaison Committee for the Defence of Trade Unions (LCDTU), which it had originally created in 1966 to coordinate opposition to Wilson's prices and incomes policy. In the period 1970–4 the LCDTU sought to pressurize the TUC into adopting a general strike against the Tories' industrial relations legislation. In December 1970 some 600,000 answered the call for strike action and mass demonstrations took place in the major cities in response to LCDTU agitation.[10] Two Communists were among the five dock workers imprisoned in July 1971 and a Communist was one of three building workers imprisoned for 'conspiracy' in 1972.[11] Naturally the LCDTU took up the cause of such militants in the struggle to destroy the Industrial Relations Act. Mass demonstrations under the slogan 'Kill the Bill' were mobilized through the LCDTU before the TUC was prepared to defy the government. Then, in March 1972, 3 million stopped work in answer to its call for a one-day general strike. In February 1972 more than 1,000 trade union delegates attended the LCDTU conference testifying to its influence among the militant rank and file.

Communists were also prominent in particular disputes. At Upper Clyde Shipbuilders (UCS) in 1971, Communist shop stewards led the opposition to the proposed closure of the four yards. In so doing they transformed the conflict into a struggle for the 'right to work'. The yards were occupied by the work force and a work-in began, which among other things greatly undermined government propaganda concerning the strike-prone character of union militants. The stewards made skilful use of the media and promoted the dispute as a turning-point for the whole trade union and labour movement. Today the UCS struggle is seen by some Communists as a brilliant application of the strategy of erecting a broad democratic anti-monopoly alliance. The Communist stewards, it is argued, not only kept the workers of four shipbuilding yards united but attracted the active support of the community, local politicians, shopkeepers, UCS management, the local church and national trade union and labour leaders, as well as the rank and file. UCS is now seen as the origin of the Heath government's U-turn on industrial relations policy and the victory of the 1972 miners' strike. It directly inspired some 190 factory occupations and work-ins between July 1971 and December 1975.[12]

Internal division and decay

Though no Communist would doubt that the party played an honourable role in defending basic trade union rights in these years, divisions began to appear over other aspects of its industrial policy as early as the mid-1970s. Two issues in particular increasingly became a source of faction within the party. First, how should the party assess the strike wave of the early 1970s and the bouts of trade union militancy thereafter (such as in the winter of 1978–9)? Secondly, how does the party's industrial work relate to its programme, and the objective of construct-ing a broad anti-monopoly alliance? A vocal minority argued that the traditional role of supporting workers in industrial struggle and defend-ing existing trade union gains was not enough so long as this militancy re-mained merely economistic and sectional.

Communist support for such struggles was very often simply a reflex response that stemmed from the party's accustomed role as a purely oppositional force. Though most of the party's trade union militants and most of the leadership were at home with such politics, some of the party's economists (in particular David Purdy, Pat Devine and Bob Rowthorn) argued that the tide of wage militancy in the early 1970s had been a defensive response to the worsening economic situation and one that had added to the inflationary problem. Worse still, the Left had failed to advance a credible solution to the economic crisis with the result that when a Labour government was returned in 1974 the initiative quickly passed to the movement's right wing.

Until the first Thatcher government was elected in 1979 these heretical doubts were confirmed to a minority of the party's intellectuals. The party's official position supported the Alternative Economic Strategy (AES) which the party had pioneered from the late 1960s.[13] By 1974 a variant of the AES appeared in the Labour Party's election manifesto but it was, of course, never implemented. The Communist version demanded nationalization of the banks, 'key' multinationals, a variety of finance institutions and North Sea oil. It called for withdrawal from the EEC, selective import controls, planning agreements backed by the threat of nationalization and restrictions on capital movements. While capital was to be further restricted by price controls workers would benefit from free collective bargaining, from a major state-directed investment programme designed to create jobs and to provide for modernization of the economic infrastructure, and from increased public expenditure on the social services. It was emphasized that the whole programme would be financed by incursions against the ruling class and cuts in defence expenditure (where it was not self-financing).[14] But the AES's detractors in the CPGB accused it of being irredeemably statist, in-flationary and politically naive. Let us examine the reasons why.

The party's response to Wilson's Social Contract in 1974 was to denounce the deal with the Trades Union Congress as a 'con-trick' from which nothing could be expected in return for pay restraint except reduced living standards.[15] The party thus announced its opposition to all wage restraint. But it also demanded increased public expenditure on housing, pensions, health care, job creation and all the rest of the social services. However, these policies lacked credibility in the view of those 'Gramscians' in the organization who believed that instead of making general propaganda for socialism, the party ought to be addressing the real problems of the British economic crisis. On this reasoning the party would only begin to operate as a leading force when it was able to advance specific socialist solutions to specific economic problems. In particular it was argued that there was no escaping the conclusion that inflation was indeed related to wage militancy – the latter was 'the only consistent explanation for the emergence of *persistent* inflation as the major economic problem of modern capitalism'.[16] No useful purpose could be served by blind opposition to wage controls. Instead, they reasoned, the organizations of the working class should construct their own incomes policy as a bargaining device for a greater say in economic decision-making. The unions then would exchange an illusory increase in living standards for a real increment of economic power. By these means the political sophistication of the movement is advanced and a counter-hegemonic strategy is actually set in motion. Otherwise the movement remains trapped on the treadmill of wage militancy.

Similar themes were taken up in the pages of the party's theoretical journal *Marxism Today*. Here it was argued that

What above all characterized the decade from 1966–75 was that the ruling class was unable decisively to impose a new strategic course on the working class whilst the working class. . . failed to advance beyond the bounds of corporate defencism to mount an offensive political struggle around a credible alternative economic programme of its own.[17]

Once again it was being argued that the incoherence and implausibility of the Left's own programme stemmed from its desire to plan everything except wages. But there is also an awareness here of the counterproductive demand for large-scale extensions of nationalization. Not only was this demand of the Left unpopular, it was unpopular as an instance of the statist and bureaucratic false remedies which some Communists and many radicals had begun to reject: these centralizing policies were increasingly seen as incompatible with democracy and the prefigurative politics favoured by the new social movements and the party's 'Gramscians'.

Two quite different conceptions of socialist politics now existed in the party. The 'Leninist' view, which by virtue of inertia held the majority position, was all about trade union militancy providing the solid bedrock from which the party would gain leadership positions and influence within the broader labour movement. The minority of modernizers, however, wanted recognition of the need to change habits, practices, values and institutions now in order to make socialism something more than an ultimate goal in the party's propaganda. In this perspective the party assists other movements and social forces to discover principles of action that anticipate an alternative social order, so that it is possible to challenge the hegemony of the bourgeoisie.

But it is also a view that finds the traditional organizations of the labour movement guilty of reproducing the very forms of domination that need to be overcome – especially authoritarian leadership and the exclusion of women, minority groups and a variety of issues promoted by the new social movements. Naturally, this current of thought therefore rejected democratic centralism and the domination of higher party bodies over lower tiers in the organization.[18] While in the traditional party view the organized working class was the mainspring of radical politics, the 'Gramscians' looked more favourably on those movements that seemed to subvert capitalist values – specifically conservationism, movements for decentralization, direct democracy, community and women's liberation, 'in essence . . . all socializing movements'.[19] While the fundamentalists were at best equivocal over the party's Stalinist legacy and inclined to applaud the socialist countries, the modernizers were disposed to see Left unity as thus far a victim of the party's sectarian origins and its acquiescence in Stalinism and its continued 'special relationship' with Moscow.

Whereas the party was a declining force under the dominance of the old politics, the new social movements were among the few growth points and sources of vitality on the Left. This strengthened the hand of the modernizers within the party, particularly since recruitment among students and feminists was higher than among workers in heavy industry. In comparison with the Trotskyist would-be vanguards with their insistence on hyperactivity, candidate membership procedures and rote-learned shibboleths, the CPGB was already very relaxed in the induction of new members and tolerant of dissenting opinion (though this did not extend to fractions or tendencies). Moreover, the party did not indulge in blatant attempts to manipulate independent organizations of feminists, anti-racists and the like. But most party intellectuals *were* prepared to acknowledge the ideological deficiencies of Leninism in regard to the concerns of the new radical movements. Unlike the Trotskyist sects, the CPGB through its intellectuals and academics was also sensitive to a growing body of independent socialist literature that pointed to the paternalistic and even authoritarian shortcomings within both Labourist and Communist theory and practice.[20]

Finally, the 'wets' in the party had the distinct advantage, as against their hardline opponents, of being able to point to the successful PCI as an image of what the CPGB could become if the party's long-standing commitment to a broad anti-monopoly alliance was understood as a counter-hegemonic strategy privileging cultural change rather than blind industrial militancy. For all these reasons the initiative lay with the minority of modernizers in the late 1970s.[21]

Equally important was the negative process of the decay of the party's ancient virtues.[22] The party was no longer ideologically self-sufficient – too many of its former shibboleths had been routed or surrendered without a fight for that to be possible. The old ideology, moreover, was morally bankrupt and its homeland no longer spellbinds the communist movement. Once the certainty that formerly buttressed communist convictions was undermined and the equally strong moral superiority was put in serious and permanent doubt, there then began the decay of that discipline, unity and organizational efficiency that had been the hallmark of communist politics. After 1968 these changes became more rapid, assisted, paradoxically, by the revival of interest in Marxism. From the mid-1970s the balance of forces within the CPGB shifted as the recession bit into the party's declining industrial strength and both the total membership and sales of the *Morning Star* continued to fall. The vulgar Marxists who expected the Left's political prospects to brighten as the economic situation worsened were proved hopelessly wrong; the more sophisticated strategy of the modernizers began to look a better prospect.

Stalinist legacy

Nevertheless, 20 years after Khrushchev's secret speech, in 1976 John Gollan, the CPGB's retiring general secretary, reflected on the 'problems of socialist democracy' without advancing one inch on his predecessor, Harry Pollitt. The size of the ideological gap now opening within the party can be gauged from the fact that Gollan perceived Soviet problems past and present as problems of growth. Even Stalin's admitted crimes could not disturb, so we are told, 'the basic foundations of the Soviet system', a system whose superiority over capitalism was both economic and, 'with power in the hands of the working class', political.[23] The debate that followed only served to demonstrate an enormous range of opinion within the CPGB on the nature of the Soviet Union, Stalin's record, Lenin's role in creating the preconditions for Stalinism and much else besides.[24]

Undoubtedly the rather imprecise formulations of the party programme – a blend, one might say, of Stalinist origin and of retrospective Gramscian construction – kept both sides in the organization for rather longer than might otherwise have been the case. The energies of these opposing forces went into the creation of a new draft of the *British Road* which appeared in February 1977 and was debated publicly until the thirty-fifth congress in November of that year. With the exception of a group of around 700 who resigned to form the pro-Moscow New Communist Party, the new draft managed to accommodate all shades of party opinion. In place of an anti-monopoly alliance the party now talked of the need for a broad democratic alliance: all the old arguments were now illustrated by reference to the 'new social movements'.

But if this was some sort of victory to the modernizers, the hand of their opponents was clearly visible as well in references to the superiority of actually existing socialism and (that Stalinist invention) the Marxist–Leninist ideology. Likewise, the programme referred to the 'key and decisive responsibility' of the communist party – code for the 'leading role of the party' – and made clear the party's commitment to democratic centralism.[25] But no sooner was this programme adopted than a further lengthy period of introspection was begun as the party's 'wets' sought to change the organization's Leninist norms.

Two more years elapsed before the Commission on Inner-Party Democracy reported to the thirty-sixth congress in November 1979. While the main report, as in 1957, made only verbal concessions to the critics of democratic centralism, six of the 16 commissioners submitted a minority report, which attested the major ideological changes experienced since then.[26] The minority acknowledged that the party's heritage included 'those bureaucratic, anti-democratic distorting practices which have come to be known as Stalinism.'[27] Its ongoing practices in terms of the election and exercise of leadership, they argued, were out of step with the party's programme. Branches were still not encouraged to take initiatives, the party was far too rigidly centralized for that and this concentration of political power at the top of the organization, they observed, was augmented by the rarity with which mistakes were openly recognized and the leadership seen to learn from experience. The dissenters also pointed out that the leadership was largely a self-recruiting elite, since it was the Political Committee that determined promotions to the larger Executive, which otherwise reproduced itself by means of a 'recommended list' of approved candidates. The dissenters proposed instead that the Executive should be elected directly by the party conference and that to facilitate the expression of different trends of opinion it should be possible to circulate written papers in pre-congress periods. The minority report also argued for greater 'horizontal communication' between branches and scope for dissident members of the Executive to explain their position to the ranks.

Thatcherism

These proposals would obviously have democratized and decentralized the party and moved it towards a cleaner break with its Stalinist and Leninist past. But the attempt by the self-styled Eurocommunist wing to force the pace of change was defeated in 1979 because it was not yet united on this issue or able to win over the party 'centre' and full-timers. Better progress was made via the appointment of Martin Jacques as editor of *Marxism Today*. Jacques here announced his intention to open the journal to non-party contributors and focus the articles on analysis of topical issues in Britain.[28] Not only was all this done – to the exclusion of items concerned with Marxist theory, socialist and communist history – but the CPGB's theoretical journal boosted its circulation to around 12,500 – three times its former number and certainly a higher figure than the party membership.

With the election in 1979 of the Conservative Thatcher government, *Marxism Today* used the talents of non-party socialists to set the agenda of Left debate. In particular it promoted the argument that Thatcherism had exposed the ideological weaknesses of the Left by usurping the language of individual rights and liberty, by championing a popular anti-statism and an array of cultural issues ignored by socialism. The failure of the Left to develop socialist answers to the pressing concerns of the British people was supposedly connected with its failure to change behaviour, values and relationships whilst overestimating the ability of politicians to act on behalf of people's interests. These were two sides of the same social democratic legacy in which the whole Left was implicated, in so far as it favoured statist measures and ignored the demands for devolution, local democracy and genuine participation coming from the grass roots. Clearly this was a criticism of all those who diagnosed Labour's defeat of 1979 as a punishment needlessly inflicted on the movement by right-wing leaders who simply refused to promote a socialist programme.

In fact the CPGB historian Eric Hobsbawm chose the Marx Memorial Lecture of 1978 to pose the question. 'Has the forward march of Labour been halted?'. Thus, even before Labour's electoral defeat, at a time when it still held office and trade union membership had reached a post-war peak, a gulf in perceptions and standards was opening within the Left. On one side was the small 'Eurocommunist' Left, persuaded of the necessity for innovations in policy and approach; on the other side were the much larger forces of the traditional Left loosely coalesced behind Tony Benn in the campaign to democratize the Labour party. This larger force included so-called 'Stalinists' and Trotskyists as well as militants in the Labour Party. They all believed that the Left was now stronger than ever and capable of bringing about a socialist government once the last barrier – in the shape of the Labour Right – was overcome. In contrast, Hobsbawm and those around him in the 'Eurocommunist' wing of the CPGB talked of a 30-year crisis of the labour movement. This was characterized by a decline of the manual working class, a growth in sectionalism at the expense of class solidarity and a long-term fall in the Labour vote and membership of socialist organizations. While Hobsbawm specifically drew attention to the largely sterile economistic militancy of the period 1970–4, his opponents in the debate that followed asserted that the labour movement had never been stronger and that 'wage battles . . . will, through militancy, challenge contemporary capitalism'.[29]

As the argument developed, the 'Eurocommunist' wing became more obviously critical of the strike weapon and, by impugning the motives of shop stewards and strikers, ran into head-on confrontation with the CPGB traditionalists and the *Morning Star* which acted as the latter's mouthpiece. The challenge to traditional Leftist assumptions had since the late 1960s also included the contention that socialist debate was too narrow and socialist practice guilty of reproducing features of an oppressive society. The electoral success of Thatcherism reinforced these arguments. After May 1979 the Eurocommunists – with considerable assistance from non-party intellectuals – argued that Thatcherism was an authoritarian populism bent on a radical reversal of the collectivist drift of post-war Britain. If this project was at all possible, it was argued, it was because the Right had never been challenged successfully at the level of popular beliefs and values and was now harnessing a range of fears to construct a new reactionary common sense.[30] When proponents of this analysis later concluded that 'the most crucial task' was to concert the anti-Thatcher forces and create 'the broadest possible set of alliances' many Communists saw this as evidence that their own 'wets' had dropped socialism from the agenda and were even ready to court the despised Liberal–Social Democratic Alliance.

The spectacular defection of a member of the CPGB's Executive, a former Communist president of the National Union of Students and star of the 'wets', to the Social Democratic Party must have crystallized these fears and highlighted the party's lack of cohesion and ideological rigour.[31] It was not necessary to belong to the party's pro-Moscow wing to worry that the organization had virtually opened its doors to anybody but was no longer able to induct recruits and formulate and enforce a clear line. Moreover, the modernizers, while full of doubts and questionings on socialist fundamentals, had now embarked on a project that only made sense, if it made any sense at all, for a mass party such as the PCI. Even those in the party who rejected the emphases of the 'Stalinists' were not wholly persuaded that an organization so electorally insignificant that it was regularly beaten by even tinier groups could base any future hopes on a proposal to participate in a broad electoral front unless it supplied the distinctive industrial militancy always associated with the Communist Party. In fact the party's industrial organizer, Pete Carter, was another outspoken critic of the limited alternative vision of industrial militancy, trade union sectionalism and the politics of the 'hard left'.[32] His own vision of the unions learning from the politics of conservationism, participatory democracy, feminism and anti-racism, was denounced in turn as 'a repudiation of the previous 60 years of Communist Party strategy'.

Factional struggle

It was undoubtedly the successes of Thatcher in 1979 and especially 1983 that more than anything enabled the party's 'Eurocommunists' to enlist the support of the organization's leadership and therefore that section of the membership consisting of party loyalists. Together these forces constituted a majority for change in the party which could be used to displace the traditionalists from their redoubts within the organization. These were now castigated as Stalinists and depicted as a dead weight blind to the necessity of ideological and organizational change. Theirs was the politics, it could be argued, that had brought the party years of decline resulting in moral and political marginality. The party conference of 1981 criticized the *Morning Star* – the mouthpiece of this traditionalist current – for its failure to reflect adequately the new emphases of the programme adopted in 1977. The *Morning Star*, for its part, chose August 1982 as the right time to denounce openly the politics of *Marxism Today*, which had recently referred to the 'perks and fiddles' of shop stewards.

The public row that was about to begin displayed a small sample of the divisions that now racked the party. It is not too much to say that the CPGB had been profoundly divided and demoralized for the previous 10 years. Organized fractions only sprang up after 1979, however, when the festering internal debate suddenly acquired urgency and movement by virtue of Thatcher's electoral success and systematic class offensive. I have so far perforce emphasized the sources of change within the organization; but obviously the Thatcher governments were living proof of the significance of class politics – and this was what the 'Eurocommunist' stress on non-class issues seemed to neglect in the eyes of many party members who were not in the least old-fashioned Stalinists.[33] Of course, the latter existed and were grouped around the factional journal

Straight Left, which received the support of some 20 per cent of the delegates at the thirty-eighth national congress in November 1983. These stood for unconditional support for the Soviet Union and argued that the CPGB had taken a revisionist course since 1956. For these party members the new social movements were thoroughly petty-bourgeois and a long way removed from real communist politics.

Another group has organized around the *Morning Star*, led by its editor Tony Chater – one of those who denounced the Soviet invasion of Czechoslovakia in 1968. Something like 17 per cent of the delegates at the thirty-eighth congress supported this faction, which is characterized by a Panglossian confidence in the virtues of trade union militancy rather than sycophancy towards the 'socialist' countries. Indeed its real sin in the eyes of the modernizers is its refusal to acknowledge the need for ideological renewal. Characteristically the *Morning Star*'s response to Labour's 1983 electoral defeat was to prescribe an even larger dose of the Alternative Economic Strategy (AES) for the next Labour Party manifesto. Within two years the 'Eurocommunist'–led party would jettison the AES altogether.

Finally, the implosion of the CPGB gave birth in 1981 to an opposition faction that traces the source of the present malaise back to Stalin and the Popular Front. Those grouped around *The Leninist* find Stalin guilty of bringing opportunism and centrism into the heart of communist politics. This, it is argued, calls for a reappraisal of the whole history of the CPGB and the communist movement – a process that will surely take some of those involved to Trotskyism. Already by November 1986 *The Leninist* celebrated the sixty-ninth anniversary of the October Revolution with a rally at which it shared the platform with Mike Banda, erstwhile defender of 'orthodox Trotskyism' in the Workers' Revolutionary Party. But so far *The Leninist* combines criticism of the Soviet Union with the injunction that the 'socialist' countries must be defended against imperialism.

With all this in mind, it can readily be understood why the thirty-eighth congress of the CPGB in 1983 was such a turbulent affair. Delegates were presented with a faction paper *Congress Truth* which provided an alternative recommended list of candidates for the executive committee. Forty per cent of the delegates supported this unprecedented move. Nevertheless, congress also voted to dismiss Tony Chater and his assistant editor David Whitfield (155 votes to 92) from their controlling positions at the *Morning Star*. They refused to step down and shocked the leadership in June 1984 by retaining their positions when a majority of the paper's shareholders voted to support their line. This was only possible because the *Morning Star* is owned by an independent cooperative, the People's Press Printing Society (PPPS), but it revealed accurately the true dimensions of the split now confronting the party.

By November 1984 opposition majorities managed to dominate proceedings at the North West District Congress and the London District Congress. At the former the national leadership of the party was taken by surprise and was unable to react until the damage had been done and a 'Stalinist' slate elected for the district. To forestall a repetition of this in London, General Secretary Gordon McLennan attempted to dissolve the congress, but 125 delegates refused to follow him out of the congress hall. This was now open warfare.

The *Morning Star* group meanwhile announced a 'survival plan' involving the purchase of a new printing press costing £750,000 – and this at a time when its anticipated deficit for 1984 stood at £200,000. The CPGB was not consulted on these matters; indeed it was now described as an 'outside body' by its own newspaper. The party responded by expelling Chater and Whitfield and suspending 22 members of the London District Committee. A special congress was called for May 1985 but already a purge had begun designed to smash the opposition factions. The *Morning Star* stepped up its campaign against the leadership with articles by founder members Andrew Rothstein and Robin Page Arnot declaring 'CP Executive Wrecking Action' and 'Eurocommunist Opportunism'. Workers at the *Morning Star* sympathetic to the party leadership were removed. The party was forced to launch a new weekly, *Focus*, which it distributed free to all party members.

The special congress of May 1985 secured two to one majorities for the leadership but the party failed to repossess the *Morning Star*. The June 1985 meetings of the PPPS in Manchester, Glasgow and London supported management committee nominees by a three to two majority. Influential allies spoke for the opposition. Arthur Scargill praised the *Morning Star* and denounced *Marxism Today* along with the CPGB's industrial organizer, Pete Carter, for respectively 'compromising with the class enemy' and 'vilifying' the National Union of Mineworkers (NUM). Carter had argued that the 1984/5 miners' strike would obstruct the election of a Labour government. It had been conducted, so the argument ran, in a spirit of narrow intransigence and without sufficient regard for, or recourse to, the broad alliance of support groups that the strike had summoned up. So far as the opposition was concerned the strike demonstrated the continued salience of class politics and the need for communist intervention.

But despite the prominence of Mick McGahey in the miners' struggle – and McGahey's support for the party's Eurocommunist leadership gave it badly needed credibility – the 1984/5 campaign was the first in which the party actually *lost* members, including Malcolm Pitt and Jack

Collins, president and secretary respectively of the Kent NUM. Indeed party membership fell alarmingly from 15,000 in 1983 to 11,000 in 1985 to 9,000 by January 1987. Much of this shrinkage can be attributed to the effects of demoralization and the purge that followed the special congress of May 1985. In the course of this purge borough committees were disbanded, branches dissolved and various advisory committees on industrial organization liquidated. Members were subjected to a loyalty test, if they bothered to reapply for membership after their branch organizations had been destroyed. Ironically the first purge in the party's history was conducted by its Eurocommunist democrats. Among the victims were Ken Gill, president of TASS and chairman of the TUC in 1985; Bert Ramelson and Mick Costello, former industrial organizers for the party; Derek Robinson, a leading shop steward in the car industry and an early victim of 'Thatcherism' at British Leyland's Longbridge plant. The party also lost leading feminists such as Elizabeth Wilson and Angela Weir as well as one of its few black members of the leadership, Winston Pindar. In all, 2,000–3,000 members either left the party or were removed from it between the special congress and January 1987.

Many of these are now organized on the outside by the Communist Campaign Group which intends to oust the 'Eurocommunist faction in control of the Communist Party'. This is a distinct possibility, though much depends on the ability of the present leadership to arrest the party's decline. A sizeable opposition persists within the party in spite of the purge. The demise of the party as an instigator of radical campaigns, as a champion of internationalism and as an organizer of militant trade unionists gives this opposition plenty to complain about. 'Class politics' as they see it provides a viable basis for a small but effective party: the 'Eurocommunist' perspective is much more ambitious than this, but it always threatens to leave the CPGB with much less.

Appendix *Membership of the Communist Party of Great Britain*

1945	45,435
1955	32,681
1965	33,734
1966	no figures
1967	no figures
1968	32,114
1969	30,607
1970	29,356

1971	28,803
1972	28,505
1973	29,943
1974	28,378
1975	28,529
1976	26,242
1977	25,293
1978	no figures
1979	20,599
1981	18,458
1983	15,691
1985	12,711
1986	11,000
1987	9,000

Notes

1   Harry Pollitt, *Looking Ahead* (CPGB, London, 1947), p. 90.
2   *The British Road to Socialism* (CPGB, London, 1951), p. 14.
3   The best account by a British communist of the state monopoly capital thesis is Sam Aaronovitch, *The Ruling Class* (Lawrence and Wishart, London, 1961).
4   Pollitt, *Looking Ahead*, p. 43.
5   *New Reasoner*, no. 2, 1957; see the essay on Harold Laski by Stephen Hatch.
6   Michael McCreery, *The Way Forward: a Marxist–Leninist Analysis of the British State, the CPGB and the Tasks for Revolutionaries* (Working People's Party of England, London, n.d.).
7   For further information on this see John Callaghan, *British Trotskyism* (Blackwell, Oxford, 1984).
8   See Fourth International, *Women's Liberation and the Socialist Revolution* (Pathfinder, Sydney, 1979).
9   E. J. Hobsbawm, 'Syndicalism and the Working Class', in *New Society*, 5 April 1979, pp. 8–10.
10   *Comment*, 19 December 1970, vol. 8, no. 51, p. 802.
11   Jim Arnison, *The Shrewsbury Three: Strikes, Pickets and 'Conspiracy'* (Lawrence and Wishart, London, 1974).
12   John Foster and Charles Woolfson, *The Politics of the UCS Work-in* (Lawrence and Wishart, London, 1986).
13   See Conference of Socialist Economists (CSE) Working Group, *The Alternative Economic Strategy* (CSE Books, London 1978).
14   For a recent defence of this programme see Communist Campaign Group (CCG), *Which Way for Labour?: A Communist Perspective for the Labour Movement* (CCG pamphlet, London, April 1986).
15   Bert Ramelson, *Social Contract – Cure-all or Con-trick* (CPGB pamphlet, London, n.d.).
16   Bill Warren and Mike Prior, *Advanced Capitalism and Backward Socialism* (Spokesman pamphlet no. 46, Nottingham, n.d.), pp. 8–9.

17 David Purdy, 'British Capitalism Since the War', Pt 2, in *Marxism Today*, October 1976, p. 316.

18 Mike Prior and David Purdy, *Out of the Ghetto* (Spokesman, Nottingham, 1979), p. 13.

19 Ibid., pp. 90–1.

20 This is the theme of many of the contributions to *Politics and Power* (Routledge and Kegan Paul, London). See also Alan Hunt (ed.), *Marxism and Democracy* (Lawrence and Wishart, London, 1980); G. Hodgson, *Socialism and Parliamentary Democracy* (Spokesman, Nottingham, 1977); F. Claudin, *The Communist Movement* (Penguin, Harmondsworth, 1975); R. Selucky, *Marxism, Socialism and Freedom* (Macmillan, London, 1979); Stuart Hall, 'The Great Moving Right Show', in *Marxism Today*, January 1979. After 1979 the number of books concerned to 'rethink' socialism along pluralist decentralized lines greatly increased.

21 It was in *Politics and Power* that, from 1980, like-minded Labour and Communist intellectuals pursued their rethinking of socialism. Although it only lasted until the end of 1981, its four issues managed to question everything from nationalization to the very existence of capitalism.

22 This theme is eloquently pursued by Raphael Samuel in 'The Lost World of British Communism', in *New Left Review*, 154, November/December 1985, and *New Left Review*, 156, March/April, 1986.

23 John Gollan, 'Socialist Democracy – Some Problems: the Twentieth Congress of the CPSU in Retrospect', in *Marxism Today*, January 1976, pp. 5/6.

24 See *Discussion on Socialist Democracy* (CPGB pamphlet, London, November 1976).

25 *The British Road to Socialism*, 5th edn (CPGB, London, March 1978), pp. 3 and 25.

26 The minority consisted of Dave Cook, Pat Devine, Josie Green, Maria Loftus, Veronica Luker and Joanne Richards.

27 *Report of the Commission on Inner-Party Democracy* (CPGB, London, 1979), pp. 5–46 and 47.

28 Editorial, *Marxism Today*, September 1978.

29 Martin Jacques and Francis Mulhearn (eds), *The Forward March of Labour Halted?* (Verso, London, 1981), p. 21.

30 Hall, 'The Great Moving Right Show'. This was the opening shot in the argument. Subsequent contributions appear also in Stuart Hall and Martin Jacques, (eds), *The Politics of Thatcherism* (Lawrence and Wishart, London, 1983).

31 This was Sue Slipman. Jimmy Reid, David Purdy and a number of other prominent Communists – mostly intellectuals – left the 'soft' wing of the CPGB for the Labour Party in the 1970s.

32 Pete Carter, *Trade Unions, the New Reality: the Communist View* (CPGB, London, 1986).

33 See, for example, Ben Fine, L. Harris, M. Mayo, A. Weir and E. Wilson, 'The British Women's Movement', in *New Left Review*, 148, November/December, 1984.

14 Conclusions

Meindert Fennema

Twenty-five years ago, very few people would have given much for the future of the non-ruling communist parties of Western Europe. The revelations concerning the excesses of Stalin's rule in the celebrated 'secret speech' delivered by Khrushchev at the CPSU's twentieth congress in 1956 and the Soviet invasion of Hungary in the same year had long-lasting effects, especially in Western Europe. They demoralized both leadership and rank and file of the communist parties and isolated them from the rest of society. Moreover, the Sino-Soviet split, which had come into the open by 1962, destroyed the unity of the international communist movement and created splits in communist parties all over the world, especially in north-western Europe.

Membership was declining, as was the electoral appeal of these parties. Youth movements, such as the Provo movement in the Netherlands, still in its infancy, did not seem to be attracted to the communist parties, which they regarded as conservative, humdrum organizations.

Ten years later, in the early 1970s, the picture had completely changed. The student movement, and the subsequent workers' revolts in Italy and France, had changed the political landscape in Western Europe. They had been the locomotive of new social movements all over Europe and had led to an influx of new members into most of the ailing communist parties. Furthermore, the trade union movement was radicalized under the influence of the massive strikes in Italy (1967) and France (1968) – a radicalization that was to affect other countries a few years later.

Under these circumstances it was difficult for most social democratic unions to maintain the traditional tough line against 'communist infiltration'. Marxism had resurfaced as an academic debate, and although traditional Marxism–Leninism was not very popular in intellectual circles, the benevolent reception of the Leninism of Gramsci and Althusser led to a reopening of the debate with traditional communism. An additional area in which communist parties could score points was the debate over multinational corporations that swept through universities and trade unions. The general protest against the behaviour of the 'multis' which did not seem to be bound by any laws, human or divine, formed the basis for a renewed interest in the phenomenon of imperialism. The classical theories of Lenin, Bukharin and Luxemburg provided the theoretical anchorage for a fresh and empirical approach to the study of imperialism.

A major turning-point in this story was the Vietnam War, which tended to give new lustre to the 'sister parties' of the Vietnamese Workers' Party. Even if the campaign against the Vietnam War was not started by the communists themselves, they were among those who harvested the political fruits. At the same time, not only did the Allende government in Chile show that a democratic road to socialism with loyal communist support was feasible, but its overthrow in 1973 also made clear that US intervention could hardly claim to be defending democracy. Through these different but related developments the image of communism improved, and the gulf that separated the communist parties from other left-wing movements narrowed accordingly.

The *rapprochement* between different formations of the Left was speeded up by an internal development in the larger communist parties. Partly as a result of the political developments recorded above, and partly as a result of the Sino-Soviet split, the PCI, the PCF and the PCE jointly moved to a 'Eurocommunist' position, formalized by a summit meeting in Madrid in March 1977. Deliberately distancing themselves from the Soviet Union, these parties accepted some of the tenets that had hitherto been maintained by social democratic parties: the parliamentary road to power, the need to struggle for power positions within the state apparatus and the need for a pluralist political system even under socialism. This last in particular, expressed by the farewell to the dictatorship of the proletariat, was a major departure from the classical Bolshevik position.

Nor did these changes in policies and rhetoric seem to have resulted from a position of weakness. On the contrary, the PCI was doing well under the leadership of Berlinguer, reaching 34.4 per cent of the vote in the general elections of 1976; the PCF had embarked on a *Programme commun* which, at least at the time of its inception, had seemed to benefit the united communist party at least as much as the still divided *Parti socialiste*; and finally the PCE, under the audacious and experienced leadership of Santiago Carrillo, seemed, in the Spanish *apertura*, to be heading for a position in Spain that equalled that of the

PCI in Italy. Carrillo's call for 'reconciliation', echoing Berlinguer's 'historic compromise', would certainly benefit, so it seemed, the party with such a magnificent record in the struggle against Francoism.

The only large parties that still stuck firmly to their orthodox principles – the Portuguese Communist Party and the Greek KKE – also did well. The PCP did not initiate the Portuguese revolution which nearly brought the ruling class to its knees, but it participated actively in it. The KKE, which faced a serious Eurocommunist challenge during the colonels' regime from 1967 to 1973, had regained its dominant position by the 1977 elections in relation to the KKE of the Interior. The KKE polled some 10 per cent of the vote, whilst the coalition headed by the KKE-Interior obtained no more than 2.76 per cent.

No matter what strategy was pursued – pacting with the Christian Democrats as in Italy, or with the Socialists as in France, or forming more restricted electoral fronts as in Portugal – the larger communist parties did remarkably well. This was true even of the Finnish SKP, which had suffered from a severe split in 1969, when a large minority marched out of the party's fifteenth congress. The SKP recovered from its electoral loss in 1970 (from 21.2 to 16.6 per cent) and by 1975 was polling 18.9 per cent of the votes in parliamentary elections.

Not in all countries did these new developments in the 1970s lead to an improvement in the electoral position of the communist party. The German DKP, newly founded in 1968, had been unable to attract electoral support. The Irish Communist Party, reunited in 1970, was unable to attract voters either in the Irish republic or in Northern Ireland. But these exceptions may well be explained by specific factors such as the divided nation in Germany, and the deep political and religious cleavages in Ireland. The voting system no doubt also had an impact on the performance of smaller parties, and is one factor among many in the poor electoral results of the CPGB. Apart from these marginal parties, communist parties did well in the 1970s, electorally, organizationally and ideologically.

Another ten years later, in the early 1980s, the communist parties in Western Europe were in a deep crisis; and the strategies pursued to stop the decline, despite their variety, did not seem to have much impact. The Spanish party consistently pursued its Eurocommunist line, whilst expelling some popular leaders, such as Manuel Azcárate. Nevertheless, the PCE had come to be completely paralysed by a struggle between Carrillistas and Gerardistas which seemed to be no more than a personal vendetta and to touch upon no political issue. The PCE, which had polled 9.2 per cent of the vote in 1977 and 10.8 in 1979, dropped to 4.1 per cent in the 1982 elections. The party organization suffered correspondingly, and since 1979 the PCE has lost 60 per cent of its members.

The PCF oscillated between a united front policy and a return to isolation. The *Programme commun* of 1972 collapsed in September 1977, and the party went back into the fortress, to embark upon a pro-Soviet line and an attitude of hostility to the Socialist Party. Euro-communism was replaced once more by Gallo-communism.[1] However, this strategy did not halt the party's electoral decline, and in the presidential elections of April 1982 Georges Marchais received only 15.3 per cent of the votes cast. The PCF was thus forced to support Mitterrand, and when eventually it was permitted to participate in the new government it was on conditions imposed by its socialist partners.

This new united front could not last, and when in 1984 the PCF ministers resigned, the party once again went back into the fortress and to its Soviet allegiance, to the accompaniment of a vociferous dissent. Unity was maintained, but this did not prevent an electoral decline to a mere 11 per cent in the European elections of 1984, and to some 9 per cent in the 1986 parliamentary elections. Even the PCI, which stepped carefully out of the historic compromise without taking a new consistent position, lost in the local elections of 1985 and fell back to some 30 per cent of the vote.

Most parties experienced a more dramatic electoral decline (see figure 14.1). The Dutch party dropped unexpectedly from 4.5 to 1.7 per cent in 1977, and in 1986 disappeared from the parliament; the Belgian party dropped in 1981 from 3.6 to 2.3 per cent. There have been exceptions: the Portuguese party is still going strong under the leadership of Alvaro Cunhal (despite a slip from 18 to 15.5 per cent in the 1985 elections), but its influence upon government policies is negligible. The same can be said of the Greek KKE, which under the pro-Soviet leadership of Florakis maintains its position as the third party of the political system with more than 10 per cent of the vote. For most parties, however, there has been a general decline in membership and electoral success since 1979 and, even worse, the crisis has also touched upon their ideology and organizational structures. Whereas in 1962 at least the party members and most of their leaders still had faith in a 'radiant future', this is no longer the case.

How did this dramatic change come about? Each of the chapters of this book has dealt in one way or another with this question. In this concluding chapter an attempt will be made to summarize the answers given, with an emphasis on the general trends in Western European communism.

Perry Anderson has argued that there have been two 'founding moments' in the history of the international communist movement, in which there took place a mass transfer of loyalties of large sections of the working class towards communist parties.[2] The first runs from 1919 to 1923, and the second from 1942 to 1945. It could be suggested that the period from 1970 to 1976 had the makings of a third such 'founding moment', if of somewhat more restricted scope, in which there was a marked upswing in support for the communist parties of Western Europe. This time, however, it was in many cases not industrial workers that were involved, but sections of the new middle classes, especially students and those working in the state sector – for example teachers, nurses and welfare workers.

Like the two earlier 'founding moments', this period in the early 1970s was characterized by a global expansion of communist regimes. The first founding moment was, of course, triggered off by the 1917 Russian revolution, which brought millions of people under socialist rule. The second founding moment was defined in Western Europe by the Second World War and the popular struggle against German occupation, and in Eastern Europe by the accretion of a number of Eastern European countries to the socialist camp, some of them of their own accord, others because they happened to be on the eastern side of the line established at Yalta. The Chinese revolution in turn brought a new part of the world into the socialist sphere, which as a result then encompassed one-third of the world's population.

In the third period a new wave of social revolutions and radical military coups shook the world's capitalist nations. The Cuban revolution in 1959 had a profound impact on the European Left, as did the Algerian war of independence, the electoral victory of Salvador Allende in Chile, and, as mentioned above, the victory of the Vietnamese over a high-tech American army. In Laos and Cambodia communist takeovers followed, just as the domino theory had predicted. In Africa, after the collapse of the Portuguese government in 1974, revolutionary movements came to power in Mozambique and Angola, whilst the African National Congress strengthened its position in relation to the Pretoria regime. The subject of rather less comment in Western Europe was the establishment of a number of radical military regimes that styled themselves Marxist–Leninist (at various times and with varying degrees of commitment and credibility) in the Sudan, Somalia, Ethiopia, the Congo and Benin.

The reasons for the failure of Western European communist parties to convert that upswing in their fortunes in the 1970s into long-term gains lie relatively far back in time, and must be sought, in the first place, at the time of the second 'founding moment' of Western European communism, in the years immediately following the Second World War, which were to have so profound an effect on the course of European history.

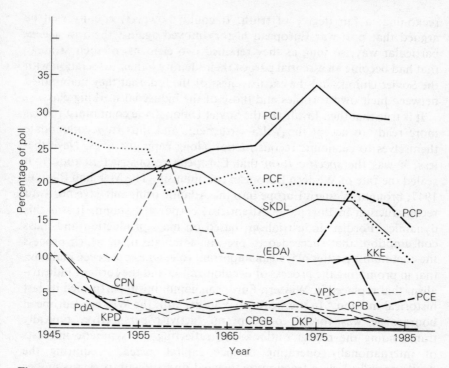

Figure 14.1 Electoral performance since 1945 of the communist parties treated in this book. The graph is drawn from the figures in appendix 1, where the other Western European communist parties are also covered. For abbreviations, see pp. ix–xii.

A declining social base

The communist parties of Western Europe emerged from the Second World War as genuine mass parties whose power, due to their international alliance with the Soviet Union and to the prestige that the Soviet Union's economic progress had acquired, exceeded their electoral strength which was itself substantial, running in 1945 from 10 to 25 per cent.

Although some of these parties participated in post-war cabinets, by 1948 all of them had lost considerable support and had become politically and ideologically isolated. One can argue, as has Fernando Claudin, that this was partly due to their lack of revolutionary spirit, which made them miss chances for a socialist revolution.[3] This puts in rather blunt form the argument that the communist parties have only themselves to blame for their present plight – an argument that must contain, on any reckoning, a fair degree of truth. It could, however, equally well be argued that post-war European history moved against them in a very particular way, so long as they retained two elements of their strategy that had become an essential part of their identity – their association with the Soviet Union, and the exclusiveness of the link that they maintained between their own fortunes and those of the industrial working class.

It is true that their loyalty to the Soviet Union made communist parties more ready to accept the Yalta settlement, and thus to accommodate themselves to economic reconstruction along capitalist lines. Nevertheless, it was the *specific form* that European reconstruction took that sealed the fate of Western European communism. The Marshall Plan, in 1947, brought Western Europe into the Atlantic orbit and gave post-war reconstruction in Europe an Atlanticist, corporatist stamp. It was this dynamic, 'Fordist' industrialism, based on mass production and mass consumption, that succeeded to pre-war colonialism, in which process the communist parties played an important role. One could even maintain that in promoting the process of decolonization and the form of industrialism that replaced it, Western European communism performed its last historical mission.[4] In the words of Van der Pijl, the Western European bourgeoisie was forced to adopt an 'activist perspective, typically transcending the rentier outlook and reflecting the synthetic interests of internationally operating finance capital instead, requiring the "euthanasia" of class fractions associated directly with previous modes of accumulation'.[5]

The expansion of this new form of industrialism required a certain integration of the working class into the political system. Hence there was a tendency for governments and industry to compromise with the parties of the working class. However, it was not the communist parties that reaped the fruits of this 'historic compromise', however hard, in some cases, they tried to prove that they were reliable allies in the post-war reconstruction. The PCF in particular went a long way in showing loyalty to the industrial interest. It induced the French worker to work hard and prevented industrial action wherever it could. It even supported the maintenance of a French colonial empire. But all in vain.

Industrialists and governments had at least two good reasons not to trust the communists. Most important was, of course, the latter's affiliation with the international communist movement and their loyalty to the Soviet Union. This made them unreliable allies in a programme of national reconstruction within an Atlantic framework. The second reason, and one that is often overlooked, was that the communist parties had their strongholds in traditional industries that were the first to be dismantled in the process of modernization. Communists had strong bases in mining, shipbuilding, the docks, the timber industry. Syndicalist tendencies remained strong in these areas.

It was therefore the social democratic and Christian democratic parties that were preferred as the representatives of the working class in post-war Europe. It was these parties that could present the fruits of industrial reconstruction as their crop, thereby attracting a large part of the working class who preferred a modest increase in living standards (which at least until 1952 consisted mainly of promises) to the hazardous prospect of revolutionary politics. The losers in this post-war political and economic constellation, the communist parties, were forced into a defensive strategy, criticizing the corporatist policies of social democrats and Christian democrats.

The communist parties, by thus perforce being uncontaminated by the compromise that integration had led their social democratic rivals to accept, maintained a certain moral and ideological prestige, but that prestige evaporated when they stubbornly defended the domination of Eastern Europe by the Soviet Union, and the Stalinist show trials that accompanied it. They rapidly lost support amongst the intelligentsia, and were forced to expel many militants from their own ranks.

Having been driven from the broader political arena, the communist parties withdrew into a narrow syndicalist one. Here they were in some instances quite successful in defending the workers' economic interests, but more often than not the political fruits of this struggle too were captured by the social democrats. Moreover, since the communist strong-holds were in the traditional sectors, they fought what was eventually to be a losing battle. They were able to slow down the process of dismantling these industries, and to negotiate better conditions for the workers that were to be laid off, but they were unable to reverse the process. In the meantime they proved utterly unable to secure a new base in modern sectors, such as the chemical industry, electrical equipment and electronics, which were rapidly expanding and introducing new forms of labour relations and management techniques. It was in these sectors that social democratic and Christian democratic unions became most successful.

In the ideological domain Keynesian theory reigned supreme and Marxist theories of crisis appeared more and more outdated. Thus, by 1968 the communist parties had become fossil formations, a refuge for workers who were excluded from the Keynesian compromise and for all those who, having been traumatized by the fascist occupation were condemned to live in the past. The communist parties, notwithstanding their appalling Stalinist record, maintained the support – often silent and only financial – of some resistance fighters, those whose relatives had met their deaths in the concentration camps and some members of the intelligentsia. They had become parties of the war-time resistance.

The trajectory of the Spanish and Portuguese parties, for obvious reasons, was rather different. Owing to the Franco and Salazar dictatorships, they were to remain resistance parties for another 30 years. Their record in that role was heroic, and for a long time they were practically the only organized opposition in their countries. Although their strategy as illegal parties may not have been perfect – as has been eloquently argued in the case of the PCE by Jorge Semprún – it is difficult to see how, in the given circumstances, they could have done much better.[6] In any case, they were unable to deliver a decisive blow to the dictatorships in Spain and Portugal. The downfall of the Salazar dictatorship resulted from a belated and uncontrolled decolonization process. The Spanish *apertura* was triggered off by the slow death of Franco, but the basis had been laid by the modernizing fraction of the Spanish bourgeoisie, secretly organized through Opus Dei, which had been leaning towards the United States already under Franco. The sad history of the PCE after 1976 seems to be an accelerated repeat of the history of the other Western European communist parties since 1945.

The Soviet invasion of Afghanistan played ideologically the same role now as had been played earlier by the interventions in Hungary and Czechoslovakia. Significantly, the orthodox communists in the PCE (as indeed in the PCI) were called 'Afghans' by their Eurocommunist comrades.

The history of the Communist Party of Portugal after the failed revolution of 1975 is one of consolidation and defence of the agrarian reforms and of the economic interests of agrarian labourers. The Portuguese revolution, which was carried out as much by certain sectors of the armed forces as by the PCP, seems to have succumbed to the dominance of European social democracy and to have lost its propulsive force.

The resurgence and the crisis of communism

From the dark years of the cold war, and through the aftermath of 1956, the communist parties of Western Europe have been thrown back on to the defensive everywhere, and – to use an expression that has appeared frequently in these pages – they withdrew 'into the fortress'. Excluded from government and socially isolated, they were seen as, and indeed became, a deviant hard-line opposition. As the chapter on the Finnish SKP points out, a sphere of culture was created as a cocoon in those hard times, in which hobbies, cultural and sports activities and even the upbringing of children were all carried on. The communist parties became, whether they wanted it or not, anti-system parties *par excellence*. This was a position of weakness because, whilst they had a strong influence in certain sectors, through a network of front organizations, they had little influence in the wider political arena. However, the reverse was also the case, and that formed their strength: the communist parties were not receptive to the 'Americanism' that was making its way through the mass media and, needless to say, through the very success of the Keynesian compromise in the 1950s and 1960s. Social democratic ideology became the dominant ideology of the Left in Western Europe, and there was a general consensus that capitalism had been abolished in a peaceful way.

Sticking fanatically to their own point of view, the communist parties were to become, in the 1970s, a pole of attraction for certain groups that also wanted to break way from the dominant ideology and its institutions. There were, of course, other available sources of anti-system ideology. Anarchism retained its appeal, as did different forms of Leninism, notably Trotskyism and Maoism, to which many students in revolt turned.

Those who embraced the communist parties did so partly because of the working class base of those parties. But there were other attractions at the time. They were big parties – at least in relation to the Trotskyist and other formations – or at least big enough to represent a powerful force in society. Especially for those radical reformists whose revolutionary ideals accommodated a wish to get something done in practical terms, the communist party was an attractive organization. And the greater the step that one had to take in order to become a communist – organizationally, ideologically, or socially – the more the party became a pole of attraction for those who rejected bourgeois society *in toto*. Finally, being a communist meant belonging to an international movement which, although discredited by political repression in socialist countries and by the Sino-Soviet split, still had an important appeal, in view of the liberation wars that were being fought under the banner of communism and with the material support of the Soviet Union. Thus all communist parties attracted in the 1970s a great number of student militants, many of whom had gone through an anarchist or Maoist phase.

It was at this point, in the mid-1970s, that a division appeared between those who wanted to maintain the purity of the 'fortress' position and those who wanted to compromise in order to obtain tangible results; a split between proponents of an isolationist and those of a united front strategy, a split that was perceived as one between radicalism and reformism, and which was to haunt the European communist parties from the 1970s on in the guise of the debate on Eurocommunism. During the cold war, almost all the communist parties of Western Europe had been able to avoid this issue, since they had been forced into a radical, anti-system, isolationist stance. Paradoxically, the attractiveness of this latter position for the student and other radical youth movements now made it untenable for the parties themselves, since they had to convert their organizational and electoral successes into political results. This required collaboration with other left-wing parties, and with the social democrats in particular. Yet any such collaboration reactivated the historical trauma of the split within the European Left that had been brought about by the creation of the Comintern, and had been exacerbated by subsequent events.

The PCI evaded collaboration with its historical enemies by opting for an alliance with the Christian Democrats in order to outflank the Socialists. It proved in vain. In 1983 Craxi's Socialist Party outmanoeuvred the PCI and embarked upon a policy of social modernization, together with fierce attacks on the positions of the working class. The PCF's united front with the Socialists, its collapse in 1977, and its revival and final breakdown in 1981 and 1984 have been recorded above.

In Spain, the PCE took 11 per cent of the poll in 1979, but in 1982, when the Socialist PSOE under Felipe Gonzalez was embarking upon a programme of modernization that could hardly be said to favour the workers, the PCE's share of the poll dropped to 4 per cent.

The Finnish SKP had entered the government in 1966 but split over this issue into majority and minority wings and suffered a heavy defeat in the 1970 elections. It slowly recovered its electoral strength during the 1970s, but dropped again in 1983 from 18 to 13.8 per cent of the votes cast and was ousted from the government.

The Dutch Communist Party was left without a single seat in the parliament in 1986, after 50 years of parliamentary representation. In most smaller parties developments were not so spectacular, the option of a formal alliance with the social democratic labour parties being less apparent because anti-communism remained a strong force in their countries. This was particularly the case in Germany, Switzerland and Ireland, but to a lesser degree also in the Netherlands, Belgium, Great Britain and the Scandinavian countries.

It was particularly in these latter countries that the reformism-versus-radicalism dilemma posed itself in terms of collaboration with other radical groups, such as pacifist, ecological and Trotskyist formations. It was here that success in attracting new sources of support forced the communist parties to widen their appeal.

The main problem that the communist parties faced in the 1970s, however, was neither tactical nor even strategic, but structural. The organizational and electoral success brought about by the attraction of new groups to the communist parties could do nothing to prevent the eventual decline of their traditional working class constituency. Thus, the workers were not so much chased away by the influx of intellectuals or by discussions on Eurocommunism, as has often been claimed by the traditionalists within the communist parties. They were eliminated gradually in a process of industrial restructuring that was accelerated by the economic crisis. In these circumstances the social base of the Bolshevik parties gradually crumbled, and this was reflected in their electoral performance. The gradual decline had been concealed in the 1970s by the influx of new members and by new support from state-dependent sectors: education, health and social services and the like. Unfortunately, however, the support of these new layers was to turn eventually to a considerable extent to the social democrats.

The party that seems to have incorporated these new sectors most successfully is the Swedish. According to Hermansson,

a typical member of the Communist Party is quite different today in comparison with the 1960s. Formerly, he – male, of course – was about 45 years old, and he had entered the party 20 years previously, that is, in the mid-1940s. Furthermore, he was occupied in heavy industry, for example a pulp-mill in central Sweden or a mine in the north. Nowadays, a member is also likely to be female and she or he will be less than 40 and will have joined the party just a few years previously. He may be a worker, but it is just as likely that she may be occupied within social welfare, health care or education'. (chapter 8, pp. 146–7)

Such a change has also taken place in other communist parties, especially the smaller ones, i.e. those of Holland, Belgium and Great Britain. It is also in these parties that the political influence of these new sectors has been greatest. They all moved to a more Eurocommunist position, which made them more similar to other radical left-wing parties. Their success in this new orientation must depend particularly on the nature of the party system and the electoral system of the country concerned. The Swedish party seems to have had a success that has been denied to the Dutch, British and Belgian parties.

In the marginal parties, such as the German, the political influence of these layers has been negligible, as these parties have remained in the sectarian 'fortress' position. In these circumstances they lost most of the initial support from these new layers, as is documented in this book for the Swiss party (see chapter 12). On the other hand, the German party is still growing organizationally, even if this is not reflected in election figures.

In the large parties the influence of the new state-dependent element is evident but, given a still considerable worker constituency, not predominant. The leadership is still able to invoke the support of old rank and file members in order to maintain a traditional Bolshevik policy and structure. However, the PCI, so it seems, is slowly coming to resemble, in organizational terms, the social democratic parties. It is also one of the few communist parties in Western Europe that is not, according to Gianfranco Pasquino in chapter 2, in a state of crisis.

Up to this point, the account given here of the decline of Western European communism has emphasized those factors that have been beyond the control of the communist parties themselves. There remains the question of the extent to which the decline has been conditioned, or accelerated, by internal structural factors that the members of the various communist parties are, in principle, able to influence. This question, and the considerations on which any answer to it must rely, are addressed in the discussion of democratic centralism presented in chapter 1. This study of Western European communism concludes by returning to matters of organization, and picks up a theme that has run through the chapters of this book. In a celebrated passage from 1902, Lenin wrote that 'democracy is a dangerous plaything; no revolutionary organization could sustain it'; yet in 1905 he was claiming, in changed circumstances, that it was time to 'institute the widest democracy within the party'. The conflict between the maintenance of democratic procedures, on the one hand, and organizing for a revolutionary transformation of society on the other, has accompanied Bolshevism throughout its history. Today, the cry of the traditionalists in the Western Europe communist parties against the various renovators, modernizers and Eurocommunists that have been encountered in these pages is that their party is 'a revolutionary organization and not a discussion club'. Behind these words lies a paradox to which the concluding remarks of this study will be addressed.

A totalitarian paradox

The West European communist parties have thus been confronted with a problem of adaptation to a changing social environment, and have seen their working class base dwindle. The corollary of this has been new internal pressures stemming in good part from changes in their social composition, and, in many cases, from the perceived need to cater for a broader electorate. The problem of adaptation has been compounded by the maintenance of a traditional form of organization that has clearly inhibited the articulation of policies that rival those of the party leadership. Orthodox democratic centralism is without doubt a problem for today's Western European communist parties. This aspect of their present predicament is of particular interest, and it raises a number of important questions, the answers to which in turn affect any judgement as to whether Western European communism is now exhausted.

First of all, in terms of the capacity of these parties simply to survive, democratic centralism in its traditional form has undoubted merits. The sense of *esprit de corps* that it entails enables a communist party to face ill fortune by closing its ranks and sitting out a bad period until a change in the political environment makes it possible to raise its social profile. The importance of this point is that the health of a communist party cannot be judged by electoral results alone. The striking deterioration in the electoral performances of most Western European communist parties that is recorded in these pages is important evidence of a decline, and cannot, therefore, be ignored. But neither can the views of traditionalists in these parties when they point out that they have, after all, been here before. Time alone will show whether the traditional recipe will work again; but until time delivers its verdict, communism in this sense cannot be said to be dead. If one aspect of communism's strength has been to enable a leadership to mobilize the masses, another aspect has been the attention given to maintaining the good health of the 'guiding nucleus'. But what is concerned here is the functional aspect of democratic centralism; and what is at issue – as when Lenin wrote *What is to be Done?* in 1902 – is not democracy, but survival.

A second consideration is rather more complex, and concerns what Erik van Ree has termed 'the totalitarian paradox'.[7] Orthodox democratic centralism can be, and indeed has been, a rigorous form of disciplined organization that has enabled the leadership of a party (and therefore at times of a state) to resort to terror against the membership. At a less catastrophic level it has clearly acted as a brake on debate and on the circulation of ideas and opinions. These disadvantages are a matter of historical record and they weigh heavily on Western European communist parties that do, after all, have other available traditions to hand that cannot in the long term be ignored.

There remains, however, the positive aspect of democratic centralism, as a means of mobilizing the masses. In that sense democratic centralism has, in certain circumstances, at certain times, and in certain places, proved effective in achieving a party's social goals. To save democratic centralism, a distinction could be made between Bolshevism, as a way of mobilizing the masses, and Stalinism, as a distortion of that technique, and with it of Bolshevism. Bolshevism then could be held to have been successful in bringing about an insurrectionary revolution in Russia, China and elsewhere, and in enabling revolutionary elites to address the tasks of national construction by way of socialized forms of 'primitive accumulation'. Unfortunately for those who, by doing so, wish to save the 'good' communism as Bolshevism whilst doing away with Stalinism, things are not quite so simple. It seems that the mobilizing aspect of democratic centralism is strongly related to its iron discipline. Such, at least, has been the case with Maoism. Those who wished to see Maoism as a form of Bolshevism without terror could only have been disappointed by revelations about Mao's cultural revolution. Correspondingly, we have seen in the chapters on Dutch, Spanish, British and Belgian communism that with the disappearance of orthodox democratic centralism these parties have also lost most of their mobilizing potential, even among their own members.

Investigation into this intriguing problem is certainly necessary in order to decipher the specific relations between the two aspects of democratic centralism. The question must be whether Bolshevism in this sense, and with it orthodox democratic centralism, have any political value outside the context of insurrectionary revolution in agrarian societies and of a programme of economic development from a disadvantaged start. E. H. Carr has pointed to the contradiction between Lenin's views on organization and the traditions of the Western Europe communist parties:

The very conception of 'the masses' as a vast reservoir of oppressed and unorganized proletarians . . . reflected the backwardness of the typical Russian industrial worker. But the same conception was not applicable, or applicable only with far-reaching qualifications, to countries where the problem was not to imprint a revolutionary consciousness on the *tabula rasa* of politically unconscious masses, but to penetrate and transform a political consciousness already highly developed in the bourgeois democratic tradition.[8]

It is not at all surprising therefore that reformers in the Western European communist parties should wish to throw out the Leninist baby with the bathwater of Stalinism. It remains an interesting fact, none the less, that the mobilizational features of democratic centralism have apparently played an important role even in industrial Western Europe. It could be argued, for instance, that the attraction of Bolshevik forms of organization among students at the beginning of the 1970s was partly due to the highly paternalistic university structures, where students were excluded from participating in the making of decisions that affected them. In those circumstances, they formed an 'undifferentiated mass' in which Bolshevik notions of mobilization had a certain relevance.

It should also be pointed out that even differentiated, bureaucratic organizations in Western Europe are not blind to the political advantages of a requirement for solidarity as constrictive as that associated with orthodox democratic centralism. This is most obvious in trade union organization.

All these considerations can be put forward by anyone who so wishes in defence of orthodox democratic centralism. They all, however, represent a sacrifice of democracy that might be held to be justified in certain kinds of circumstances, but it is clear that not all members of today's communist parties are any longer prepared to make those sacrifices. Since the aim of this book has been to chart the present predicament of these parties, the conclusion must stand that orthodox democratic centralism has been one of the causes of that predicament, in that it has made too many sacrifices of democracy.

The salience of this conclusion once registered, there remains a question that must concern those who wish to reform a communist party, and indeed anyone who is committed to promoting radical social change. The question is, quite simply, what form of organization is appropriate for such radical action. If the communist parties stand condemned for their authoritarian ways, as they must be, it remains to be seen what new organizational recommendations will emerge, for example, from today's 'new social movements' should the urgency of their concerns ever reach the stage of overcoming their present almost obsessive group individualism.

The Western European communist parties are unlikely to disappear. The larger, 'Eurocommunist' ones will continue to exist and will carry with them the broader ideals with which socialism has always been associated. But what has been specific to them as communist parties in the political spectrum of Western Europe will have been lost. They will continue to function increasingly like the parties characteristic of liberal democracy.

Those that continue to adhere to traditional Soviet-style Marxism–Leninism as an ideology, orthodox democratic centralism as an organizing principle and support for the socialist countries as a foreign policy are likely to atrophy and remain as sectarian fossils in a rapidly changing environment. But there are other opportunities open to them. They could choose, first of all, as the Spanish, British and Netherlands parties have done, to develop an orientation towards the new social movements, which in the long run may turn out to be fruitful for both. In doing this the communist parties will doubtless lose much of their traditional ideology and constituency, but they will be able to maintain their radical tradition and their experience in mobilization. Another possible future lies in what could be termed a new internationalism, orientated towards the organization of migrant labour in Western European societies. In this case they would have to shake off their nationalistic ideology as expressed in the British, French, Belgian, Dutch (and so on) road to socialism and the immanent ethnicism involved in this strategy. But they would be able to draw on the tradition of internationalism that stood at the cradle of communism. Such an orientation would also retain the class basis of the communist parties and some of the elements of Bolshevism, as defined in the introduction to this book.

But even if none of these futures were to materialize, and the communist parties were to disappear altogether, their influence would be felt for some time to come, through the individual communist militants who, by participating in new movements and in creating new structures are bound to transmit some of the communist heritage to new generations of political activists who share their aspirations for a better society.

Notes

1 Vincent Wright, 'The French Communist Party during the Fifth Republic', in Howard Machin (ed.), *National Communism in Western Europe* (Methuen, London, 1982), p. 105.
2 Perry Anderson, 'Types of Literature', in Raphael Samuel (ed.), *People's History and Socialist Theory* (London, 1982), pp. 152–3.
3 Fernando Claudin, *The Communist Movement; From Comintern to Cominform* (Penguin, Harmondsworth, 1975).
4 This is not true for the PCF and the CPB, which participated in the post-war coalition cabinets that tried to perpetuate the French and Belgian colonial empire. Hence these communist parties were also responsible for the wars fought in Vietnam and the Belgian Congo to restore colonial rule (Claudin, *The Communist Movement*, pp. 346 *et seq.*).
5 Kees van der Pijl, *The Making of an Atlantic Ruling Class* (Verso, London, 1984), p. 146.
6 Jorge Semprun, *La Autobiografia de Federico Sánchez* (Planeta, Barcelona, 1977).
7 Erik van Ree, *De totalitaire paradox. De terroristische massademokratie van Stalin en Mao* (Van Gennep, Amsterdam, 1984).
8 E. H. Carr, *A History of Soviet Russia. The Bolshevik Revolution* (Macmillan, London, 1950), vol. 3, p. 181.

Appendix I
Communist Votes in Parliamentary Elections

Percentage share of the vote for Western European communist parties in parliamentary elections, 1945–86

Party	1945	1946	1947	1948	1949	1950	1951	1952	1953	1954	1955	1956	1957	1958	1959	1960	1961	1962	1963	1964	1965	1966
PCI (Italy)		18.9							22.6					22.7					25.3			
PCF (France)	26.2	28.6		(30.1)[a]			25.9					25.6		18.9				21.8				
AP (Iceland)		19.5			19.5				16.1			19.2			15.3	16.0			16.0			
SKDL (Finland)	20.9			20.0			21.6			21.6				23.2				22.0				21.2
PCB (Belgium)		12.7			7.5	4.7				3.6				1.9			3.1				4.6	
CPN (Netherlands)		10.7		7.7				6.2				4.8			2.4				2.6			
PCL (Luxembourg)	13.4			10.0						8.5					9.1					12.9		
NKP (Norway)	11.9				5.8				5.1				3.4				2.9				1.4	
VPK (Sweden)	10.3[b]			6.3				4.3				5.0		3.4		4.5				5.2		
DKP (Denmark)	12.5		6.8			4.6			4.8				3.1			1.1				1.2		0.8
PdA (Switzerland)			5.1				2.7				2.1				2.7				2.2			
DKP/KPD (West Germany)					5.7				2.2				c				c				c	
KPO (Austria)	5.4				5.1				5.3			4.4			3.3			3.0				0.4
KKE (Greece)[d]							10.6	9.6				48.2[e]		24.4			14.6		14.3	11.8		
PCE (Spain)																						
PCP (Portugal)																						

Appendix I (cont)

Party	1967	1968	1969	1970	1971	1972	1973	1974	1975	1976	1977	1978	1979	1980	1981	1982	1983	1984	1985	1986	1987
PCI (Italy)	26.9					27.2				34.4			30.4				29.9				26.6
PCF (France)	22.5	20.0					21.3					20.5			16.1					9.8	
AP (Iceland)	13.9				17.1							22.9	19.7				17.3				{ 9.4 (SKDL) / 4.3 (DEVA)
SKDL (Finland)				16.6		17.0			18.9				18.0				13.8				
PCB (Belgium)		3.3			3.1			3.2			2.7	3.3			2.3						
CPN (Netherlands)	3.6				3.9	4.5					1.7				2.1	1.8					
PCL (Luxembourg)		15.4						10.5					5.8					5.0			
NKP (Norway)			1.0								0.4				0.3				0.2		
VPK (Sweden)		3.0		4.8			5.3			4.7			5.6			5.6			5.4		
DKP (Denmark)		1.0			1.4		3.6		4.2		3.7		1.9		1.1			0.7			
PdA (Switzerland)	2.9				2.5				2.4				2.1				0.9				
DKP/KPD (West Germany)			(DKP) c			0.2				0.3				0.2			0.2				
KPO (Austria)				1.0	1.4								1.0				0.7				
(KKE) Greece								(9.5)f			9.4				10.9				9.9		
PCE (Spain)											9.1		10.6			3.8				4.6	
PCP (Portugal)									12.6	14.6			19.5	17.1			18.1				12.2

[a] The PCI formed in the 1948 elections a bloc with the forerunner of the PSI, the PSIUP.

[b] 1944.

[c] The KPD was declared illegal in 1956 and replaced by the DKP in 1968 which for the first time participated in the elections of 1972.

[d] Banned until 1974 elections. Figures until then are for the 'substitute' EDA.

[e] Coalition.

[f] In 1974 the two Communist parties, KKE and KKE-Interior, formed a bloc with other parties.

Sources: Klaus Von Beyme, *Parteien in Westlichen Demokratien* (R. Piper, Munich, 1982); *Chronicle of Parliamentary Elections*, IX (1975), XII (1978) (CIDF, Geneva). Figures after 1981 are taken from the *European Journal of Political Research*

Appendix II
Democratic Centralism in the Rules of Four European Communist Parties

The Communist Party of the Soviet Union   Article III.19

The guiding principle of the organizational structure of the Party is democratic centralism, which signifies:

(a) election of all leading Party bodies, from the lowest to the highest;
(b) periodical reports of Party bodies to their Party organizations and to higher bodies;
(c) strict Party discipline and the subordination of the minority to the majority;
(d) decisions of higher bodies are binding on lower bodies.

The French Communist Party   Article II.5

Democratic centralism is the basic principle on which the internal life of the Party rests. Based on the Party's revolutionary theory, democratic centralism is the condition for the ideological and political cohesion of the Party, and for its unity of action. The principles of democratic centralism are as follows:

(a) Discussion of all problems is free at all levels, on the basis of the principles accepted by communists when they joined the Party. Once decisions have been adopted by the majority, they are applied by all. The organization of fractions, and fractional activity, are forbidden because they undermine the unity of the Party and compromise the effectiveness of its action.

(b) The leading (*dirigeants*) organs of the various levels of the Party are democratically elected by the assemblies of cells, the conferences of sections and federations, and by congresses. Their activity is based on the rules of collective leadership, which is the essential guarantee of correct (*justes*) decisions, properly applied. Collective leadership does not exclude, but implies, the personal responsibility of each member of the leadership.

(c) Elected leading bodies are responsible to their electors and must give a regular account of their activity.

(d) The decisions of higher organs are binding on lower organs. This discipline, freely consented to by all communists, gives their Party its strength.

(e) Criticism and self-criticism are exercised freely without respect of persons in all organizations of the Party. When made in a frank and constructive manner they enable errors and faults to be corrected, and weaknesses and failings to be overcome.

The Communist Party of Great Britain   Article 3

To conduct organized activity, and to give leadership in all circumstances of the class struggle, the Communist Party bases itself on the theory and practice of Marxism–Leninism and must be able to act as a single unified force. Therefore the Communist Party bases its organization upon democratic centralism, which combines the democratic participation of the membership in Party life with an elected centralized leadership capable of directing the entire Party.

Democratic centralism means that:

(a) All leading committees shall be elected regularly and shall report regularly to the Party organizations which elected them.

(b) Elected higher committees shall have the right to take decisions binding on lower committees and organizations, and shall explain these decisions to them. Such decisions shall not be in conflict with decisions of the National Congress or Executive Committee.

(c) Elected higher committees shall encourage lower committees and organizations to express their views on questions of Party policy and on the carrying out of that policy.

(d) Lower committees and organizations shall carry out the decisions of higher elected committees, and shall have the right to express their views, raise problems, and make suggestions to these committees.

(e) Decisions shall be made by majority vote, and minorities shall accept the decision of the majority.

The Italian Communist Party   Article III, 8

The internal life of the Italian Communist Party is regulated according to the method of democratic centralism, in such a way as to guarantee unity of direction in the party's activity, clarity in the terms of the political debate, and the assumption of responsibility on the part of each member and leader, together with maximum participation of the membership in making political choices and in conducting the struggle, and rigorous care for their rights.

In consequence:

(a) All leading organs must be elected according to the norms and procedures laid down by the statutes, and must function in a collegial manner.

(b) All leading organs have the duty to report periodically on their activity to the Party members, in the organization that they lead.

(c) Each instance (*istanza*) of the Party, and each individual leader, has the duty of encouraging the activity of all Party members, maintaining a living link with them, stimulating the widest political debate, and guaranteeing in all organizations – with respect to decisions taken – freedom of expression of opinion to each and every communist.

(d) Decisions (*deliberazioni*) adopted in conformity with the statutes are binding on all members of the various organizations and, if they have been taken by the national leadership organs, on the entire Party. A decision taken by a majority must be respected also by the minority.

(e) In order to safeguard the unity of the Party and to defend its political discipline, fractional activities are forbidden.

Bibliography

General

D. E. Albright (ed.), *Communism and Political Systems in Western Europe* (Westview Press, Boulder, CO, 1979).

C. Boggs, *The Impasse of European Communism* (Westview Press, Boulder, CO, 1982).

R. Cayrol, 'Courants, fractions, tendances', in P. Birnbaum and J-M. Vincent (eds), *Critique des partis politiques* (Editions Galilée, Paris, 1978).

F. Claudin, *The Communist Movement; From Comintern to Cominform* (Penguin, Harmondsworth, 1975).

Communisme (L'Age d'Homme, Paris), 'Le communisme en Europe occidentale: déclin ou mutation?', nos 11–12 (1986).

R. V. Daniels, *A Documentary History of Communism*, 2 vols (I. B. Tauris, London, 1985).

R. Kindersley (ed.), *In Search of Eurocommunism* (Macmillan, London, 1981).

A. Kriegel, *Un autre communisme? Compromis historique, eurocommunisme, union de la gauche* (Hachette, Paris, 1977).

P. Lange and M. Vanicelli (eds), *The Communist Parties of Italy, France and Spain: Postwar Change and Continuity* (Allen and Unwin, London, 1981).

H. Machin, *National Communism in Western Europe; A Third Way for Socialism?* (Methuen, London, 1983).

N. McInnes, *The Communist Parties of Western Europe* (Oxford University Press, London, 1975).

L. Marcou, *Les pieds d'argile: le communisme internationale, 1970–1986* (Ramsay, Paris, 1986).

G. Schwab (ed.), *Eurocommunism: The Ideological and Political-Theoretical Foundations* (Greenwood Press, Westport, Conn., 1981).

R. N. Tannahill, *The Communist Parties of Western Europe: A Comparative Study* (Greenwood Press, Westport, Conn., 1978).

R. Tiersky, *Ordinary Stalinism: Democratic Centralism and the Question of Communist Political Development* (Allen and Unwin, London, 1985).
P. F. della Torre, E. Mortimer and Jonathan Story (eds), *Eurocommunism: Myth or Reality?* (Penguin, Harmondsworth, 1979).
M. Waller, *Democratic Centralism: an Historical Commentary* (Manchester University Press, Manchester, 1981).

The Communist Party of Belgium

De klandestiene 'Roode Vaan' (F. Masereel Fonds, Brussels, 1971)/ *'Le Drapeau Rouge' clandestin* (Fondation J. Jacquemotte, Brussels, 1971).
R. van Doorslaer, *De KPB en het Sovjet–Duits niet aanvalspakt tussen augustus 1939 en juli 1941* (F. Masereel Fonds, Brussels, 1975).
J. Gotovitch, *Archives des partisans armés* (Centre des Recherches et d'Etudes Historiques de la Seconde Guerre Mondiale, Brussels, 1971).
J. Humbert-Droz, *Origines et débuts des partis communistes des pays latins: 1921–1923. Textes établis et annotés par S. Bahne* (D. Reidel, Dordrecht, 1970).
M. Liebman, Rudi van Doorslaer and José Gotovitch, *Een geschiedenis van het Belgisch kommunisme, 1921–1945* (Masereelfonds, Ghent, 1980).

The Finnish Communist Party

A. Aalto, *SKP historiallisten tehtävien mittaiseksi in SKP:n 20. edustajakoukous*, (SKP, Helsinki, 1984).
O. Borg and J. Paastela, 'Communist Participation in Governmental Coalitions: the Case of Finland', *Quaderni* (Milan), 26/1983.
J. Iivonen, *A Ruling Non-ruling Communist Party in the West: the Finnish Communist Party*. University of Tampere, Department of Political Science, Occasional Papers 32/1983.
J. Iivonen, 'Veljeyttä yli rajojen. NKP:n ja SKP:n välisten suhteiden kehittyminen ja suhde puoluehajaannukseen', *Politiikka*, 1/1985.
L. Lehto, and J. Ruotsalo, 'Kommunisten vapautusliike', *Helsingin Sanomat*, 2 April 1982; *Soihtu*, 2/1983.
'NKP:n kirje SKP:lle', *Tiedonantaja*, 24 October 1984.
L. Lehto, and J. Ruotsalo, 'SKP:n tilanne – uhkaava katastrofi ja miten sitä vastaan on taisteltava', *Kansan uutiset*, 17 January 1981; *Soihtu*, 6/1981.
A. Saarinen, *Suomalaisen kommunistin kokemuksia* (Tammi, Helsinki, 1984).
S. Toiviainen, *Nykyinen kriisi ja hallituskysymys* (Kursiivi, Helsinki, 1978).
A. F. Upton, *Communism in Scandinavia and Finland: Politics of Opportunity* (New York, 1973).
'Ylimääräisen edustajakokouksen päätokset 16. edustajakokouksen pohjaksi', *Soihtu* 1/1972.

The French Communist Party

J-J. Becker, *Le Parti communiste veut-il prendre le pouvoir? La stratégie du PCF de 1930 à nos jours* (Seuil, Paris, 1981).
J-P. Brunet, *Histoire du PCF* (PUF, Paris, 1982).

Communisme (Paris), 7 (1985), issue devoted to *La sociologie du PCF.* (Each issue of this journal contains a *Chronique de la vie communiste.)*

S. Courtois, 'Les délégués aux congrès du PCF et l'évolution de l'appareil communiste, 1956–1985', *Communisme*, no. 10, 1986.

La culture des camarades (Autrement, Paris, 1986).

F. Hincker, *Le Parti communiste au carrefour. Essai sur quinze ans de son histoire, 1965–1981* (Albin-Michel, Paris, 1981).

A. Kriegel (with G. Bourgeois), *Les communistes français, 1920–1970*, new ed. (Seuil, Paris, 1985).

G. Lavau, *A quoi sert le Parti communiste français?* (Fayard, Paris, 1981).

P. Robrieux, *Histoire intérieure du Parti communiste* (Fayard, Paris, 1980–84) (disappointing on the recent period).

The German Communist Party

R. Ahlberg, 'Differenzen und Konflikte zwischen den kommunistischen Parteien der Bundesrepublik Deutschland', *Beiträge zur Konfliktforschung*, 3/1979, pp. 67–83.

H. Bilstein *et al. Organisierter Kommunismus in der Bundesrepublik Deutschland,* 4th edn, (UTB Leske Budrich, Opladen, 1977).

R. Ebbighausen and P. Kirchhoff, 'Zur Betriebsgruppenstrategie der DKP', *Politische Vierteljahresschrift*, (vol.13, no. 1, 1972, pp. 106–29.

R. Ebbighausen and P. Kirchhoff, 'Die DKP im Parteiensystem der Bundesrepublik', in Jürgen Dittberner and Rolf Ebbighausen (eds), *Parteiensystem in der Legitimationskrise* (Westdeutscher Verlag, Opladen, 1973), pp. 427–66.

S. Heimann, 'Die Deutsche Kommunistische Partei', in Richard Stöss (ed.), *Parteienhandbuch*, I (Westdeutscher Verlag, Opladen, 1983), pp. 901–81.

G. Langguth, *Die Protestbewegung in der Bundesrepublik 1968–1976* (Wissenschaft und Politik, Cologne, 1976) (revised edn 1983).

V. Probst, *The Communist Parties in the Federal Republic of Germany* (Haag/Herchen, Frankfurt am Main, 1981).

M. Schäfer (ed.), *Die DKP: Gründung, Entwicklung, Bedeutung* (Verlag Marxistische Blätter, Frankfurt am Main, 1978).

D. Staritz, 'Der "Eurokommunismus" und die DKP', in *Die Linke im Rechtsstaat*, 2 (Rotbuch, Berlin, 1979), pp. 133–54.

G. Walter, *Theoretischer Anspruch und politische Praxis der DKP. Eine Analyse am Beispiel der Betriebsarbeit* (Anton Hain, Meisenheim am Glan, 1973).

The Communist Party of Great Britain

R. Black, *Stalinism in Britain* (New Park, London, 1970).

The British Road to Socialism, 5th edn. (CPGB, London, 1978).

N. Branson, *History of the Communist Party of Great Britain, 1927–41* (Lawrence and Wishart, London, 1985).

J. Callaghan, 'The CPGB in Local Government' in B. Szajkowski (ed.), *Marxist Local Government in West Europe and Japan* (Pinter, London, 1986).

J. Gollan, *People's Democracy for Britain* (CPGB, London, 1952).

M. Prior and D. Purdy, *Out of the Ghetto* (Spokesman, Nottingham, 1979).

R. Samuel, 'The Lost World of British Communism', in *New Left Review*, 154 (November/December 1985) and 156 (March/April 1986).

The Communist Party of Greece

C. Chiclet, *Les communistes grecs dans la guerre; Histoire du parti communiste de Grèce, de 1941 à 1949* (L'Harmattan, Paris, 1987).

J. O. Iatrides, *Revolt in Athens; the Greek Communist Second Round, 1944–1945* (Princeton University Press, Princeton NJ, 1972).

D. Kitsikis, *Historia tou hellênotourkikou hôrou apo ton E. Venizelo ston G. Papadopoulo, 1928–1973* (Hestia, Athens, 1981).

D. Kitsikis, 'Greece: Communism in a Non-Western Setting' in D. E. Albright (ed.), *Communism and Political Systems in Western Europe* (Westview Press, Boulder, CO, 1979).

D. F. G. Kousoulas, *Revolution and Defeat. The Story of the Greek Communist Party* (Oxford University Press, London, 1976).

J. C. Loulis, *The Greek Communist Party, 1940–1944* (Croom Helm, London, 1982).

J. Meynaud, *Les forces politiques en Grèce* (Etudes de Science Politique, Montreal, 1965).

P. Nefeloudis, *Stis pêges tês kakodaimonias. Ta bathytera aitia tês diasasês tou KKE, 1918–1968* (Gutenberg, Athens, 1974).

P. Roussos, *E megalê pentaetia, 1940–1945* (Syghronê Epohê, Athens, 1978).

A. L. Zapantis, *Greek–Soviet Relations, 1917–1941* (Columbia University Press, New York, 1982).

The Italian Communist Party

A. Accornero, R. Mannheimer and C. Sebastiani (eds), *L'identità comunista. I militanti, le strutture, la cultura del Pci* (Editori Riuniti, Rome, 1983).

M. Barbagli, P. Corbetta and S. Sechi, *Dentro il Pci* (Il Mulino, Bologna, 1979).

S. Belligni (ed.), *La giraffa e il liocorno. Il Pci dagli anni '70 al nuovo decennio* (Franco Angeli, Milan, 1983).

D. L. M. Blackmer and S. Tarrow (eds), *Communism in Italy and France* (Princeton University Press, Princeton, NJ, 1975).

M. Ilardi and A. Accornero (eds), *Il Partito Comunista Italiano. Struttura estoria dell' organizzazione 1921/1979* (Feltrinelli, Milan, 1982).

P. Lange, 'Il Pci e i possibili esiti della crisi italiana', in L. Graziano and S. Tarrow (eds), *La crisi italiana* (Einaudi, Turin, 1979), pp. 657–718.

J. Ruscoe, *The Italian Communist Party 1976–1981. On the Threshold of Government* (Macmillan Press, London, 1982).

S. Serfaty and L. Gray (eds), *The Italian Communist Party. Yesterday, Today, and Tomorrow* (Greenwood Press, Westport, Conn., 1980).

S. Tarrow, *Between Center and Periphery. Grassroots Politicians in Italy and France* (Yale University Press, New Haven, Conn., 1977).

S. Tarrow, *Peasant Communism in Southern Italy* (Yale University Press, New Haven, Conn., 1967).

The Communist Party of the Netherlands

Cahiers over de geschiedenis van de CPN (The History of the CPN), vols 1–7 (Amsterdam, 1979–82).

P. Coomans, T. de Jonge and Erik Nijhoff, *De Eenheidsvakcentrale (EVC) 1943–48* (H. D. Tjeenk Willink, Groningen, 1976).

J. Divendal, A. Koper and M. van Weezel (eds), *De moeizame destalinisatie van de CPN. Documantatie over het conflict tussen de CPN en de Bruggroep – toen en nu* (Van Gennep, Amsterdam, 1982).

J. Divendal, H. de Liagre Böhl, A. Koper and M. van Weezel (eds), *Nederland links en de Konde Oorlag. Breuken en Bruggen* (De Populier, Amsterdam, 1982).

Paul de Groot, *De dertiger jaren, 1930–1935. Herrineringen en overdenkingen*, 2 vols (Pegasus, Amsterdam, 1965–7).

G. Harmsen, 'Leven en werk van Mr. Alex S. de Leeuw. Kommunisties politikus tussen de werelddoorlogen. Een bijdrage tot de geschiedenis van het nederlandse marxisme-leninisme' in *Jaarboek voor de geschiedenis van socialisme en arbeidersbeweging in Nederland* (SUN, Nijmegen, 1980).

G. Harmsen, *Nederlandse kommunisme. Gebundelde opstellen* (SUN, Nijmegen, 1982).

D. Hellema (ed.), *Crisis van het Nederlandse kommunisme* (Jan Mets, Amsterdam, 1986).

A. A. de Jonge, *Het kommunisme in Nederland. De geschiedenis van een politieke partij* (Kruseman, The Hague, 1972).

A. Koper, *Onder de banier van het stalinisme. Een onderzoek naar de geblokkeerde destalinisatie van de CPN* (Van Gennep, Amsterdam, 1982).

H. de Liagre Böhl, *Herman Gorter. Zijn politieke aktiviteiten van 1909 tot 1920 in de opkomende kommunistiese beweging in Nederland* (SUN, Nijmegen, 1973).

The Communist Party of Portugal

A general bibliography of works on Portuguese communism can be found in 'Bibliografia sistemática sobre o PCP' in *Estudos sobre o Comunismo*, vols 1–4 (1983–85).

The Communist Party of Spain

E. Berntzen and P. Selle, 'Norwegian and Catalan Communism: Relativism in the Use of Models of Electoral Behaviour', *European Journal of Political Research*, vol. 13 (1985), pp. 41–51.

J. Botella, 'L'electorat comunista a Catalunya, 1977–1980' (unpublished PhD Thesis, Universitat Autònoma de Barcelona, 1982).

S. Carrillo, *'Eurocomunismo' y Estado* (Grijalbo, Barcelona, 1977).

S. Carrillo, *Memoria de la transición* (Grijalbo, Barcelona, 1983).

F. Claudin, *Eurocomunismo y socialismo* (Siglo XXI, Madrid, 1977).

G. Hermet, *Les communistes en Espagne* (Armand Colin–FNSP, Paris, 1971).

J. J. Linz, 'A Sociological Look at Spanish Communism', in G. Schwab (ed.),

Eurocommunism: The Ideological and Political–Theoretical Foundations (Greenwood Press, Westport, Conn., 1981), pp. 217–68.

E. Mujal-Leon, *Communism and Political Change in Spain* (Indiana University Press, Bloomington, Ill., 1983).

N. Sartorius (ed.), *Una alternativa a la crisis. Las propuestas del PCE* (Ed. Planeta, Barcelona, 1985).

The Left Party Communists of Sweden

P-E. Back and S. Berglund, *Det svenska partiväsendet* (AWE/Gebers, Stockholm, 1978).

C. H. Hermansson, (Lancet) *Det monopolkapitalistiska Sverge Arbetarkultur, Stockholm, 1943).*
Vänsterns väg (Rabén and Sjögren, Stockholm, 1965).

J. Hermansson, *Kommunism på svenska? SKP/VPK:s idéutveckling efter Komintern* (Almqvist and Wiksell International, Stockholm, 1984).

J. Holmberg and M. Giljam, *Väljare och val i Sverige* (Bonniers, Stockholm, 1987).

V. Korpi, *Arbetarklassen 1 välfärdskapitalismen* (Prisma, Stockholm, 1978).

K. Lindkvist, *Program och parti. Principprogram och partiideologi inom den kommunistska rörelsen i Sverige 1917–72* (Arkiv, Lund, 1982).

S. Rydenfelt, *Kommunismen i Sverige: En samhällsvetenskaplig studie* (Gleerups, Lund, 1954).

D. Tarschys, 'The Changing Basis of Radical Socialism in Scandinavia' in Karl H. Cerny (ed.), *Scandinavia at the Polls. Recent political trends in Denmark, Norway and Sweden* (American Enterprise Institute for Public Research, Washington, DC, 1977).

G. Therborn (ed.), *En ny vänster* (Raben and Sjögren, Stockholm, 1966).
Vad gör den härskande klassen när den härskar? (Zenit/Raben and Sjögren, Lund/Stockholm, 1980).

Notes on Contributors

Juan Botella teaches political science at the Universitat Autònoma de Barcelona. His publications include 'Sociologìa de los partidos catalanes' in *Revista de Estudios Politicós* (1979), *Partits i Parlamentaris* (1980) and 'Communist Voters' (doctoral thesis, forthcoming). His main fields of research have been party systems, electoral behaviour and policies in higher education.

John Callaghan is senior lecturer in British politics at Wolverhampton Polytechnic. His publications on the British Left include *British Trotskyism; Theory and Practice* (1984) and *The Far Left in British Politics* (1987). He is at present working on a study of the ideological impact of Soviet experience on the Labour Party.

Stéphane Courtois is a research fellow at the Centre d'Etudes de la Vie Politique Française Contemporaine of the CNRS in Paris. In 1978 he defended a doctoral thesis (third cycle) on 'The Policy of the French Communist Party and its Trade Union Aspects, 1939–1944'. His publications include *Le PCF dans la guerre* (1980) and *Le communisme* (with Marc Lazar) (1987). He was co-founder in 1981, with Annie Kriegel, of *Communisme*, a multi-disciplinary journal on communism (published by L'Age d'Homme), and remains its co-editor.

Meindert Fennema studied sociology at the University of Utrecht and political science at the University of Amsterdam. His doctoral dissertation, 'International Networks of Banks and Industry' was published in 1982. Together with the Dutch historian Henri Baudet he published a study on the political and economic effects of the retreat from empire for Dutch society (1983). He is at present senior lecturer in political science at the University of Amsterdam.

Anton Fischer studied social sciences at the universities of Zürich and Tübingen before defending his doctoral dissertation at Marburg. He later trained as a psychotherapist and is at present in private practice as a psychoanalyst. His book *Der Reale Schein und die Theorie des Kapitals bei Karl Marx* was published in 1978.

Marcel Hotterbeex took his first degree in mathematics. He has been in charge of the Institut d'Etudes Juridiques Européennes, then of the Centre d'Analyse et de Documentation Politiques, attached to the regional Service de Politologie in Liège. His published works on elections include the three-volume *Description des resultats des élections du 10 novembre 1981 dans la province de Liège.*

Jörgen Hermansson is assistant professor in the Department of Government at the University of Uppsala. Since completing his doctoral thesis on 'Communism in a Swedish Way? The Ideological Development of SKP/VPK since the Comintern' in 1984, he has been engaged on projects on corporatism in Sweden, and on applications of game theory. He has published works on democratic theory, and on the General Will in Rousseau.

Matti Hyvärinen took his first degree in the social sciences. He is at present a research fellow in the postal administration of Finland, and is preparing a doctoral thesis at the University of Tampere on the student movement and on change in politicul culture. His major publication on social movements – *Alussa oli liike* (In the Beginning was a Movement) – appeared in 1986.

Dimitri Kitsikis is professor of the history of international relations at the University of Ottawa. Born in Athens and educated at the Sorbonne, his books include *Propagande et pressions en politique internationale, Le rôle des experts à la Conférence de la Paix en 1919, Hellas tês 4ês Augoustou, Hellas kai Xenoi, Sygkritikê Historia Hellados kai Tourkias, L'Empire ottoman.* For the past 20 years he has been a prominent theorist of a Greek–Turkish confederation.

Paul Lucardie studied sociology at Groningen in the Netherlands and at Frankfurt. He took a PhD in political science from Queen's University at Kingston University, Ontario. Since 1979 he has been research associate at the Centre for Documentation on Dutch Political Parties at the University of Groningen. His publications include *Nederland Stromenland: een geschiedenis van de politieke stromingen* and, with Ruud Koole, 'The Netherlands: Social Democrats and Security Policy' in *Semialignment and Western Security.*

Jukka Paastela is assistant professor in political science at the University of Tampere. His major publication on *Marx's and Engels' Concepts of the Parties and Political Organizations of the Working Class* was published in 1985. His present research is on the new social movements in Finland.

José Pacheco Pereira is assistant professor at the *Instituto de Ciencias do Trabalho e da Empresa* in Lisbon, and is now a member of parliament. He is the founder and editor of *Estudos sobre o Communismo* and has published several articles and books on labour studies and on the Portuguese Communist Party.

Gianfranco Pasquino has been professor of political science at the University of Bologna since 1975 and visiting professor of political science at the Bologna Center of the Johns Hopkins University since 1973. His most recent books are: *La complessità della politica* (1985) and *Restituire lo scettro al principe. Proposte di riforma istituzionale* (1985). Former editor of *Il Mulino*, he is on the editorial board of the European Journal of Political Research and of Comparative Political Studies. Since 1983 he has been a Senator for the Independent Left.

Denis Peschanski conducts research at the Institut d'Histoire du Temps Présent of the CNRS. His doctoral thesis (third cycle) dealt with the discourse of communism between 1934 and 1936. His present research is on the history of communism, and on France in the Second World War. He is a member of the Editorial Board of the journal *Communisme*, and headed the editorial team of *Vichy 1940–44; archives de guerre d'Angelo Tasca* (1986).

Michael Waller's research interest is in European communism, East and West. His *The Language of Communism* appeared in 1972, and *Democratic Centralism; an Historical Commentary* in 1981. He is co-editor of *The Journal of Communist Studies.* His first post was in the Department of Russian and Soviet Studies at Lancaster University, and he now teaches in the Department of Government of the University of Manchester.

Index